Greek Islands in the Sun
2nd Edition

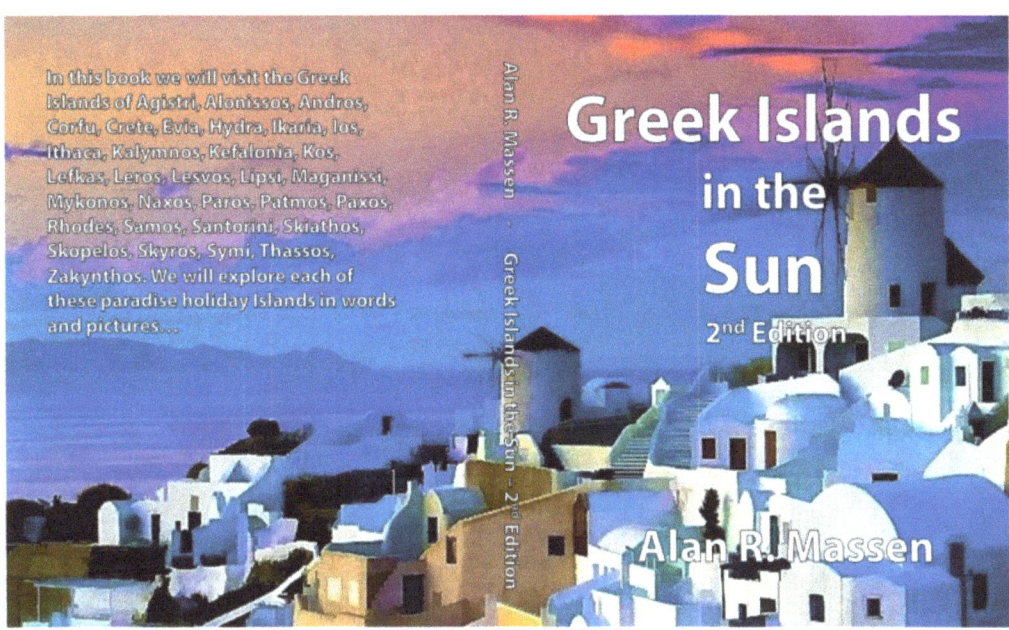

Greek Islands in the Sun is a journey to many of the beautiful paradise Greek holiday islands set in the warm crystal clear Mediterranean azure blue sea. In this book we will explore, all of the paradise holiday Islands of Greece, from A to Z. We will visit the Islands towns, villages, seashore, resorts and beaches in words and pictures.

by Norfolk Watercolour Artist Alan R. Massen
Published in Great Britain by Rainbow Publications UK

First Published in 2017 by Rainbow Publications UK
2nd Edition Published in 2019 by Rainbow Publications UK

Copyright © 2019 Alan R. Massen

The moral right of Alan R. Massen to be identified as the author of this work has been asserted in accordance with the UK Copyright, Designs and Patents Act of 1988. All rights reserved.

No part of this book may be reproduced, or stored in a retrieval system, or transmitted in any form or by any means, electronic, mechanical, photocopying, recording, or otherwise, without the prior written permission of both the author and the above publisher of this book All imagery and illustrations

© Alan R. Massen

Neither the publisher nor the author can accept liability for the use of any of the materials, methods or information recommended in this book or for any consequences arising out of their use, nor can they be held responsible for any errors or omissions that may be found in the text or may occur at a future date as a result of changes in rules, laws or equipment All manufacturers, sellers, product names and services identified in this book are used in editorial fashion and for the benefit of such companies with no intention of any infringement of trademarks. No such use or the use of any trade name is intended to convey endorsement or other affiliation with this book

Paperback Edition ISBN 978-0-9935591-8-1
Typeset in Minion Pro
Published in Great Britain by Rainbow Publications UK

About the Author

Alan was born in the city of Norwich in the county of Norfolk, England in November 1949. When Alan was still a teenager he started painting whilst attending art classes in Norwich. In his mid-teens he had two paintings accepted for a National Art Exhibition held in London and other major UK cities. Alan spent most of his working life as a professional Health and Safety Advisor and rarely picked up a paint brush until Alan, his wife Susie and daughter Ginny (his other daughter Mandy is married and lives with her husband Adrian in Sheffield) moved out of the city of Norwich into the countryside in 1993. They moved to a little village called East Lexham in the heart of Norfolk. The village was very peaceful and pretty. This helped inspire Alan to take up watercolour painting once again. In 2004 they moved to another small West Norfolk village near Downham Market where they still live today. In 2008 Alan had to retire due to ill health (bad knees) and whilst he still painted regularly he began to spend more and more time gardening. In 2013 his wife Susie suggested that he kept a gardening diary to record his adventures in the garden and capture the changing seasons, animals, birds and the successes and failures of being a gardener he encountered. By the following year Susie suggested that he should write a book from his diary and include illustrations of both the garden and his artwork.

In 2014 Alan's first book was published by Creative Gateway called **"Retiring to the Garden – Year One".** This proved such a success that Alan decided to follow this up with his second book called **"Retiring into a Rainbow"** featuring his watercolour paintings. In 2015 Alan published **"Retiring to Our Garden – Year Two"** published this time by Rainbow Publications UK. He then re-issued his first two books this time in a **"Second Edition"**. Also published by Rainbow Publications UK. In 2016 Alan published: **"Skiathos a Greek Island Paradise", "Norfolk the County of my Birth", "Art Inspired by a Rainbow", "Ibiza Island of Dreams", "Majorca Island in the Sun", "Flip-flops and Shades on Thassos", "Mardle and a Troshin' in Norfolk", "England the Country of my Birth", "Mousehole the Cornish Jewel", "Sunshine and Shades on Kefalonia", "Shades and Flip-flops on Zakynthos" and finally "Trips into my Mind's Eye"** Also published by Rainbow Publications UK..

In 2017 Alan published the following new books entitled: **"Corfu and Mainland Greece", "Crete and the Island of Santorini", "Cyprus the Pyramids and the Holy Land", "Greek Islands in the Sun", "Being Greek - The Culture of the People of Greece", "Greece Land of Gods and Men" and finally "Rainbow Art" and "A Rainbow of Art".** Also published by Rainbow Publications UK…

Books by the same Author

Retiring to the Garden – Year 1

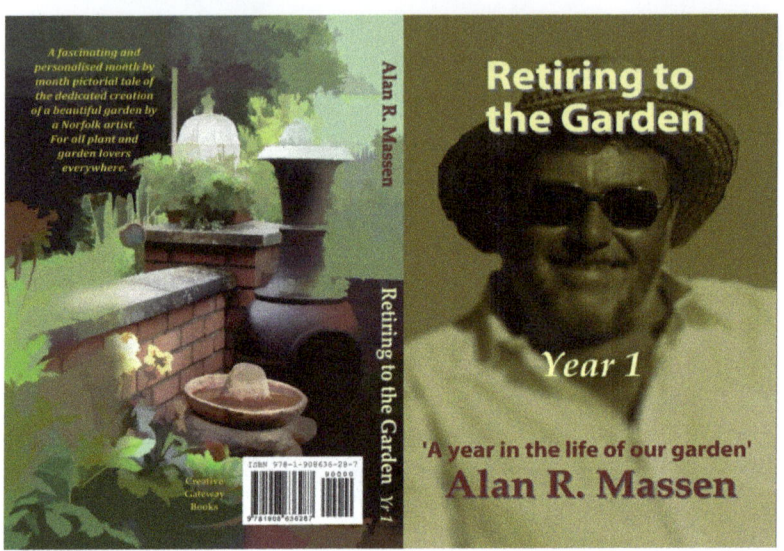

Retiring to Our Garden – Year 1 - 2nd Edition

by Norfolk watercolour artist - Alan R. Massen.
Published in Great Britain by Creative Gateway and Rainbow Publications UK

Books by the same Author

Retiring into a Rainbow - 2nd Edition

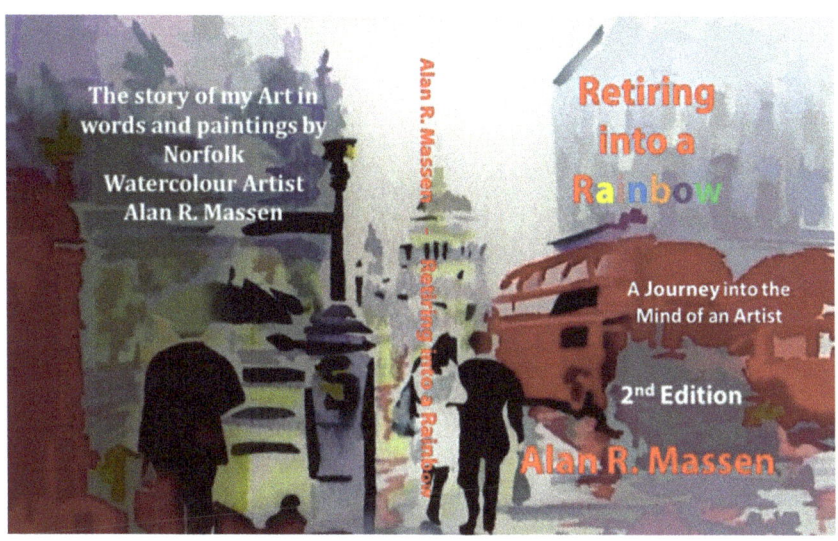

Retiring to Our Garden – Year Two

by Norfolk watercolour artist - Alan R. Massen.
Published 1st Edition by Creative Gateway and 2nd Edition by Rainbow Publications UK

Books by the same Author

Skiathos a Greek Island Paradise

Norfolk the County of my Birth

by Norfolk watercolour artist - Alan R. Massen.
Published in Great Britain by Rainbow Publications UK

Books by the same Author

Ibiza Island of Dreams

Majorca Island in the Sun

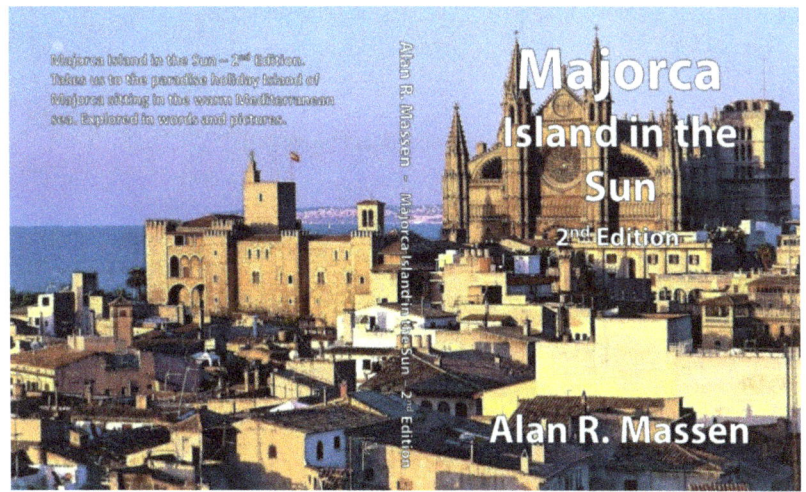

by Norfolk Watercolour Artist - Alan R. Massen
Published in Great Britain by Rainbow Publications UK

Books by the same Author

Art Inspired by a Rainbow

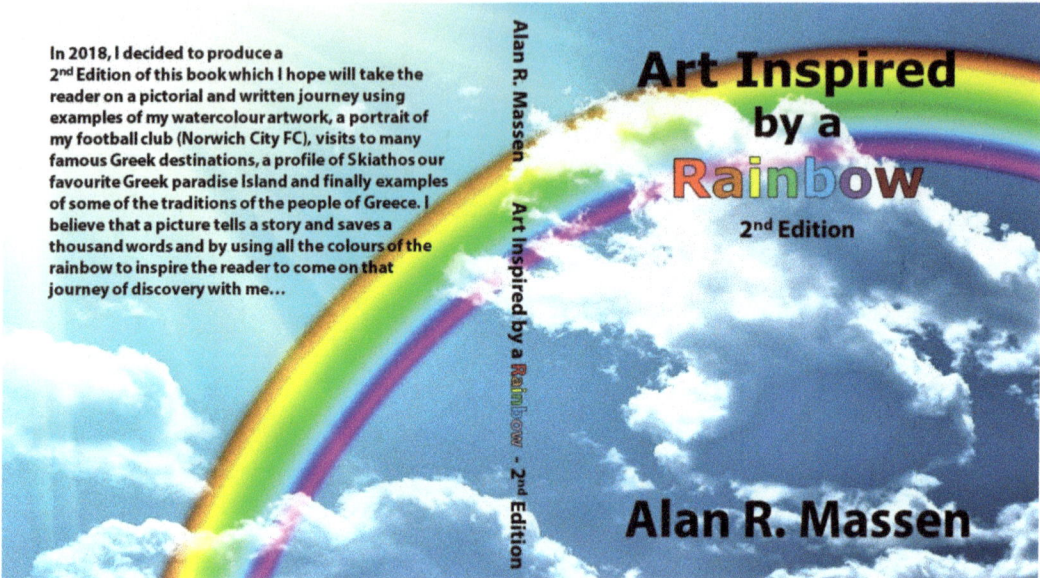

Flip-flops and Shades on Thassos

by Norfolk Watercolour Artist - Alan R. Massen
Published in Great Britain by Rainbow Publications UK

Books by the same Author

Mardle and a Troshin' in Norfolk

Being Greek - The Culture of the People of Greece

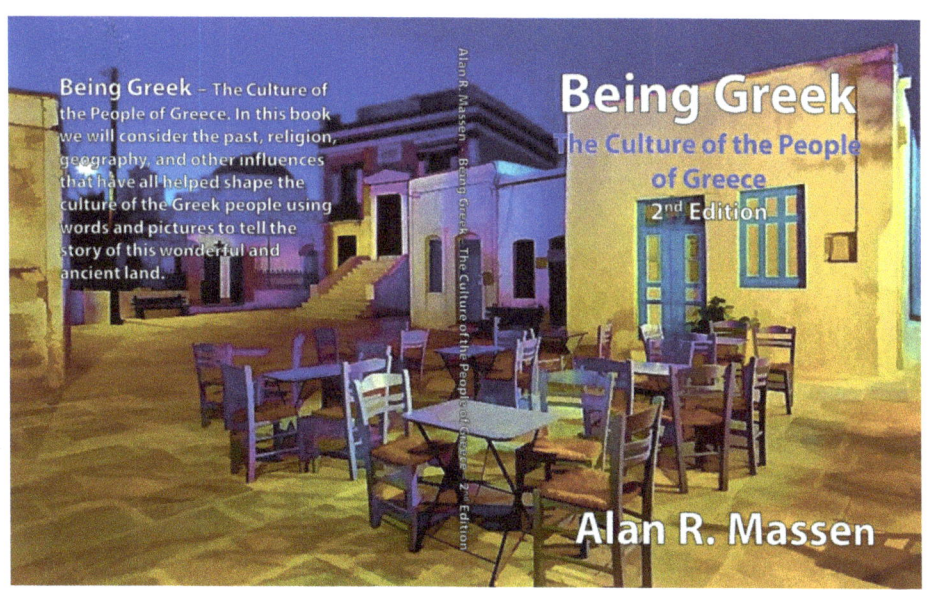

by Norfolk Watercolour Artist - Alan R. Massen
Published in Great Britain by Rainbow Publications UK

Books by the same Author

England the Country of my Birth

Greek Islands in the Sun

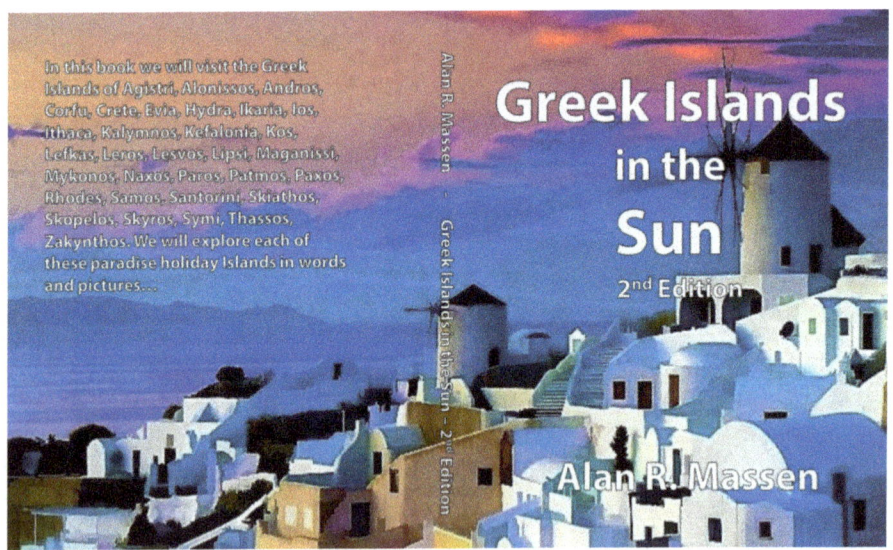

by Norfolk Watercolour Artist - Alan R. Massen
Published in Great Britain by Rainbow Publications UK

Books by the same Author

Mousehole the Cornish Jewel

Crete and the Island of Santorini

by Norfolk Watercolour Artist - Alan R. Massen
Published in Great Britain by Rainbow Publications UK

Books by the same Author

Sunshine and Shades on Kefalonia

Shades and Flip-flops on Zakynthos

by Norfolk Watercolour Artist - Alan R. Massen
Published in Great Britain by Rainbow Publications UK

Books by the same Author

Corfu and Mainland Greece

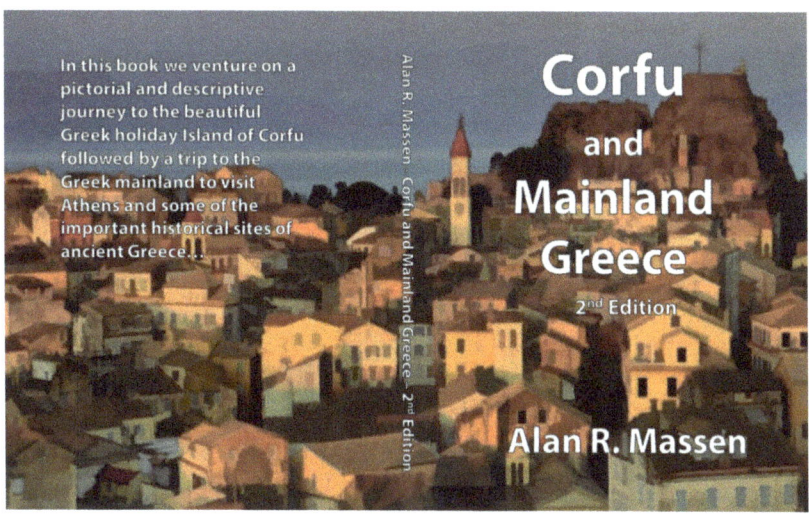

Cyprus the Pyramids and the Holy Land

by Norfolk Watercolour Artist - Alan R. Massen
Published in Great Britain by Rainbow Publications UK

Books by the same Author

Trips into my Minds Eye

Greece Land of Gods and Men

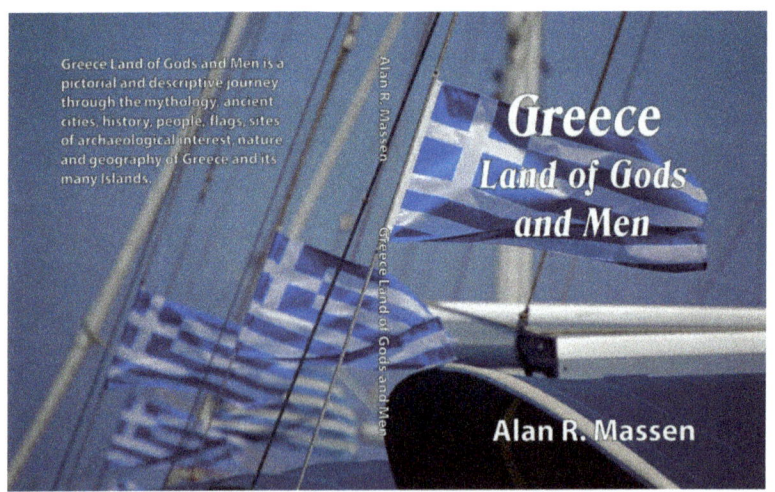

by Norfolk Watercolour Artist - Alan R. Massen
Published in Great Britain by Rainbow Publications UK

Dedication

I would like to dedicate this book to the people of Greece. They have always welcomed Susie and I with great warmth and friendliness during our many stays on the mainland of Greece and/or on many of the Greek Islands. A special mention must also go to our special holiday friends from Vienna Anna and Karl, Andrew and Lynn from Sheffield, Issy and Alistair from Scotland, all the management and staff at the Troulos Bay Hotel and the Mythos Cafe on Skiathos and finally to my wife Susie who makes every moment of our lives together special.

A big **THANK YOU** to them ALL.

Books by the same Author also published in 2019

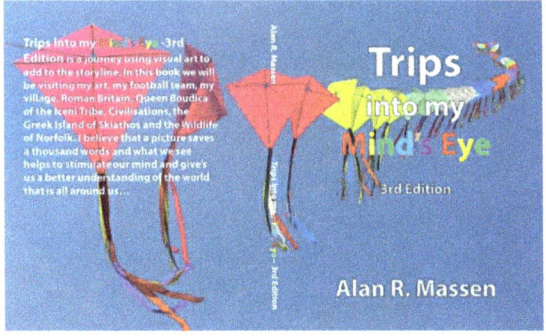

by Norfolk Watercolour Artist Alan R. Massen
Published in Great Britain by Rainbow Publications UK

Contents

Greek Islands in the Sun

Introduction	1	**Aegina**	3	**Agistri**	7
Alonissos	10	**Andros**	14	**Corfu**	21
Crete	41	**Evia**	53	**Hydra**	55
Ikaria	59	**Ios**	63	**Ithaca**	67
Kalymnos	72	**Kefalonia**	77	**Kos**	85
Lefkas	93	**Leros**	102	**Lesvos**	108
Lipsi	117	**Maganissi**	121	**Mykonos**	125
Naxos	133	**Paros**	140	**Patmos**	151
Paxos	157	**Rhodes**	160	**Samos**	169
Santorini	179	**Skiathos**	185	**Skopelos**	195
Skyros	202	**Symi**	208	**Thassos**	214
Zakynthos	223	**Acknowledgement**	232		

Copyright © 2019 Alan R. Massen

Introduction

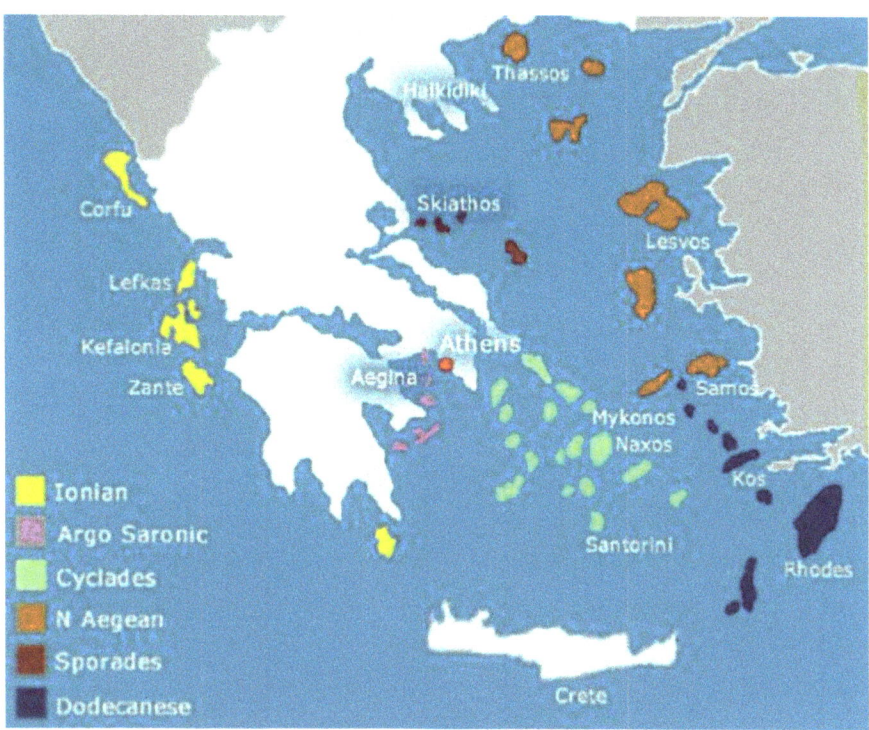

Greece is a country in the south-east of Europe. It is located between the Mediterranean, Ionian and Aegean Seas. Greece includes many Islands such as Rhodes, Crete, Skiathos, Corfu and the Dodecanese Islands. There is a wealth of accommodation in Greece to suit all travelers including budget lodging, travel lodges, bed and breakfast and hotels. Places to visit in Greece are endless and there is something to suit everyone with a wealth of historic sites, sporting venues, walking trails, museums, landmarks, monuments, festivals, carnivals and beautiful beaches everywhere. In this book we will visit the great beaches, towns and villages on many of the lovely Greek Island from A - Z that help make up the country of Greece. As you progress through the pages you will see numerous examples of my watercolour paintings and photographic artwork which I have scanned onto my computer. Then using a piece of art software, to give the pictures an impressionist style finish, a bit like the great Impressionist painter Claude Monet, to produce the illustrations used throughout this book. So if you are ready we will start our journey of discovery together. However, before we venture too far into the pages of this book, I thought, that I ought to introduce myself for those of you that have not been with me on one of my other journeys to visit some of the Spanish Islands, Egypt Land of the Pharaohs, Israel The Holy Land, many of the Greek Islands and/or the mainland of Greece with me…

Hello my name is Alan and I am married to Susie, we live in a small village called Shouldham in North West Norfolk in the UK. Together, over the last twenty years, we have been fortunate enough to have been able to have numerous summer holidays abroad. In this time, our holiday destination of choice, has usually been to go to one or more of the many Greek Islands. We have over the years holidayed on Corfu, Ithaca, Crete, Zakynthos, Santorini, Thassos, Kefalonia and Skiathos to name but a few. We have also visited the major archaeological sites on the Mainland of Greece as well as spending several days visiting the important ancient sites in the City of Athens itself. Now you know who I am let us venture out and about onto many of the beautiful Greek Islands…

The Greek Island of Aegina

The Island of Aegina lies in the Argo Saronic bay to the south of Athens. To get to the Island you need to fly into Athens and get the ferry from Piraeus Port. It is even closer to Athens' centre than some of the city's northern suburbs. Many of the 12,000 people who live on Aegina commute to the capital to work and the Island is a popular weekend retreat and a favoured retirement Island for many well-heeled Greeks. Visitors find Aegina an ideal Island base when touring the historic sites on the Greek mainland with easy transfers from Athens' airport. The main resorts may get swamped with day trip visitors, especially at the weekends and Aegina Town even suffers the suburban problems of limited street parking and night-time traffic noise. Aegina is a roughly triangular shaped Island, about eight miles by six. To the north and west are fertile coastal plains, noted for crops of pistachios, almonds and figs. Aegina Islanders who don't commute to Athens either work in the tourism industry or as farmers. To the east and south are hills that rise to the conical Mount Oros (also called Profitis Illias) and a long and rocky ridge that runs across Aegina with fertile valleys on either side. There are several important historical sights here including the 5th century BC Doric temple of Aphaia, the ruins of a village at Paliohora and the remarkable church of Agia Nektariou are all worth a visit. As one of the closest Islands to the Greek capital of Athens, Aegina has a well-developed tourist infrastructure geared mainly to the Greek weekenders who descend on the Island in droves from Athens. Most visitors head for the north coast beach resort of Agia Marina or to the east coast beaches. Sandy beaches are in short supply and the Island has more to offer in the way of interesting historical sights and good walks…

The Island of Aegina:

Aegina Town: Although a busy port, Aegina Town has a pleasant crescent shaped harbour backed by brightly painted neoclassical houses with shops, tavernas, and cafes along the water's edge. The waterfront is where everything gravitates, including most of the traffic. Dozens of bars and clubs emphasize that this is a party Island, yet quiet corners ensure plenty of genuine Greek charm. The Island-grown pistachios are on sale everywhere, most notably at the growers' cooperative by the harbour gates. Boats moored to the quay also sell fresh fruit, vegetables nuts and raisins. In the Town there are several craft shops specialising in the sale of local hand-made pottery. Tables line the main promenade at night while tasseled horses take the tourist up and down the front in carriages. The austere and much photographed chapel of Agios Nikolaos, sits alone at the water's edge. The Greek Orthodox cathedral of Agios Demetrios is where the first government of modern Greece was sworn in and north of the town at Cape Kolono is a fluted 23-ft column, the surviving remnant of a 5th century BC temple to Apollo. Recent excavations have also uncovered a theatre and a stadium. Nearby, a small, sandy beach called Avra, or Kolono, has sunbeds and tavernas.
Marathonas: Marathonas is what passes for a traditional Greek fishing village in these modern tourist days. Found about four kilometres south of Aegina Town it is almost half-way to the popular resort at Perdika. The pretty village has just 250 or so permanent inhabitants with their homes climbing up on the steep hillside where a walk uphill reaps some spectacular views of the coast and leads to good hill trails and even mountain climbing. Of the two small beaches only one is sandy while the road behind is lined with tavernas bidding for passing trade. Nearby is the imposing monastery of Panagia Chrysoliodis, which dates from the 16th century…

The Island of Aegina:

Faros: The coast road south from Aegina Town is dotted with tavernas at every sandy cove and backed by pistachio groves and eucalyptus trees, notably at Aeginitissa and Profitis Ilias, before it reaches the resort of Faros. Faros is most noted for its beautiful neoclassical buildings and a less than classical giant water park. On the edge of Faros, past the petrol station is a dirt road leading down to Sarpa beach. The visitor will find plenty of sun loungers and a small cantina by the beach. **Perdika:** The fishing village of Perdika has managed to cling on to some original Greek charm with its picturesque flower-bedecked side-streets and pleasant fish tavernas. The resort is perches on a promontory with a large marina below where luxury yachts share shelter with small colourful fishing boats. Shady tavernas sit above and behind on the high walls that line the utilitarian strip of battleship grey concrete that passes for a promenade. Excursion boats leave here for the islet of Moni that lies just offshore and there are day trips to Angistri Island which lies about four kilometres to the west. Just before Perdika is a small beach called Klima, or Klidi, noted for beach parties that attract DJs from Athens. It is well signposted off the main road to Perdika. **Portes:** The tiny sea port of Portes lies on the east coast of Aegina. It is reached along the coast road south of Agia Marina, Portes perches rather dramatically over the sea with a long beach of steeply banked stone and shingle. A little way inland is the Ekpaz Wildlife Sanctuary which houses around 5,000 animals and birds. Entry is free and visitors get guided tours throughout the day. The sanctuary has a small souvenir shop where any donation made by the visitor aids the excellent work going on there…

The Island of Aegina:

Agia Marina: Agia Marina is the busiest and biggest beach resort on the Island with a long, wide sandy beach that's gently shelving, so it's ideal for families with children, and with every sort of tourist facility. Sun loungers cover every scrap of sand along the busy shoreline. Tavernas, bars, shops and cafes are plentiful and weekending Athenians will pack the marina out with boats. Steep wooded slopes lead to the Temple of Aphiaia, one of Aegina's major attractions while the charming village of Alones, nestling in a deep green valley nearby, has scores of excellent tavernas. Also nearby is the mountain village of Mesagros. It is close to the Temple of Aphiaia which is known both for its wild flowers, some unique to the area, and for its fine ceramics. **Vagia:** Vayia, or Vagia, is a small port located about four kilometres east of Souvala. It has a small sand and shingle beach and a couple of old-style traditional tavernas. Vayia has the relaxed air of a bygone age. Eastwards, along a coastal path, are isolated coves while the neighbouring village of Agius, smothered in pines, is noted for its water jug pottery and for the church of the Apostle Crispus. **Kipseli:** In the midst of the pistachio and olive groves of north-west Aegina is the attractive village of Kipseli with a fine central square and traditional two-storey homes. The name Kipseli means 'beehive' and local tales have it that the village was renamed following protest over the former village name of Halameni which meant 'ruined'. Kipseli is at the heart of the most prosperous area of the Island with extensive orchards and farms stretching over the green plain. The village is noted for its huge number of chapels, another reflection of the area's great wealth in times gone by…

The Greek Island of Agistri

Agistri, also called Angistri, is a small, pine covered Island close to Aegina in the Saronic Gulf that lies south of the Greek capital of Athens. To get to the Island you need to fly into Athens and get the ferry from Piraeus Port. It is very small, with an area of about 13 sq km, making it the smallest of the inhabited Island in the Saronic group. Agistri is a quiet backwater, free of cars and with little in the way of nightlife outside of the few hotels in the three main settlements of Skala, Milos and Limenaria. Milos is where most people live but Skala is the most developed of the Island's resorts and the main tourist centre. Agistri is home to fewer than 1,000 people with holiday beds for perhaps 1,000 visitors. It has a single 10 kilometre road but no cars and just one bus. Agistri is also very hilly with about half of the hills covered in fields of citrus and olives and the rest cloaked in dense pine forest. Apart from walking and sunbathing there is little to do here. Most beaches are pebble and shingle with the best of the sand at Skala and Halkiada, the latter noted as being the first official designated naturist beach in Greece. Agistri Island is located in the Saronic Gulf only 45 minutes sailing time from the Athens port of Piraeus. A regular ferry service to the mainland makes Agistri a very popular weekend retreat for Athenians. The Island is largely un-spoilt, it's a tiny Island with few good beaches. Most visitors stay in the main port of Skala which has many good restaurants and the best beach on the Island…

The Island of Agistri:

Skala: Skala is the Island's main tourist centre and the main port of Agistri. It is a bustling little place, Skala also has many restaurants and bars both around the beach, which lies to the north of the harbour, and in the village itself. The impressive blue dome of Agia Anargiri church stands out from the resort's rather plain buildings where it overlooks the beach. Fine, gently shelving sand and shallow water makes this beach popular with families and, as the only natural sand beach on the Island, it can get very crowded in the high season, especially when day visitor boats arrive from Aegina and Athens. Skala beach is quite narrow, just a couple of rows of sun loungers at the deepest part, but it is quite long with a variety of watersports. Low trees and scrub back the beach to the west where it gets much less busy. At the headland it turns to stone and shingle and runs on all the way to Mylos. Skala village has a handful of shops and a good selection of tavernas, bars, cafes and a couple of nightclubs add to the mix.

Halikiada: South of the harbour at Skala a scenic path threads past some modern villas at Skiliri and beyond the Agistri Club Hotel to the secluded beach at Halikiada. It takes about 20 minutes to walk to what became the first official naturist beach in Greece, despite strong objections from the church. A steep and relatively difficult scramble down to the beach has been made easier by a new path or visitors can tackle the rather precipitous headland for easier access. Strong Saronic currents keep the waters here turquoise clear and clean while the beach is mostly pebble and rock. There are no facilities but casual camping, although technically illegal, is still fairly common. A cave at the back of the beach is sometimes lived in over the summer…

The Island of Agistri:

Milos: The only road out of Skala heads north along the coast to the Island capital and port at Milos or Mylos, also called Megalochori. The road is lined with restaurants, rooms to let, isolated shingle coves and the occasional long, flat stretch of stone. Milos is a quiet village of stone-built houses sitting on a steep hill above the small harbour and a tiny, man made beach. It has a few basic tavernas, shops and traditional kafenion. West of Milos, walking trails lead into the pine covered hillside and to the village of Metochi that has a small chapel and splendid views. On the coast road a sign points to Dragonera beach, a favourite spot for casual campers where a cantina opens in the summer. **Limenaria and Apiossos Islet:** The paved road south of Milos crosses the Island to Limenaria, a small village surrounded by olive groves and noted for the golden dome that adorns the village church of Agia Kriaki. It is about as traditional Greek as you can get so near to Athens, it has a shop that doubles as a taverna selling local crafts and an ancient olive mill in the central square. There is no beach here and a sign that says 'to the beach' points to a cement diving platform overhanging a sheer drop to the sea. Strong currents make diving here safe for strong swimmers only and it's a difficult scramble back up the steep rocks. About a kilometre east, just past the chapel of Agios Nikolaos, is the substantial salt lake from which Limenaria gets its name. A dried out salt pan in the summer, it turns into a blue saltwater lagoon in winter, suitable for paddling and swimming. There is a small taverna nearby. A couple of rocky beaches lie to the north of the lagoon in the remote and secluded coves at Marghisa and Biarama. Most visitors head south to the attractive sand and shingle beach at Apiossos on the tiny picturesque offshore islet reached along a narrow stone causeway. A small taverna opens in summer and facilities include sun loungers and watersports. The beach can get rather crowded with early arrivals bagging the best spots. Offshore is the larger, uninhabited islet of Droussa...

The Greek Island of Alonissos

Alonissos is one of the Islands of the Sporades chain that lie off mainland Greece's east coast. To get here you can fly to Skiathos then get the ferry to the Island. Alonissos has a tranquil atmosphere with lots of old-world Greek charm. Recently, signs of change are apparent as more visitors have discovered the Island. New accommodation has sprung up in the main resorts while a newly surfaced road offers easy access to even the remote beaches. Alonissos boasts some of the cleanest swimming in the Mediterranean Sea. The Island has very green, fertile and heavily wooded hills crossed by well-marked walking trails. There are regular daily ferries from Skiathos to Alonissos. Alonissos is rightly famous for its clean sea water, green landscape and beaches wrapped around by pine trees. The beaches are mostly stone, rock and shingle and many are difficult to reach down steep dirt tracks. The best are strung along the south-east coast with access off the Island's only paved road. Only a handful of these beaches have a substantial taverna or summer cantina. **Patitiri:** The Island's main port at Patitiri is little more than a cement quayside and a couple of streets running inland up the steep hillside. The harbour used to be lined with wine presses - 'patitiri' translates as wine press - and locals lived in the hillside village Chora above. But an earthquake wrecked the hilltop homes and disease destroyed the vines. Villagers left the Chora to live in hastily built cement houses in Patitiri and nearby Votsi. Flowers, vines and coats of paint brighten up the shops, cafes and tavernas that now line the harbour. Beyond the harbour is a narrow stretch of coarse sand. There are wooded hills on three sides and good swimming in the shallow, rock-strewn crystal clear clean seawater…

The Island of Alonissos:

Palia Alonissos (Chora): Chora, otherwise known as Palia Alonissos, is perched on the hilltop above Patitiri and approached either by road or a walking trail from the port, now paved, lit and signposted. Chora was the Island capital until the 1965 when an earthquake forced the villagers out, some forcibly. The derelict houses were then snapped up for holiday homes and now Chora is again abandoned for the winter. The village has narrow streets and fortified stone houses, originally built to withstand attack from pirates. At Chora's highest point a series of small squares host cafe bars and tavernas that open up for the summer season offering impressive views over the whole Island. An old windmill and some preserved threshing floors are more interesting for their views than their architecture. Chora sits on a hill at the southern end of the Island and several steep narrow tracks lead down in almost every direction to small beaches and coves below. The tracks can be difficult to find and the beaches are not always easy to find and some tracks are very steep. **Mourtias:** Has a delightful small quay at the northern end of a small cove of shingle and stone. Trees at the back offer some natural shade and there is good swimming in the sea among the rocks. A trio of tavernas offer plenty of refreshment. **Marpouenta:** Is the most popular of the beaches around Chora thanks to easy access. In the summer crowds cram the small coarse sand and shingle bay and early arrivals get the best spots. Flat rocks beyond at Plakes offer sunbathing and a camp site called Camping Rocks nearby has a small taverna and toilets. **Rousoum Gialos:** The steeply banked shingle and pebble beach has apartments and villas behind a low stone wall. Rocks at the southern end add interest and it has an attractive little harbour to the north. A trio of shady tavernas line the back of the beach which, being south facing, gets full sun for most of the day…

The Island of Alonissos:

Votsi: The tiny beach at Votsi has great visual appeal and is actually two small bays, it is the northerly one that wins the photographic prizes. A narrow stone and shingle beach that is under a towering cliff looking out over the sea so clear that boat shadows play on the sandy sea bottom far out into the bay. Access is down a short, but steep, rough track which is both narrow with a sheer cliff behind. **Chrysi Milia:** Fine sand makes a rare appearance at Chrysi Milia beach beyond the headland north of Votsi where pines trees line the seashore. The descent is down a long and winding track through pine woods which seems to be leading nowhere until it hits the shore. The flat beach has soft sand that gently slopes into a clear turquoise sea with rocky pools at the far end of the beach. The beach soon fills up though, even in the low season. **Kokkinokastro:** The bay at Kokkinokastro has an arresting red cliff promontory (it gives the beach its name). Access is via a narrow gully at the end of a steep goat track where winter rains carve deep ruts into the path. Nearby archaeological excavations have unearthed the site of ancient Ikos with evidence of the oldest known prehistoric habitation in the Aegean. The beach is long and the water shallow. Nearby is a pleasant pebble stretch at Tzortzi Gialos with shallow water and a beach cantina in the summer. **Leptos Gialos:** Leptos Yialos is a couple of bays north from Kokkinokastro. Access is down a steep track from the main road. The beach of white pebble enjoys a lovely setting, just a small south facing scoop of stone backed by pine trees that tumble right down to the shore to give plenty of shade. A couple of tavernas will stay open late for those who like to linger in the clear turquoise waters for a late swim. A few sun loungers are scattered along the shore and there are boats for hire from the shore…

The Island of Alonissos:

Steni Vala Port: The tiny fishing port of Steni Vala is little more than a quayside lined with tavernas, a shop and a bar however, the setting is idyllic. The approach from the south is spectacular with wide sea vistas and the nearby deserted Island of Peristera offshore. Taverna fare is above average thanks to the demands of visiting yacht flotillas but popularity has pushed up prices as well as the standards. The village is the headquarters of the Hellenic Society for the Protection of the Monk Seal and visitors may see seals recuperating in the small rescue centre at the end of the harbour wall. There are no beaches here but small bays lie hidden along the coast at Glyfada, Glifes and Tzortzi that can be reached on foot or by boat. A daily bus service runs from Patitiri in the high season and there is a camping site near the shore. **Agios Dimitrios:** The road hugs the coast north of Steni Vala through the Kalamakia area lined with rock and pebble beaches, some long and flat although none with any tourist facilities. The road rises and journeys along the cliff tops to provide panoramic views over the huge triangular white stone beach at Agios Dimitrios with the large islet of Peristera just offshore. Agios Dimitrios beach consists of two large beaches of white pebble either side of an attractive, beach cantina. Swimmers beware each beach has sharp and slippery stones that drop quickly into the sea that has stones on the sea bed for some distance from the shore. Sun loungers edge the south beach where a small jetty invites boats to tie up and the wide swathe of large white stones and pebbles seem to stretch to the horizon. The north beach is a little quieter, although neither beach could be said to be very busy…

The Greek Island of Andros

Andros Island is one of the most northern of the central Cyclades group of Greek holiday Islands and a popular choice for weekending Greeks as it's a short hop from the mainland and on a good ferry route. The Island of Andros has a character all of its own, if a little one-dimensional. Variety may not be the Island's long suit but it has plenty of good points. It has a popular tourist beach resort at Batsi, another less popular at the capital of Hora and the rest are very remote beaches scattered around the Islands coast. Hora is located on a spectacular finger of rock with the sea lapping the cliffs on both sides and the main street dotted with cafes, restaurants, shops and galleries. Natural springs give rise to lush green valleys nestled between majestic mountain peaks. The best of Andros Island's beaches can be spectacular but they are all relatively remote. An extensive network of donkey paths criss-cross the interior, making this an ideal destination for hikers. Although some paths can be choked with scrub and thorns, many are well maintained. Andros is easy to reach from mainland Greece as ferries leave Rafina every day and the Island of Andros is usually their first port of call. Andros is a long, thin Island just off the east coast of mainland Greece. Neatly divided by a mountain ridge there is the beach resort of Batsi to the west and the capital town of Hora in the east. Other beaches are dotted around this large Island and the bests beaches tend to be the remote ones…

The Island of Andros:

Batsi: The Island's main resort at Batsi is built on two hills overlooking a fine natural harbour with a splendid beach of soft, golden sand. Shady trees line the road behind with a clutch of hotels and tavernas opposite. Shallow water makes it safe for children and there is lots of shade at the northern end. At the southern end, the beach meets the harbour wall and a string of tavernas edge a small square. Yet more tavernas line a balcony above offering fine views over the bay. A family resort, Batsi has plenty of shops, bakeries, grocers, banks and a splendid outdoor cinema. The only drawback is that Batsi's popularity with weekending Greeks does tend to push up prices. Hillside alleyways create a maze of steep walks in pleasant shade where spring water often streams down deep gullies on either side of the path. Escape from busy weekend crowds is offered on the other side of the bay at the sandy strip of Fanormos, within easy walking distance, or by following tracks over the headland to some of the secluded coves beyond. **Agia Marina:** Just south of Batsi and within easy walking distance, is a trio of small beaches at Agia Marina. The nearest is a narrow nondescript strip of gravel and stone beneath vertical cliffs. Over the headland, and surrounded by a large hotel complex, is the best of the beaches, a narrow strip of sand and stone with a summer cantina beneath the cliff. Access is down very steep steps from the hotel and Agia Marina beach barely has room for half a dozen umbrellas so it can get quickly packed in the summer. The sea is strewn with rock slabs with deep water beyond, so it's not ideal for children. A small stream runs down to the sea at one end. The furthest beach of the three is a narrow, exposed strip of gravel and stone…

The Island of Andros:

Kiprianos: The coast road twists and turns north out of Batsi skirting a couple of small, sandy coves, best visited on foot as there is nowhere to park on the narrow highway. The attractive cove at Kiprianos is easily spotted because of the small blue and white chapel of Kyprianos which overlooks the tiny inlet of sand and stone. Close up, the chapel is little more than a cement block, like a garage with a bell tower, but it looks quite pretty sitting on a rock outcrop over the sea draped in lashings of blue and white paint. There is room here for a few cars to park and it's just a short scramble down the cliff to the small beach of stone and a little sand. **Psili Ammos:** The first decent stretch of sand north of Batsi is found at Psili Ammos, or Chrisi Ammos depending on which map is consulted. A long stretch of pure white sand with a few stones is backed by low dunes that provide shelter from the wind and relief from the noise of the main road nearby. A ramshackle beach bar puts out loungers in the summer and the beach gets a summer clean-up when duckboards are laid out between the rows of sunbeds. More facilities are offered at a couple of roadside tavernas - just a short walk north to the headland where another sandy strip at. Dunes bank up behind the beach here and sunbeds are laid out for tourists in the summer months. **Liopesi:** Just south of the main port of Gavrio are several small bays easily accessible from the main road that runs behind them. Most are little more than small rocky inlets with a few scruffy patches of gritty sand but they still make attractive spots for those who prefer a quiet getaway place to sunbathe? One of the more interesting inlets is at Liopesi which is blessed with a distinctive and much photographed rock formation. There are nearby coves to explore and the picturesque setting features heavily in many of the Island's tourist brochures…

The Island of Andros:

Agios Petros: North of Kypri is a long stretch of scruffy sand bisected by a small stream. The beach at Agios Petros, largely sand with a few stones, is a popular place in the high summer when beach bars open and sunbeds come out. The road runs close behind and there is good parking while hotels on the headland offer facilities for eating and drinking. **Gavrio Port:** The main Island port of Gavrio is a scruffy, ramshackle sort of place that holds little of interest other than its beautiful position. Swathes of concrete cover the dock and a large cement car park with bus and coach terminal does nothing to improve the scene. A dozen or so utilitarian cafes and tavernas line the road behind the quay, serving as waiting rooms for ferry passengers. The surrounding hills are very beautiful and good walking trails can be found in the area. **Beaches North of Gavrio:** Beyond Gavrio, and across the bay to the north, are a clutch of decent beaches that are well worth a visit, especially for visitors with their own transport and a decent enough map. The road leads around the bay to the small, but pleasant, beach at Charakas. Alternatively, the road over the headland ends at the splendid beach at Felos where tamarisks back onto a beautiful arc of golden sand. **Beaches East of Gavrio:** There are several remote beaches to the east of Gavrio but access can be difficult on the long and winding mountain roads. A turn inland from the road north out of Gavrio leads up into the mountains through the villages of Pano Felos and Frouesi before petering out into a rough track that drops gently to the coast along a river valley full of ancient Andros waterwheels. At the end of the track is the splendid white stone beach of Zorkos set inside a small horseshoe bay, quite exposed to the wind and with shade provided only by the surrounding steep cliffs…

The Island of Andros:

South Coast Beaches: The road from Stavopedra to Hora pretty well splits Andros Island in two. The main centre of interest is Hora which perches on a long and dramatic promontory. There are only a few beaches dotted around the coast. **Hora Town:** The Island capital of Andros Town, known locally as Hora, is like a white blanket thrown over a long, narrow 400 metre long promontory that ends at a small rock islet. On the islet are the ruins of a Venetian fortress connected to Hora by a picturesque, if precipitous, stone arch that was rebuilt in 1956 after the original was destroyed in a storm. Further out to sea is the Tourlitis lighthouse, impressive on its large rock. Hora is bisected by the long traffic-free street of Georgiou Empirikou, dotted with shops and cafes and small artists' studios. Three quarters of the way along the street is the main square with cafe tables set out around a fountain beneath the dappled shade of a huge plane tree. Hora boasts several large neoclassical buildings, evidence of the wealth of its former citizens. The Archaeological Museum was founded in 1981 and includes a statue of Hermes of Andros - a first century copy of the original discovered on the coast at Paleopoli. Most unusual is the Gouldandris family's Museum of Modern Art with works by Greek artists as well as eminent modern masters such as Picasso, Braque and Matisse. Nearby is the much photographed chapel of Agia Thakassini built on an offshore rock. In the town is a large plinth that has a large bronze statue on it dedicated to the Unknown Sailor, donated by Russia. Wealthy donors have also funded the Kairoa Library which has some 3,000 rare titles. To the south-west of town is the pretty village of Menites and its marble fountains with lion head spouts while at Apoika, to the north-west, is the Sariza spring where mineral water is bottled and exported throughout Greece. At nearby Stenies, popular with wealthy Greeks, is an attractive beach called Gialia, backed by eucalyptus trees and a very good fish taverna…

The Island of Andros:

Faneromeni Castle: The road south out of Hora eventually leads to Ormos Korthi but first passes the beautiful beach of Sineti with sharp white sand edging a small and attractive bay. This is the start of a nature trail that leads down the long narrow valley of Dipotamata and takes in 22 of the Island's famous watermills. Most are now ruined heaps of rubble but the trail leads over stone bridges and through some delightful scenery. Limestone outcrops above the village of Kochlou are topped by the ruins of Faneromeni Castle. A dirt track leads out of the village up to the former fortress, now little more than a heap of stones. Many structures that were once underground are now visible after the roof collapsed. Along the valley trails are many fine houses, several dovecotes, a pretty church and some wonderful views. The road winds down to Kocklou, one of the prettiest villages on Andros. On the opposite valley slope is a road leading to the village of Mesa Vouni and a track to the monastery at Panachrantou.

Ormos Korthi: The village of Ormos Korthi, or simply Ormos, is the main town in southern Andros and it lies along the edge of a huge wide bay with splendid hills rising all around. The road follows the curve of the bay and a paved esplanade is edged with a concrete sea wall. Over the wall a line of rocks have been put in the sea to act as a breakwater. At the far end of the esplanade a succession of concrete wharfs providing shelter for boats. Ormos has a good folk museum which holds exhibitions in the summer as well as staging performances of traditional music and dancing…

The Island of Andros:

Grias Pidima: Just north of Ormos Korthi are a trio of small beaches. Signs in Ormos point to the best at Grias Pidima. The first beach is Milos, a favourite of windsurfers, then Vidsi which has a small, nondescript shingle beach. Finally comes Grias Pidima, or Old Lady's Leap, where a singular stone column stands tall in the sea. Legend has it that a pregnant woman was persuaded by besieging Turks to open the gates to Faneromi Castle. Amid the slaughter that followed the guilt-stricken woman threw herself from the cliff and the pillar of stone is the result. **Aidonia:** There are many fine houses to admire as well as many dovecotes and chapels in the village. The village of Aidonia has a beautiful fountain with a vaulted roof and some flamboyant marble decoration. At Moskionas there is a delightful church and at Agia Triada a complex of ancient stone houses, built in the traditional Island style. The road rises up into the hills at Apatia where small villages like Megalo Chorio, Morakes and Tzeo offer some pretty scenery. This is one of the best places to view the terraced fields that ripple down the hillsides almost everywhere. Along the valley floor are some abandoned windmills and above Tzeo is one of the best examples of a dovecote on the Island…

The Greek Island of Corfu

A holiday favourite since Victorian times Corfu has its own airport and is located in the Ionian Islands that lie off the north-west coast of mainland Greece. This was one of the first of the Greek Islands to be "discovered" by holiday firms and many of the Island's beach resorts have embraced the demands of the package tour operators. The Island of Corfu is blessed with many beautiful bays of golden sand and pretty fishing villages that have been somewhat unfortunately been overrun with hotels and happy-hour karaoke bars however, there are still some of the loveliest beaches and most romantic villages in the Greek Islands to be found here. The most popular holiday hotspots are concentrated in the resorts that surround Corfu Town and along the Island's north coast. Visitors looking for more sedate resorts will find them all around the long coastline away from the main town while many villages deep within the Island's lush, green interior, have escaped the holiday hotel boom altogether. Whatever holiday you prefer there are plenty of beautiful resorts on the Island. Corfu is also a popular destination for independent travellers and there are plenty of accommodation available everywhere on the Island. One of the most popular beach holiday Islands in Greece, Corfu is pretty much awash with good beaches. Strangely, some of the most popular are not the best. Dassia and Ypsos, for example, are major holiday favourites despite having relatively poor beaches, although they do benefit from being near Corfu Town. Big sand beaches make their mark on the north coast, notably at the resorts of Roda and Sidari. West coast beaches are quieter but further apart and the further south you go, the wilder they get. The east coast has a clutch of resorts with Kavos a favourite with teenagers…

The Island of Corfu:

Corfu Town: Kerkyra, or Corfu Town, is as pleasant a provincial town as you will find anywhere in Greece. Venetians, French and British have all had a hand in developing Corfu Town and the results are both impressive and attractive, especially since public buildings were given a major clean-up in 1994. This is a large town of 40,000 inhabitants that is dominated by two forts. The 13th century Neo Frourio (New Fort), with its dungeons and impressive turret battlements, is far more interesting than the older 6th century Paleo Frourio (Old Fort). The focal point of Corfu Town is the Spianada, a public square and park which is one of the biggest in Europe. In the square evening crowds can take a pleasant stroll as children play happily on the grass central area which bizarrely was once an English cricket field where matches are still played even today. North of Corfu Town square is the French-designed Liston arcade, built to resemble the rue de Rivoli in Paris and is today packed with elegant cafes and restaurants. It is a pleasant place for a stroll but expect to pay top prices in this tourist hotspot. The food can be somewhat bland and the service may be brusque at times. Nearby is the Georgian Palace of St Michael and St George which houses the wonderful Museum of Asiatic Art, one of the largest and best collections in the world. In fact Corfu Town is known for its many museums of quite weird collections. The Ionian Bank houses a Museum of Banknotes and you can even find a Serbian War Museum (the Balkan Wars of 1915-1917, not the more recent one). The Byzantium Museum is housed in a restored 15th century church and the Solomos Museum is dedicated to the Island's poet. Also of note is the impressive St. Spiridon's Church, home to the long preserved bones of Corfu Island's patron saint. Corfu Town is a real gem and worthy of a full days visit. Now it is time to visit the resorts on the rest of the Island of Corfu...

The Island of Corfu:

Kontokali: The dreary highway that threads north from Corfu Town through a commercial wasteland eventually leads to the marina and ferry port of Gouvia and is not the best introduction to the Island of Corfu. But just before Gouvia, and almost merged into it, is the busy resort of Kontokali which defies its cement-paved surroundings to offer some subdued nightlife, several good tavernas and fine views over the Bay of Gouvia. Kontokali village has several shops, restaurants and the remains of a castle. The narrow village streets lead down to a couple of sand and pebble beaches. The beaches have shallow water between a couple of groins and a watersports area is cordoned off to prevent accidents. The beach to the north of Kontokali is smaller and gets greater use from the locals. Further north along the coast are the ruins of an ancient Venetian shipyard. **Gouvia:** Massively developed with tourist hotels, the resort of Gouvia, about 8 km north of Corfu Town, boasts a huge yacht marina that overlooks the spectacular Komeno Bay. Gouvia is and remains one of the most popular holiday destinations on Corfu Island although it is sometimes difficult to see why. Set among olive groves and pine forest, Gouvia with its marina makes for an impressive sight that hides what is a fairly dull resort. Despite a good selection of bars and restaurants and a lively night atmosphere there is not much else or do during the day but to head off somewhere else. The beach is a bedraggled strip of pebble hidden under sunbeds, the drop into the sea is steep and so it's not a great beach for families. The waste outlet pipes into the sea don't add much ambiance to the seashore either. Lots of souvenir shops are concentrated along the short, narrow street that is Gouvia centre. The impressive Corfu Shell Museum has an outstanding collection but it is precariously positioned on a busy highway. Gouvia is on the main local bus route which enables visitors to explore other northern sandy beach resorts…

The Island of Corfu:

Cape Komeno: Curving around the bay from Gouvia is the once picturesque promontory of Cape Komeno. Now dominated by a large hotel and bungalow complex. The cape has little to please the eye these days unless you are a sucker for luxury hotel life. Visitors looking for a base to explore the north-east of the Island will find Komeno well sited to do this. The promontory is little more than scrub and rock but there are splendid views over the bay to Corfu Town, to the yacht marina in Gouvia to the south, whilst to the north is the Gulf of Dassia and the holiday resorts of Dassia and Ipsos. The hotel complex has sea on both sides and there are many small inlets and bays for sunbathing. Most beach coves are shingle and stone but come with changing cabins and showers. **Dassia:** The resort of Dassia, also spelt Dasia, has a large cluster of bars, restaurants and shops on either side of a very busy main road. Hotels line one side of the road and apartments the other but with the constant heavy traffic making it a nightmare to cross. A network of footpaths lead down to Dassia beach which is a long strip of stone and sharp shingle with just a little sand, about 200 metres long and 30 meters deep with the shallow waters backed by dramatic pine and olive topped cliffs. A long cement path runs down the back of the beach but there are no showers or toilets provided. At the southern end is a small bay with a ruined Venetian boatyard, but it's a bit of a scramble to get there to see it. Dassia resort proper has a wide range of restaurants and bars, although it's mostly uninspired tourist fare. Many shops are given over to selling souvenir trinkets but the locals are well known throughout the rest of Corfu Island for their friendliness. Surprisingly, Dassia has little night-life despite the high tourist numbers, so visitors often go to nearby Ipsos for more clubbing action. Ipsos is about 15 minutes on foot with fine sea views all the way…

The Island of Corfu:

Ipsos: Ipsos, or Ypsos, is a firm favourite with British package tour operators as Ipsos boasts wall-to-wall burger outlets and karaoke bars. The beach is a narrow, long strip of shingle and sand backed by a very busy road. There are watersports galore from the beach with jetties every 50 yards or so. Showers and toilets are available and there is lighting along the main Ipsos road where families must run a gauntlet of traffic to reach the tavernas and cafes across the road opposite the beach. Ipsos is not an Ibiza or Faliraki so the nightclubs generally close by around 4 am. The tavernas sell basic, low-priced meals and bars boast giant TVs, all-day English breakfast, pool tables and have noisy gaming machines. Stay in Ipsos and if you want more than just a tan and a hangover you may be disappointed. If it's cheap, cheerful and noisy you're after then Ipsos could be just right for you. The neighbouring resort at Pyrgi is just an extension of Ipsos; a little less hectic, a bit cheaper and they even have Greek food on the menu now and then. You will; find a stark contrast in the hills close by where the lovely village of Agios Markos is a step back in time and a step up in quality. **Barbati:** The long, straight and narrow kilometre of white pebble beach at Barbati is set away from the main road in a fine bay cloaked in pines. Barbati beach is relatively quiet until boat loads of day trippers arrive from Kerkyra and Ipsos. There are showers and toilets at the back of the beach alongside tavernas, cantinas and beach bars. There is plenty of parking close to the beach. The water is shallow on the east-facing beach but it does drop off steeply just a little way out to sea. On the beach rocks at both ends provide interest and there are sunbeds and watersports as available. Barbati village is set on the steep hillside between the main road and the beach with terrific views over the bay and has plenty of shops. The night-life is low key but Corfu Town is only 20 minutes away on the local buses. There is no taxi rank here but locals will be happy to phone one for you…

The Island of Corfu:

Nissaki and Krouzari: The shingle and stone beach at Nissaki is very pretty, sitting in a horseshoe bay with a taverna at one end. Nissaki is Greek for 'islet' and so it once was before quarrying joined the islet to the shore and created the beach. Do not confuse this beach with nearby Krouzari beach, which is much bigger. Nissaki beach is ideal for those who like it quiet, enjoy lovely views and want little more from a holiday than a taverna, beach, sea and a sunbed to relax on. The resort is noted for its excellent tavernas, three close to the beach and two in the village itself. There is also a cafe and a mini-market. The neighbouring beach at Krouzari is a long strip of steep sloping shingle. There are showers, changing rooms and toilets and the trees behind the beach provide natural shade. There are also the usual sunbeds and watersports you would expect on a developed beach. **Kaminaki:** Visitors to Kaminaki are greeted by a delightful, romantic bay of shingle and sand in an idyllic setting enclosed by olive groves and well sheltered from the wind. The beach has sunbeds, a shower but no toilets. There is a beach taverna and another taverna on the cliffs above. A mini market provides basic village shopping. It is a steep drive down the hill from the village to Kaminaki beach where there is limited parking available. Kaminaki is a good place to chill and relax in. **Agni:** Agni is found at the end of a very steep and twisting lane off the main coast road north-west of Corfu Town. It is a small bay of pebbles with the odd patch of sand. Three tavernas open in the summer, all with views across the sea to Albania. Jetties have been built to accommodate the boats that regularly pull in here. Agni beach shelves deeply and the sharp underwater rocks make this an unsuitable beach for children. Apart from the tavernas the resort has no facilities. Agni has a beautiful and peaceful setting with a relaxing atmosphere…

The Island of Corfu:

Kalami: The beautiful bay at Kalami has a long beach of white shingle with sunbeds and showers and toilets provided. The resort has strong literary connection with the Durrell's (Lawrence and Gerald). Once a quiet retreat, Kalami is now home to one of the biggest self-catering complexes on the Island of Corfu. It sprawls up the hillside, although expertly planted wisteria hides most of it. The beach is of stone and pebble and Albania sits just two kilometres offshore. On the headland towards Kouloura there are sheltered coves with flat rocks for sunbathing, but they can only be reached by boat. Kalami village itself has mini-markets, shops and a couple of tavernas. **Kouloura:** Around the headland from Kalami is the pretty fishing village of Kouloura. The beach is just a narrow strip of sand and shingle under the cliffs opposite the harbour. Kouloura enjoys a beautiful setting that oozes peace and tranquillity. The local rocky coves offer great snorkelling and sunbathing opportunities. Much visited by boats, the bay can get dirty with fuel on the sea in the summer and sea urchins are a problem for people walking bear foot on the rocks. As there are no watersports, no bars, no clubs, one taverna and the nearest shop is a 20 minute walk to Kalami this resorts is heaven on earth some would say. **Kerasia:** The 300 metre sweep of shingle at Kerasia is in a beautiful spot and ideal for those wishing to escape the crowds. Surrounded by olive and pine trees the beach is flat and the water shallow, although it dips sharply after a few metres. Kerasia has a single beach taverna and a small shop but not much else, although sunbeds are for hire and there is plenty of parking. Prince Charles is an occasional guest of the Rothschilds, who have a large estate nearby but you are unlikely to find yourself sharing the beach with royalty…

The Island of Corfu:

Agios Stefanos: Agios Stefanos is a lovely, isolated and secluded cove with a small, but attractive, pebble beach, not to be mistaken for the resort of the same name on the north-west coast. There are four tavernas on the beach and two more in the village. There is also a mini-market and a few gift shops in the village. An upmarket resort of luxury villas that dot the surrounding hills come tagged with very exclusive prices. The beach is a prime target for day-trip boats, Agios Stefanos can get busy very quickly. Sunbeds line the beach but the shingle drops very steeply into a deep sea, so it's not very suitable for children. Neighbouring coves include the pretty Kerasia beach and horse riding is on offer at the nearby Emeritus Nature Reserve. The narrow, winding road down to the beach is steep and difficult, not least because of the repeated urge to stop and take photos all the way down. **North Coast Beaches:** The north has the best and the worst of the Islands landscape. The first 10 km or so out of Corfu town the landscape has a sprawl of hotels and apartments relieved only by occasional vegetation. Further north and the highway peters out and the scene changes dramatically. You are greeted by an impressive rocky coastline which is backed by the greenest of hills and a more typically Greek atmosphere that has small pebble coves and dazzling turquoise waters all around. **Avlaki:** The long and splendid bay of Avlaki often gets missed by visitors thanks to its better-known neighbour Kassiopi and some poorly signposted roads. The narrow 800 metre-long beach is mostly shingle with sunbeds, boardwalks and a shallow sea for a few metres before dropping off sharply. Avlaki is very quiet, but with more lively resorts only a short walk away. Visitors can also opt for a boat trip to Kerkyra. There are canoes for hire and a sailing school, a couple of tavernas and a bar but no shops. A couple of small coves of rock and shingle lie beyond the headlands at either end of Avlaki beach…

The Island of Corfu:

Kassiopi: The small but busy seaside resort of Kassiopi has traditional tavernas and relaxed friendly locals. The resort has a pretty waterfront but much of the village is thick with souvenir shops while a quartet of mini-markets meet the visitor's basic shopping needs. Four beaches can be reached along footpaths around the headland. The main Kassiopi beach is pebble and has showers and toilets. The other beaches have no facilities and better beaches can be found south at Avlaki and Koyevinas which are about 20 minutes drive. Boats trips leave daily from the harbour for Corfu Town and to other sandy beaches along the coast. There are castle ruins overlooking the harbour. **Agios Spiridon:** This was a tiny, peaceful bay until a hotel complex was built. The sandy beach is set in a small bay with rocks on either side. A longer and better beach lies about 500 metres west. The shoreline on both beaches is shallow with rock pools to add interest and with sunbeds, showers, toilets, changing rooms and a cantina that opens in the summer is ideal for families. Agios Spiridon village has a couple of mini-markets, a tourist shop and three good tavernas. A nearby lagoon is home to the showy sea daffodil but please do not pick any as they are now very rare in Greece. **Almyros:** East of the protected wetlands of Antinioti, where birds nest in the wide lagoon, is the huge sandy beach of Almyros. The western end of the seven-kilometre long sandy beach is quiet with dunes and shallow water while the east has the hotels, tavernas and restaurants. The beach is ideal for families and has beach sports and windsurfing. There are more pebbles in the centre of the beach which also has a sharp drop into the sea. In places the beach is mainly wide but there are also areas where there is just room for a single line of loungers. Almyros is a good spot for visitors who like the combination of lively and quiet. Escape the crowds by walking west. There are also good sea views across to the Albanian hills…

The Island of Corfu:

Acharavi: The approach to Acharavi not very appealing however, first impressions can be deceptive. The village itself is tucked away from the main road, a quiet crescent of traditional tavernas and cafes behind the western end of Almiros beach. The beach is sand and pebble and shelves gently into the sea. It's a clear favourite with families although stones lie underfoot so it's wise to have footwear for children and adults alike. The village offer a wide range of facilities including doctors, bank, post office and mini-markets. In the hills behind the village walkers can get onto the Corfu Trail and other excellent walking paths that lead up to Mt Pantokrator. There are some remains of a Roman baths nearby. A good water park (Hydropolis) is 10 minutes walk away. **Roda:** Roda is a small, pretty village with a large number of bars, restaurants and small shops. It is about three hour drive from Corfu Airport mostly along twisting roads. It looks very much like an English seaside town with karaoke and bingo on offer in scores of British-theme pubs, many run by ex-pats. Access to Roda beach is down steps from the main road where there is limited parking. The beach is sandy with pebbles at the eastern end with shallow water that is ideal for children. Roda has made recent improvements by planting some palm trees and adding seafront benches and regular daily cleaning of the beach. Peace and quite Roda is not but a midnight noise restriction helps mitigate the nightly music volume but the main Sidari road is still very busy 24 hours-a-day…

The Island of Corfu:

Sidari: The big guns of the British package holiday firms have used Sidari as a destination for many years and the once pretty village square is now overdeveloped in a hectic maze of happy hour bars, Brit-style pubs and trinket shops. Sidari has three beaches. The first and least popular is near the old fishing harbour to the east. The central beach is a long sweep of sand with a vast array of watersports. To the west is the famous Canal d'Amour area, where sandstone cliffs are eroded into spectacular formations and where the small sandy coves are as attractive as they are usually overcrowded. The resort's main street is narrow and busy. The restaurants and bars that fringe it offer a diet of bingo, TV football and chips. Sidari is much like a Greek Blackpool. Sidari nightlife is cheap and cheerful too, and enlivened by endless karaoke bars. The Sidari area is notorious for mosquitoes so do not forget the insect spray. **Peraloudes:** Peraloudes is a handsome village of traditional tavernas and cafes providing access to very quiet beaches and some lovely walks. The main Peroulades beach is just a narrow strip of sand below vertical cliffs that require a perilous descent down scores of winding cement steps. The taverna above Peroulades beach offers stunning sunset views and gives the place its alternative name of Sunset Beach. **West Coast Beaches:** From rocky cliffs to long sandy beaches, the west coast has more to offer those looking to get away from the crowds on Corfu. There is less tourism in the west as it is in the east and south of the Island. It still has its low points but they are far less widespread. As the high mountains give way to farmland, and Corfu Town gets nearer, the landscape becomes less interesting but going in the other direction and away from the crowds visitors are rewarded by some of the most beautiful landscape and some of the best beaches to be found on the Island of Corfu…

The Island of Corfu:

San Stafanos: The low-key resort of Agios Stefanos is also called San Stafanos to distinguish it from the village of Agios Stefanos on the north-east coast. Gentle hills roll down to a 500 metre flat and sandy beach that has remained fairly quiet even in the high summer season. Shallow water and gently sloping sands make San Stefanos a favourite for families and there are sunbeds on the beach which, at 70 metres deep, is big by Corfu standards. This is an ideal bucket and spade beach. Agios Stefanos resort beach has some watersports and a children's play area. Tucked away from the main traffic routes and only approached along narrow lanes the resort tends to be quieter than most. It has some good tavernas and small family hotels as well as the usual selection of shops and bars. Some outstanding scenery is on offer for hill walkers in this part of Corfu. **Arillas:** Arillas beach is flat and sandy and with very shallow water, so it's great for families and it is backed by low rolling hills, except at the southern end where high cliffs loom. Beyond a rock outcrop at the northern end is an unofficial naturist sandy beach in a sheltered cove. Walks along the headland from Agios Stefanos to the beach Arilas, or Arillas, are popular, with fine views and splendid sunsets to enjoy. The islet of Gravia is just offshore and is reachable by swimmers of a good standard. Sunbeds, watersports, boats for hire and a water taxi to other resorts along the coast are all on offer on the beach. The resort has a wide selection of mini-markets and a few shops selling souvenirs. Cafes and tavernas line the long promenade…

The Island of Corfu:

Agios Georgios: Agios Georgios is a sprawling resort at the mouth of a wide wooded valley. Not to be confused with Agios Georgios to the south. The long and gently sloping beach is one of the best on Corfu and is therefore a popular destination for young families. The beach is very long at 1.4 kilometres and also wide at 140 metres with families with children in the centre of the beach and the naturists to the north with a few enjoying the narrow and less crowded south end of the beach. There is a river running through the main resort where there is also the usual supermarkets, tavernas and bars. In the village mountain bikes can be hired and there is even a small bowling alley. Afionas village is on the headland which has spectacular views over the bay and the 13th century fortress of Angelkastro is only a 30 minute car ride away. **Paleokastritsa:** Paleokastritsa is a firm favourite with British holidaymakers. Couched in lush countryside, it is one of the most scenic resorts on the Corfu. It is also very hilly and the lack of footpaths can make walking quite dangerous, especially at night. The resort is spread over three large bays and they are big enough to accommodate all of the resorts visitors. The main beach is a narrow horseshoe crescent of shingle backed by a large hotel and car park. The water is deep but sunbeds are plentiful with showers and toilets also available. Boat trips leave regularly to go to the many nearby caves, grottos and small beaches. The usual tourist watersports are also on offer including scuba diving. The other two bays - a smaller but sandier one to the north and another sandy strip around the headland are serviced by boat taxis and take the overspill from the main beach. The resorts tavernas are notoriously expensive and there are a few music bars on the edge of the resort. Overlooking the bay is a 13th century monastery. The monastery has some impressive icons, a carved wooden ceiling and even a bizarre sea monster. The paved gardens have remarkable sea views but there are even better views at nearby Lakones and the villages beyond…

The Island of Corfu:

Liapades: Liapades, or Liapathes, is a picturesque resort set in a sheltered bay, dominated by a large hotel complex. The beach at Liapades is mostly soft sand with a few stones and the waters are very shallow, ideal for children. Large rocks either side of the bay add interest and there is parking close to the beach. The village is about a kilometre inland from the beach, but still worth a visit. It's a typical Greek village of narrow streets and whitewashed homes and has some good tavernas. **Ermones:** Ermones is a small 300 metre cove surrounded by steep hills that are covered with hotels and apartment blocks. German tour operators dominate here. It is a steep descent to the beach and the Ermones Beach Hotel boasts a small funicular railway to ferry the guests down the almost vertical cliffs. The beach is sand and shingle, clean but is divided by the river Ropa that cuts its way over the beach to the shore. The beach shelves gently, so it's safe for children, and rocks invite exploration at either end. Sunbeds, toilets and showers are available on the beach with parking available high above the beach that is then reached via some very steep steps that could be difficult to negotiate for some visitors. On the beach there is windsurfing and boat hire on offer. The beach has three tavernas and three more on the high ground above. The hotel discos provides the only entertainment in the evening and for shopping there is just one mini-market. This beach is great for a bucket and spade holiday where children can play and swim safely and parents can rest easy…

The Island of Corfu:

Mrytiotissa: Author Lawrence Durrell once described the tiny sands at Myrtiotissa as "perhaps the loveliest beach in the world" which is going it a bit. The beach is relatively difficult to reach requiring a scramble down the cliff face from the village at Vatos, the narrow but pretty stretch of sand has some mighty boulders scattered around and is overlooked by scrub covered cliffs. Once this beach was a well-kept secret, the beach is now regularly invaded by day-trip boats and gets seriously crowded in the high summer months. Even today, the beach still has great charm, despite the crowds, although it is best enjoyed at the end of the day when the boat trippers have all left. Mrytiotissa beach is still quiet enough to be a favourite haunt of nudists, but these have tailed off as the beach has grown in popularity. The beach cantina is noted for its excellent snacks. **Glyfada:** Reached down a steep, winding road, Glyfada has a one kilometre beach of golden sand that shelves gently to the sea and is very popular with families. There are the usual sunbeds and watersports provided on the beach. Glyfada beach is hugely popular, especially with Italians, and it can get very crowded in the high season. The small car park that sits nearby can soon reach full capacity and finding a place to park can be difficult later in the day. Families with young children need to be mindful that although the waters are shallow at first they deepen sharply the further out you go and the sea is notorious for having strong currents at the northern end, with warning flags for swimmers. Facilities like showers and toilets and a beach taverna are available along with all the watersports you expect on a big popular beach. On the headland is a large rock formation that is a popular spot for diving displays by the young Italian visitors…

The Island of Corfu:

Pelekas: The hilltop village of Pelekas sits on the west coast, south of Glyfada and almost opposite Kerkyra, around 15 km from the capital Corfu Town. The beach, also called Kontogialos, lies below the village and it is a 10 minute walk down the hill to a wide crescent of sand with its sunbeds, showers and toilets. There are four tavernas and a hotel behind the beach as well as boat rental and a variety of watersports on offer off the beach. The fishing harbour to the south adds interest and the beach of Yaliskari is just around the headland which has amazing rock formations. Pelekas village itself has an authentic Greek character and is noted for the lovely views of the sunsets over the sea. On top of the hill is the Kaiser's Throne, a lookout tower built on an outcrop of rock that was a favourite viewing spot of Kaiser Wilhelm II of the sunsets. **South Coast Beaches:** The Island of Corfu southerly beach resorts are found below a line drawn from Kerkyra in the east to Pelekas in the west. The eastern side of the long peninsula was the first to attract package holiday companies. By way of contrast the western coast is both wild and uninhabited, yet still wildly popular, mostly among the Greeks themselves. **Agios Gordios:** The resort at Agios Gordios is noted for its 600 metre long sandy beach and for having a relaxed atmosphere. The soft sand and shallow water is ideal for families and children. Empty coves can be found north and south and attract naturists. Some interesting beach rocks at the southern end with the Ortholithi, the trademark standing rock in the sea. The main Agios Gordios beach can get quite busy and there are beach tavernas and watersports on offer. A single road leads inland lined with tavernas, shops and mini-markets. Parking can be a problem as the narrow road dead ends at the beach and has little room for turning a car. The bus to Corfu Town runs five times a day in the summer season and is reliable enough for a day out. The small, protected, sandy beach of Yaliskari lies to the north. Pine trees sweep down to the water and a couple of cantinas provide good food and drinks…

The Island of Corfu:

Paramona: About six kilometres south of Agios Gordios is the beautiful beach of Paramona that sits below the village at Agios Mathaois. It is only a small and narrow strip of sand but it is in an idyllic setting. Paramona has developed as a small resort in recent years with holiday hotels, apartments and some beach tavernas being provided. There is some parking on the road and there are sunbeds and showers provided on the beach. There are some more remote beaches that lie further south at Prasoudi and Skidi but these require a 30 minute walk through olive groves to get to. Prasoudi beach has become popular in recent years because it is blessed with fine golden sand and a couple of beach cantinas which are noted for their seafood. The standing rocks that are offshore add interest with parking at the taverna, although it is then a steep scramble down to the sands. **Lake Kossison:** South of Paramona the hills are left behind and becomes flat and open when you reach the ruined Byzantine fortress of Gardiki which overlooks the salt water lagoon at Limni Korissa or Lake Kossison as it is also known. The lagoon is now a nature reserve and is home to turtles, lizards and migrating birds. The lake and nearby seashore that has wide, soft sand that run for miles. The lake and sea are separated by a narrow strip of dunes and a rough road. The Kossison Lake was created by the Venetians who flooded the marshy plain with sea water so they could, after evaporation had taken place harvest the remaining sea salt, a much sought after commodity in Venetian times. Today, this is a wild and unspoiled area with few visitors, although a mobile cantina springs up in the summer to serve basic snacks and drinks near the Gardiki end of the beach…

The Island of Corfu:

Agios Georgios (St George): Agios Georgios is more often called St George to distinguish it from its namesake in the north. This is a popular beach resort. The north end of the long beach is called Issos beach and it's overseen by a large hotel complex. The south end is known as Golden Beach which merges into a string of sandy stretches variously known as Maltas or Marathias and Santa Barbara. Agios Georgios itself has plenty of popular tourist attractions such as tavernas and bars, karaoke, wide screen TVs, beach sports, doughnut sellers and souvenir stands. Paragliding and jet skis are popular at this long and straggling resort that has become a firm favourite with British holidaymakers. A walk to the inland village of Argirades will reward you with astonishing views, some lovely cafes and a taste of the traditional Corfu village lifestyle. **Kavos:** The Kavos resort is a single busy street with no pavement but with scores of music bars, dance clubs and karaoke cafes that are very noisy from 11.30 pm to sunrise. Club and bar touts are the usual problem as they try to forcibly drag you in. Visitors complain that drinks are watered down. Unfortunately food in Kavos is almost exclusively pizzas, burgers, kebab and chips. Theft is common and walking at night is dangerous on the narrow road as half-wit boys outgun each other on quad bikes. Some may say that it all makes for a very exciting atmosphere on the narrow Kavos drag as youngsters spill out of the bars to dance in the street. The beach at Kavos is notoriously poor, covered in rotting seaweed, beer cans and other less savoury items left by the drunken night clubbers. Boat trips are a way to escape Kavos and those to Parga, Paxos and Blue Lagoon are well worth taking if this resort is where you are staying! Do not consider going to Kavos out-of-season as the place shuts like a clam when the teenagers leave…

The Island of Corfu:

Lefkimi: The lovely village at Lefkimi is well off the beaten track and is a step back in time. Donkeys are still used as transport and you may even spot the odd Greek in traditional costume. Lefkimi village has two striking churches, Agios Theodoros is found in the main square and the distinctive orange dome of Agios Arsenos can be seen for miles around. Some ancient Venetian salt pans are nearby. The village has a long harbour serviced by a river and boat trips visit regularly. Small beaches and fishing harbours can be found at nearby Petriti and Boukari. **Moraitika and Messonghi:** The resort at Moraitika has now virtually merged with neighbouring Messonghi is about 30 km south of Corfu Town. The shingle and sand beach is always busy with the massive Messonghi Beach Hotel nearby. The resort at Messonghi, once a quiet backwater village, has been swallowed up by its neighbour and is now considered to be the more peaceful end of the resort as it is off the main road so it tends to be quieter. The beach is long and sandy but it has more shingle and pebble than its neighbour. There are sunbeds and showers on the beach with several beach-side tavernas. There is a large mini-market in the centre of the village and several small tourist shops. Visits to the nearby hillside village of Khlomos are popular. Visitors can also head up one of the steep lanes to the un-spoilt village of Ano Moraitika where whitewashed houses are covered in flowers and visitors can enjoy some excellent food and wine in the village tavernas…

The Island of Corfu:

Agios Ioannis: Agios Ioannis is a tourist resort that sits on the east coast about half way between Messonghi and Benitses. This is one of the most attractive areas of the Island and has plenty of amenities. Agios Ioannis beach is relatively small, about 200 metres long, mostly shingle but with some good sandy areas and with a quay at the southern end. Its shallow seawater makes it good for families and children. A small parade of tavernas and bars, some shops, a mini-market are built along the back of the beach. Plenty of hotels have sprung up too and many of them have commandeered sections of beach. Watersports are available and a bus service goes to Moraitika and Benitses if you fancy a change of scenery. Agios Ioannis is just beyond a road tunnel 5 km past Benitses. **Benitses:** Benitses was once the favourite haunt of the cheap holidaymaker but it is slowly reverting to a more grown-up way of life. The resort at Benitses is about a kilometre long, strung along the east coast about 12 km south of Corfu Town. The southern end still clings precariously to its ignominious past with a string of brash music bars and cheap tavernas. Benitses old town has much charm and the houses are fairly drowning in cascades of beautiful flowers. Most of the beach at Benitses is pebble and shingle with a very steep drop into the sea so it is not great for families with children. There are the usual sunbeds and plenty of watersports such as paragliding, water skiing and pedaloes as well as small sea jetties that are good for diving off. Many tavernas at the harbour end of Benitses have improved so much in recent years that they are now even frequented by the locals. Benitses can make a good choice for those seeking a good Island base with lively nightlife and plenty of late-night bars…

The Greek Island of Crete

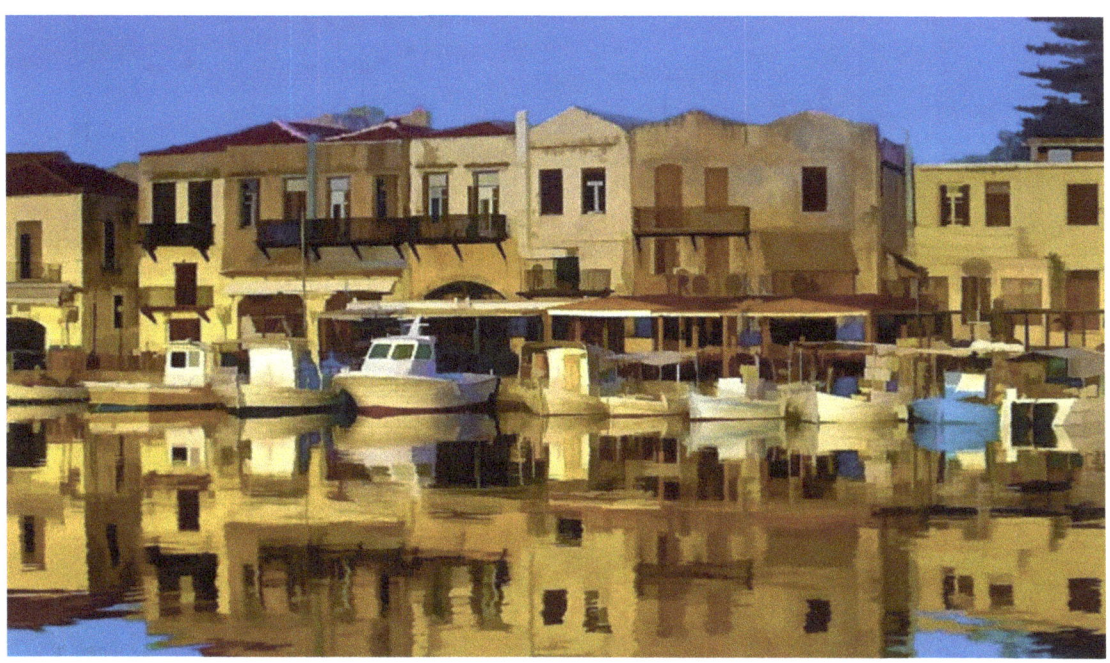

The holiday Island of Crete, or Kriti has two things that distinguish it from most other Greek Islands which are its magnificent mountains and a remarkably rich culture and history. Crete is the fifth largest Island in the Mediterranean, with a population that is mainly confined to the north coast by the huge mountain ranges that make up the backbone of this long, slender Island. Most of eastern Crete is busy with tourism but the west of the Island has magnificent mountains, the more rugged coastline and the less crowded beaches. Crete has an international airport. The long hot summers and the warm, mild winters ensure that Crete attract visitors throughout the year. Those heading inland will find monumental mountains, an abundant archaeological heritage, spirited social history and some spine-tingling scenery. Those looking for a Greek beach holiday will find that beaches vary from quiet, deserted coves with a single beach cantina to long swathes of golden sand packed with sunbeds and every kind of tourist facility. In short a holiday on the Island of Crete has just about everything for everyone, while the locals have a well justified reputation for their friendliness. The beaches of Crete are strung like washing along the north and south coasts with a mountain range between. The northern beaches are the more popular, served by a major highway that runs the full length of Crete. The far west beaches are more remote and spectacular while those over the mountains to the south are quiet and peaceful…

The Island of Crete:

Rethymnon: Crete's third largest city Rethymnon, about 60 kilometres from Chania, has the usual urban sprawl but what a difference is found in the heart of the city with its aristocratic air of arched doorways, crumbling balconies and faded facades. Charming Venetian buildings nestle next to the slender minarets of Turkish mosques and almost every street has an abundance of cafes and restaurants intermingled with craft and antique shops. The most picturesque part of Rethymnon is the old Venetian harbour where romantic, if pricey, taverna tables line the quay and the Venetian lighthouse stands sentinel on the long harbour wall. The beach lies to the east, a large flat triangle of palm fringed packed sand backed by hotels, shops and cafes. The sea is generally calm and shallow. The Fortezza is the jewel in Rethymnon's crown. The largest fort ever built by the Venetians is an impressive sight and at the main entrance there is a good archaeology museum where exhibits include helmets, bronze axes, and coins along with many finds from Minoan tombs. Other notable city sites include the Arimondi fountain, built in 1623, and the slender Nerantzes Djani minaret attached to a former Venetian church and visible from almost anywhere in the city. Nightlife in Rethymnon can be fairly lively but there are plenty of waterfront tavernas for a quiet, romantic meal. By day there is a 'pirate ship' cruises to see dolphins, caves and offshore islets. Rethymnon Carnival has three weeks of parades in the run-up to Lent. The Renaissance Festival is in July/August with music and drama while the Wine Festival, in July, has music, dancing and barrels of local wine and therefore not to be missed…

The Island of Crete:

Panormo: Panormo, also called Panormos, is an extremely attractive village on the north coast of Crete about 21 kilometres east of Rethymno that manages to blend Cretan character with low-key tourism. A trio of beaches are all of firm sand. There is a small harbour beach; the popular 'middle beach' with a taverna; and the hotel beach to the west. All three are protected by stone breakwaters making swimming safe even when there's a strong northerly wind. The beaches are gently sloping and therefore, ideal for children. There is a dive centre on the western beach and some low key watersports. If you prefer more seclusion head west past the Marine Grecotel for a sprinkling of pebble coves. There are several tavernas, a few pleasant bars, two decent mini-markets, a bakery, newsagents and a welcome absence of tacky souvenir shops all of which makes for an extremely pleasant small resort with lots of character. There' are regular bus services to Rethymno and Iraklion and a ' little road train' from Panormos offers a choice of two morning tourist trips inland into the Cretan countryside. **Georgioupolis:** Three rivers run into the sea at Georgioupolis which lies about 21 kilometres west of Rethymnon and 39 kilometres east of Chania, and flat sand stretches east from the village for almost seven kilometres. The main river runs into a small harbour where derelict boat hulks lie rusting. A second cuts through the middle of the long sandy beach and a third reaches the sea at a small cove to the west. The village has grown into a moderate sized resort. The resort is pleasantly shady thanks to massive eucalyptus trees and high curtains of bamboo that sprout at every turn. The flat beach is exposed to the northern winds but the sand is good and fine, if flat and featureless as it snakes off into the distance. The best of the beach is at the western end where a long stone walkway reaches out to a tiny chapel perched on the rocks. Marshy flats lie behind the sands, an ideal habitat to see birds and even turtles…

The Island of Crete:

Almyrida: Almyrida beach is just around the headland from the slightly more popular Kalives. A sandy beach curves around in a wide crescent from a small breakwater which serves as a simple harbour. Almyrida is a pleasant family beach resort, within striking distance of Chania, with a bakery, mini-market, car rental and a string of tavernas along the shore. The fine, golden sand shelves gently at both ends but it's stony underfoot in the middle so shoes may be useful. A line of tamarisks behind the beach provides some natural shade. A growing number of apartments, and more recently a small hotel have been built here that has affected the resort's tranquillity but it is still an attractive spot to stay. There are several coves along the cliff path to Kalives and there are also some good walks in the area with views over the bay of Souda. Inland from Almyrida lie the hill villages of Kokkino Horio and Plaka, notable both for being used as locations for the filming of the movie Zorba the Greek and for their fine tavernas that are set in shady tree-lined squares. **Kalives:** The resort village of Kalyves, also spelt Kalives, has a main street that runs parallel to the coast lined. The beach at Kalives is very fine. It sweeps around the medium-sized bay with a small harbour at one end and with a hotel with a fake windmill, at the other. The sand here is deep and soft and it is backed by trees and benches that line the narrow road behind which are some good tavernas and shops. The sand at Kalives slopes steeply to the sea in places and currents can be strong so children must be watched carefully but this is still a very good family beach. Kalives is a working village so there is a good selection of shops with a bakery, ironmongers and even a barrel maker, as well as tavernas and cafes. Just outside Kalives is the remarkable Koumos or Stone House, a private home where the buildings are covered in small stones in a Gaudi-style extravaganza…

The Island of Crete:

Akrotiri Peninsula: The large peninsula of Akrotiri, north-east of Chania, is a mix of suburbia, bare wilderness and mushrooming luxury resorts. The regional airport and nearby military base are in this area while the resorts of Kalathas and Stavros have fine sandy beaches that are both full of apartments and villas. The rest is pretty much a barren wilderness. The beach resort of Stavros sits at the northern tip of Akrotiri with two sandy beaches beneath a large rock outcrop. This is where many scenes were shot for the movie 'Zorba the Greek'. Inland are a few monasteries that are a popular target of tour buses. Nearby is a hermit cave called Arkoudiotissa, after a huge bear-shaped stalagmite found inside, and beyond that is the cave of the hermit St John, approached down 150 steps carved into the rock. **Chania City:** The capital of Crete until 1971 Chania is Crete's most charming city and for many it's best-loved. The centre is a wonderful mix of Turkish and Venetian architecture that, for the most part, miraculously survived the bombers of World War II. Laid out like a crucifix, the Agora market, built in 1911, is a delight with everything from buckets of sliced pig heads to gift wrapped herbs, from delicate mountain tea to children's comics. To the east is the busy outdoor leather market in Odros Skridlof and the splendid archaeological museum, housed in the old Venetian church of San Francesco, with its Minoan pottery and artefacts. North of the museum lies the heart of Chania - the two Venetian ports. The eastern harbour has the slender Venetian lighthouse and the squat Mosque of the Janissaries built in 1625 with strange egg-shaped domes and spider leg arches. Behind the mosque lies the Kastelli quarter with seven recently restored vaulted shipyards of the Venetian Arsenal built around 1600. The rectangular west harbour is generously lined with tavernas and cafes and tipped with the unattractive fortress of the Firkas Tower. There is a small strip of beach at the western end of the Venetian walls called Nea Chora that is very popular with the locals and has cafes and sunbeds…

The Island of Crete:

Agioi Apostoloi: Agioi Apostoloi is the first beach west of Chania. It actually has three good sandy beaches and is very popular with the locals especially at weekends. It is named after the small chapel that sits at the head of the peninsula that has three linked bays of fine golden sand with clear, shallow seawater making it a great beach for families with children. The biggest beach is Chrissi Akti or Golden Beach, so called for its soft golden sand. The beach has sunbeds, beach tavernas and cafes, music bars and water sports. There is a small, shady park of pines, palms, oleander and eucalyptus close by. Trees stand at the back of the beach and on the headland. The other two beaches are just a stroll away and are just as fine and can be a little quieter. **Agia Marina:** Agia Marina is a big popular beach west of Chania. It has a long coastal ribbon of development behind the long flat sandy beach. It sits on a very busy coastal road where tavernas, bars, gift shops and supermarkets line the road touting for the passing tourist trade. The beach is wide, flat and exposed, with all the usual facilities expected of a beach resort with loads of sunbeds and watersports galore. At dusk an array of nightspots, bars and clubs open making this, along with Platanias, one of the longest beach bar strips on Crete. **Platanias:** The busy resort of Platanias has a long sandy beach and is backed by low dunes and a very busy main road. The beach is clean and sandy and there are plenty of sunbeds and watersports. Visitors are never far from a taverna or bar. The Blue Flag section of the beach is near the main Platanias village. Further west the beach turns to shingle backed by banks of bamboo and there are quieter spots away from the crowds. The road behind is lined with tavernas, rental outfits and souvenir shops and traders selling pottery and cheap leather goods. The old village of Platanias perches quietly up on the hillside and is visited by the Platanias tourist train. There is also a water park nearby…

The Island of Crete:

Gerani: The beach resort at Gerani or Kato Gerani is much less developed than its busy neighbour, Platanias, although there are a number of big hotels. Gerani extends from the Platanias Bridge to the village of Pirgos Psilonerou and it is a lot quieter than its neighbour. All of the night-life offerings of Platanias are just a short walk away and there are regular local buses to Chania. Gerani has a long pebble and sand beach with plenty of facilities. The nearby inland hamlets at Pano Gerani, Modi, Loutraki and Manoliopoulo are good examples of traditional Cretan villages. **Kolymbari:** The small fishing port of Kolymbari lies at the base of the Rodopou peninsula and is relatively free of mass tourism, although a number of tour operators do use the resort. A long pebble beach has been artificially improved with lorry loads of sand, and a pleasant seafront promenade is lined with tavernas, shops and waterfront cafes. It also has a small and pretty harbour. **Kastelli Kissamos:** Confusion over several other Kastelli's on Crete has led to this fishing village being called Kastelli, Kissamos or both. Located 42 km west of Chania the resort marks the end of the main east west Crete highway and it sites at the edge of a very large bay. Kastelli Kissamos has a long, pebble and sand beach and several good tavernas. Local excavations unearthed a 2nd century floor mosaic here and there is a good archaeology museum. About 8 km inland is the old village of Polyrenia, as quaint a Cretan village as you will find with a history that predates the Romans. Kastelli Kissamos was the centre of fierce fighting in the Battle of Crete, and the use of pitchforks and knives by the Cretans who took on the Nazi paratroopers earned savage reprisals, including the execution of 200 villagers…

The Island of Crete:

West Coast Beaches: The far west coast of Crete provides some of the most remote, dramatic and some would argue finest, beaches on the whole of the Island of Crete. Many are spectacular and are used on many of the Island's postcards. Even just a drive down the dramatic coastline is worthwhile. But facilities here are few and far between so many visitors prefer to join one of the many day trips offered by the Islands coach tour firms and/or boat owners. **Gramvousa Islet:** Far off the beaten track, the striking spike of islet of Gramvousa, once the haunt of pirates, is now a favourite target of day-trippers. Spectacular sand bars and shallow seawater stretch out to the islet off the beach at Balos where the ruins of a large Venetian fortress sits which was built in 1582 but destroyed six years later when lightning set off a gunpowder store. The castle was rebuilt in 1630 and garrisoned by English and French soldiers in 1828. Today only the ruins remain. It is possible to walk out to the Island across the sandbanks, though this should never be attempted when it is very windy. Wild and uninhabited, Balos beach is best visited by boat. **Falasarna:** To the west of Kastelli is some of the finest, coastline in Crete. Tracks leading down from the main road to Falasarna beach certainly provide wonderful views of wrinkled rocks, clear blue sea and white sand. The view is somewhat spoilt by the rows of green plastic greenhouses full of tomatoes and cucumbers. There are several wide sandy coves here. The main Falasarna beach is at the northern end of the bay and is a long stretch of clean sand with rocks and rock pools to add interest. On the cliff tops above are some tavernas and apartments. Wooden steps lead down to the beach where the shallow sea and large rock pools are ideal for children. The northern end of the beach is quieter, away from the tavernas with scrub covered dunes and the sheltering cliffs behind…

The Island of Crete:

Elafonisi Islet: The tiny uninhabited islet of Elafonisi looks like a desert Island paradise but the beauty generates a relentless influx of daily coaches and visiting boats. Visitors can wade out to the islet along a shallow reef through the sun-warmed seawater that rarely reach more than a metre in depth. It is a magical place if you can avoid the crowds. The beach is flat white sand and the shallow waters take on a pink hue from the protected coral reefs that grow here. The coast is littered with coves, bays and rock pools. A couple of small beach cantinas open in the summer and a walk north will reveal secluded coves of naturist sunbathers. The area is rich in rare plants and animals, including frogs, lizards and snakes. The beach is also a breeding ground for sea turtles and the last European stop for birds migrating to Africa. Those visiting by road will pass through the impressive Topolia Gorge and the neighbouring mountain villages of Topolia, Elos, Kefali and Vathi that are all worth an extended stop. **South Coast Beaches:** Much of Crete's south coast is composed of sheer cliffs that plunge sharply into the sea from the Lefkas Ori Mountains above. But what beaches there are, are among the best in Crete and they enjoy some of the best weather too, facing south and well protected by the mountains behind. The weather is so mild here that resorts such as Paleochora have a tourist season that lasts through the winter. **Paleochora:** The resort at Paleochora lies on the south coast of Crete about 73 km from Chania with a harbour on one side, a long, sandy beach on the other with ancient Venetian ramparts towering above. The Venetian fortress that sits on the tip of the small peninsula was destroyed by pirates in 1539 but subsequently restored and is now open to the public. West of the fort is a big sandy beach with plenty of sunbeds and stands of tamarisk at the back for natural shade. Further west it gets quieter with sheltered coves further along the coast. To the east of the port is a small beach of pebble and stone with a clutch of tavernas and cafes around the small port. Boats leave here for Gavdos Island, the most southern part of Europe. Paleochora is one of the few Greek resorts that remain open to tourists all through the winter months…

The Island of Crete:

Agia Roumeli: Agia Roumeli is the gateway port for walkers heading in and out of the hugely popular Samaria Gorge which runs north into Lefka Ori and up to the Omalos Plain. Agia Roumeli has a long, thin strip of pebble and shingle that drops very steeply into the sea. Sunbed umbrellas offer the only shade at this very exposed spot. **Loutro:** Little more than a stopping place for passing boats the port at Loutro has no road access and all visitors arrive on daily boats. Perched in a horseshoe bay and overshadowed by looming cliffs. Loutro beach is just a small and exposed strip of pebble and shingle west of the harbour. Touted as the ideal out-of-the-way resort Loutro can get rather crowded. A bank of tavernas line the shore near the harbour ready to net any passing trade. **Glyka Nera:** About 4 km west of Chora Sfakia is the remote and beautiful beach of Glyka Nera, also known as Sweetwater or Freshwater beach. It is a beach of white pebbles with very clear and fresh water that bubbles out of the ground from nearby springs. A small beach cantina opens in the summer with basic food and drink and there are sunbeds and umbrellas for protection but there is nothing in the way of natural shade here. The beach is popular with naturists and most arrive by boats. There is a coastal footpath from Chora Sfakia that takes about 30-40 minutes to walk and a much more difficult path from Loutro, in the west, that takes about 60 minutes. Boats leave Chora Sfakia at about 10 am and return for pick-ups at about 4.30 pm everyday in the summer season. **Anopoli:** Those who fancy a glimpse of old Cretan culture, away from mass tourism, then the hillside village of Anopoli, in the mountains behind Loutro and Glyka, is the place to head for. Anopoli is a village of about 350 inhabitants on a small, fertile plateau at the foot of the White Mountains or Lefkas Ori. The villages here are very friendly and welcoming to visitors…

The Island of Crete:

Chora Sfakia Port: Many visitors make the hair-raising descent to Chora Sfakia Port to get a boat to the Samaria Gorge. It is not for the faint hearted with precipitous zigzag bends full of reckless local drivers and a steady stream of tour coaches. Hemmed in by mountains, the seaside village of Chora Sfakia lies about 74 km from Chania. This is the ferry port for walkers heading to Agia Roumeli and the Samaria Gorge. A row of cafes and souvenir shops lines the narrow street that leads west from the small harbour and there is a small pebble beach around the headland with a beach cantina and sunbeds. Also nearby is a long pebble beach at Vritomartis which boasts a licensed naturist resort and hotel. The Sfakia region of Crete was once noted for banditry and it was once said that no Sfakian ever left home without a gun. Local families were often embroiled in bloody feuds and even today the roadside signs are used for targets for gun practice. In World War II, Sfakian's were instrumental in helping evacuate retreating Allied troops from the Island, an action for which the Germans made them pay dearly. A monument on the harbour wall commemorates the evacuation while a memorial above the village honours the local families who were then summarily executed by the occupying Nazis. **Frangokastello:** A wide flat plain lies beneath the mountains from Chora Sfakia to Plakias. Behind a long flat beach stands the castle of Frangokastello, a severe rectangle of brown and orange stone. Imposing from the outside, the castle is little more than a shell inside and a full tour takes no more than a few minutes. The beach lies in front of and beneath the castle, a fine stretch of gently shelving white sand with a few rocky outcrops at one end and a sheltered boat bay at the other. The sea here stays very shallow for a good 100 metres out. A few sunbeds are scattered about around a beach taverna beneath the castle and there is plenty of natural shade from stands of tamarisks trees that run the full length of Frangokastello beach. Frangokastello makes for a tranquil spot, with the added bonus of a towering backdrop of blue grey mountains…

The Island of Crete:

Plakias: The former fishing village at Plakias, 92 km from Chania and 36 km from Rethymnon, has undergone a bit of a tourist boom in recent years with apartments scattered over the wide coastal plain. Despite the influx, the resort remains low key with some restaurants and bars, a few shops and, more recently, a couple of discos. Plakias is set in a large bay with a 1 km beach of sand and pebble backed by shoreline tavernas. The beach is mainly pebble near the resort but gets much sandier as it stretches east and there are showers and sunbeds provided. **Preveli:** It is picture postcard perfect at the beach of Preveli where a spectacular lagoon lies between the sea and a steep gorge and a long spit of shingle provides room for sun loungers. Access to Preveli beach is difficult and not suitable for those with mobility problems. Steep steps drop from the car park on the cliff top directly above and it is a long trek down the narrow gorge to the seashore. Many sensibly arrive at Preveli beach by boat. **Agia Gallini:** With its picturesque setting and compact village layout Agia Gallini, 114 km from Chania and 54 km from Rethymnon is a favourite with many package holiday companies. The taverna-lined harbour provides focus while the narrow streets that climb up the hill are thick with the usual cafes and souvenir shops. Agia Galini is very touristy but it has not sacrificed all of its charm. However the predominance of English signs in a Greek resort can be depressing. It is also a long walk to the beaches which lie around the headland to the east. The first beach is small and, although very pleasant, is often crammed to capacity. There is a longer stretch of coarse sand beyond it to the east. Further east still is a coastal plain that is mainly hidden beneath acres of polythene greenhouses and also a concrete sprawl of agricultural buildings given over to the semi-industrial growing of tomatoes and cucumbers…

The Greek Island of Evia

The Island of Evia is located off the eastern coast of Central Greece and is one of the most popular and unique of all of the Greek Islands. The Island has extremely easy access from the mainland by road and then either using one of the connecting road bridges or using a ferry . Second in size only to the Island of Crete, Evia is a wonderful holiday destination and is ideal for all types of holidays throughout the year. The stunning landscape and scenery, fusing both the dominating mountains and the blue crystal waters of the Aegean Sea and the Evoikos Gulf, Evia is a treat for both the heart and mind. It is a place where you can enjoy holidays filled with interesting activities, wonderful sites, as well as a place to unwind and relax in. Evia is best described as being an Island with three main parts being the north, central and the south of the Island. Each has its own inspiring landscape, rich vegetation and colourful scenery, interesting history, ancient sites and place of interest, as well as so much more. The Island of Evia is the perfect destination for those who seek a traditional Greek Island holiday. On Evia there are many beautiful villages and towns scattered all across this charming Island, each offering visitors a look into both the past and present traditions of this truly unique and picturesque Island. For those who enjoy the beach and the sea, Evia has some extremely beautiful beaches all around the Island. During the summer months, the beaches of the Island are popular with both the locals and visitors alike. There are many different activities that visitors can enjoy, such as hiking, water sports, horse riding, climbing, mountain biking and many others. Evia is also the perfect place for visitors who simply wish to lie back on the beach and relax in a tranquil and beautiful setting…

The Island of Evia:

Evia has wonderful beaches, a pleasant climate, renowned monuments, many thermal sources and tasty food and is, therefore, a popular and nearby destination for the inhabitants of Athens. The Island extends over an area of 3,580 km2, its coastline is 48 km long and it has 220,000 inhabitants. From archeological evidence in several parts of the Island (Istiaia, Kirinthos, Psachna, Amarynthos, Artaki, and Karistos etc) has shown that the Island of Evia was inhabited from the Paleolithic Era. Important archeological finds have been excavated from this period. Ruins dating back to the Early Helladic period have been found in Lefkanti, Vasiliko and in Manika, Chalkida, while in Oreoi and Aliveri ruins of the Middle Helladic period have been unearthed. Finally, tombs and ruins of post Hellenic and Mycenaean eras have been excavated in many areas of Chalkida. The ancient cities of the Island of Evia established important colonies in the Mediterranean Sea (Chalkidiki, Asia Minor, Southern Italy), while Eretria was one of the most powerful cities during the Classic period. During the Byzantine era, the Island of Evia was very prosperous and formed part of the Department of Greece. During the Ottoman occupation, Evia was under Turkish control and it only came under Greek control on the 13th of June 1830. In 1922 after the tragedy of Asia Minor (Greeks being expelled from Turkey) a lot of refugees installed themselves permanently on the Island of Evia in Nea Artaki and Nea Lampsakos, as well as in refugee settlements in Chalkida and Amarynthos. During the Second World War, the Island of Evia was bombarded by the Germans because of the strong resistance being put up by the local Islanders. After the war the Island has been linked to the mainland by a new bridge and has seen a dramatic increase in visitor numbers to the paradise Greek Island of Evia…

The Greek Island of Hydra

Hydra, or Ydra, lies just 37 nautical miles south of Athens between the gulfs of the Saronic and Argolis. It has something of an artistic pedigree as well as being a popular weekend destination for Athenians. Hydra is one of the easiest islands to get to from Athens either by using one of the Flying Dolphins or the high-speed Flying Cat. Hydra, pronounced 'eedra', was 'discovered' in the late 1950's by artists such as the Canadian singer Leonard Cohen and its harbour-side cafes have frequently entertained celebrities, ranging from US writer Henry Miller to British pop-star Mick Jagger. The long, thin Island is characterised by its rocky interior, virtually uninhabited with just the odd farmhouse to accompany its few, remote and deserted monasteries. Beautiful 18th century mansion houses are a reminder of Hydra's past as the home of wealthy merchants and shipbuilders when, during the 18th and 19th centuries Ydra boasted a huge commercial fleet. Today, strict building laws protect the Island's traditional architectural styles and help preserve its serene beauty. Donkeys and boats are still the only form of transport as cars and motorbikes are banned on the Island. Hydra may have no notable beaches, and much of its woodland has been lost to forest fires, but it's still a Greek Island that oozes charm while rich Athenians make up a large proportion of its regular visitors. Hydra is not a great Island for beaches. The dominant features are a heavily indented rocky shoreline backed by bare mountains, pine carpeted valleys and the odd farm. Almost all 2,500 inhabitants live in and around the main port of Hydra. Half a dozen small pebble beaches are strung along the north coast while the south has only the odd cove…

The Greek Island of Hydra:

Hydra Town: Hydra Town has a crescent-shaped harbour fringed by tavernas, cafes, boutique shops and mini-markets, often packed with yachts and other sailing craft. Steep stone streets lead up from the harbour lined with stout grey houses and impressive mansion houses, most of them topped with red tiled roofs. Once heavily populated by wealthy merchants and shipbuilders, Hydra's imposing mansions are not seen in such abundance on any other Greek Island. Many homes are tall and narrow, a consequence of steeply rising land, and many have been restored by rich Athenians who opted for bright colours on shutters, doors and walls. The most populated area is the oldest, Kiafa, which sits high above the port with fine views over the bay. There are arched bridges across some streets to connect the houses and some stone windmills at the summit complete the scene. The Church of the Assumption of the Virgin, in the centre of Hydra Town, has a notable three-storey bell tower made of Tinos marble. Founded as a monastery in 1643, only the church and a few monk cells remain. The Kountouriotis museum is housed in a former mansion house and has engaging exhibits of Hydra's maritime heritage. Through the archway under the waterfront clock tower is the Byzantine Museum with its extensive collection of religious artefacts. **Mandraki:** The beach at Mandraki lies about two kilometres east of the port at Hydra along a wide and level coast road that's lined with small stone houses and villas. Footpaths branching off the main road lead up to the remote monasteries perched on the surrounding hills and sea views usually include a taxi boat making its way to Mandraki. The bay, backed by steep rugged hills and dotted with a few pine trees and lots of scrub, has two beaches. One is a small sheltered cove below a taverna, mostly pebble and rock with sun loungers and some shade from trees. Water taxis dock at a small jetty. Around the bay is a larger sandy beach. There is sand here, rare for Ydra, but it is gritty sharp stuff. It has sunbeds and watersports and a shallow pool near the jetty that all helps to make this a popular choice for families with children…

The Greek Island of Hydra:

Spilia: Grey rock has been blasted from the hillside at Spilia, just west of at Hydra port, to create terraced cement decking where tables and loungers are positioned over the sea. The water at Spilia is clear and a deep blue colour, ideal for diving and swimming, although it's a lot easier getting in than out. Alluring sea views include offshore islets and Spilia is a good spot to enjoy some romantic sunsets, even though it can be to the background bleat of pop radio pap. **Kamini:** Above Hydra port is an area known as the "Four Corners" with houses around a small square where the Canadian poet/singer Leonard Cohen had a home. A steep stepped route through here leads to the small picturesque fishing port. There are two beaches here. Megalo Kamini (Big Kamini) is the least popular as the beautiful little pebble beach at Mikro Kamini (Small Kamini) has the shallow water that's popular with families. Both have sunbeds and watersports. **Vlychos:** West from Kamini the road leads to Vlychos, or Vlihos, a pretty beach with a small jetty where taxi boats from Hydra can tie up. The walk from port takes about 40 minutes. The grey sand and pebble beach is large with a taverna and a summer cantina. Sun loungers are laid out in the season and the gently shelving sands make it a popular spot for families. White cube houses tumble down the hillside, many of them holiday homes built close to the sea to get the best sea views. The village has a couple of tavernas and a ruined 19th century stone bridge. Nearby is the tiny chapel of Agios Xaralampos. **Bitsi:** The beach at Bitsi is in a very beautiful setting at the western tip of Hydra in a deep south-west facing bay and reached only by one of the taxi boat that sail daily from Hydra port. Pine trees coat the hillside right down to the shore where a small beach of white pebbles has tree-shaded rocks on either side and a summer cantina which sets out sunbeds along the seashore…

The Greek Island of Hydra:

Agios Nikolaos: Just beyond Bisti, another small beach cove called Agios Nikolaos which is only accessible by Island water taxi or by private boat. Agios Nikolaos is one of the largest bays on Hydra and it is a favourite port of call for caiques, although it takes nearly an hour to get there from the port at Hydra. Another drawback of this beach is the relative lack of natural shade, although there are sunbeds and umbrellas for hire. A small cantina offers basic food and drinks in the summer but there are no facilities here out of season. Visitors must be sure to arrange a boat pick up from here as well or they will face a long, steep and tough hike back over the mountain. **Limnioniza:** Limnioniza is the only beach on the south side of the Island of Hydra. It can be reached by boat or on foot across the Island backbone ridge on a well-marked trail from Hydra port that passes through Agia Triadha. The beach is in a long cove of white and grey pebbles and has shallow clear seawater. It has very little natural shade although sun loungers and umbrellas are for hire on the beach during the summer season. In the summer a cantina opens at the back of the beach and there are also some watersports on offer including water skiing and kayaking. There are several good walks very close at hand behind the beach with woodland footpaths well marked. Caiques run regularly to the beach in the summer and the trip from Hydra port takes about 30 minutes…

The Greek Island of Ikaria

Ikaria, also spelt Icaria, lies is the most southern region of the North Aegean Islands group and just off the Turkish coast about 20 kilometres south-west of the Greek Island of Samos. Visitors can travel to Ikaria island by ferry or plane from Athens. Flights to Ikaria are available only in summer, while ferries run all year round. Since ancient times, Ikaria has been famous for its dark red wine, its thermal springs and for the legend of Icarus who flew too close to the sun, melting his wings of feathers and wax. Ikaria is a large Island and not featured heavy on the tourist Island hopping trail. It has a mass of mountains with steep mountain cliffs that plunge down into the sea along a coastline that has very few sheltered bays or good harbours. The Island of Ikaria is popular amongst tourists that visit the Island and, although few in number, the best of the Ikaria beaches can compare with any to be found on any of the Greek Islands. Larger villages are confined to Ikaria's coastal plains as the interior is so rocky and rugged and its mountain villages are therefore, small and remote. The best beaches are on the north coast and vary from long swathes of fine sand to sheltered coves of pebble and stone. Ikaria is an Island for those seeking a traditional Greek holiday that is off the beaten track that gives a taste of the authentic old world Greece, away from the maddening crowds. Accommodation on Ikaria ranges from self contained villas to all-inclusive holiday hotels. Ikaria is an Island blessed with some of the best beaches in the Aegean. They range from long sandy stretches with seasonal tourist attractions to deserted pebble coves. Visitors can expect peaceful landscapes and spectacular shores with a rugged mountain backdrops. The best sandy beaches are on the north coast of the Island but the south offers several beautiful and secluded coves…

The Island of Ikaria:

Agios Kirikos Port: Agios Kirikos is the Island's main port and administrative centre on the north-east coast and, although well provided with trees and gardens, it's is not what the casual visitor might call picturesque. To the east of the ferry quay is a small strip of pebble used more for beaching fishing boats than for sunbathing. In summer water taxis shuttle visitors to the hot springs at nearby Therma. About a kilometre west, just past a couple of nightclubs, is Tsoulka beach. The tree-fringed pebble beach is just off the main road and has a beach cantina. A little further west is a long, narrow strip of rock and pebble at Xilosirtis, with a small jetty and a summer cantina. About a kilometre east, on the coast road to Therma, is a secluded sand and pebble cove at Prioni with access down a very steep path. Boats in Agios Kirykos port offer excursion trips to the Island of Fourni which has beaches, tavernas and good walking trails. **Therma:** Therma is set in a narrow rock cove with a row of cafes, the shore shaded by a line of attractive tamarisk trees and looking out over a small, quiet beach of sand and shingle split by a thin jetty. The hot mineral springs are nearby. **Fanari:** Fanari, also known as Faros, lies at the eastern tip of the Island and has a sand and pebble beach and runs for about two kilometres curving round the eastern headland. Tamarisks provide natural shade alongside a couple of large tavernas and a beach bar. The Island airport is close by but is completely invisible from the beach and flights are few enough to be more of an interest than being a nuisance. Nearby are the ancient ruins of Drakano with an acropolis among the remains of ancient walls and houses. **Evdilos Port:** Evdilos is the north coast port of Ikaria, about 40 kilometres from Agios Kirikos and reached along the Island's only main road. It is one of the more traditional settlements on Ikaria which has tavernas on the harbour-side, stone built houses, narrow streets and old mansion houses…

The Island of Ikaria:

Akamatra: Akamatra is a beautiful village, just south of Evdilos, full of attractive houses with a very picturesque square, a folklore museum and several small chapels. The central square has a 500 year-old oak tree, once used as a gallows. Close by is the Alama cave, full of stalactites and stalagmites, and at nearby Arethousa is the much photographed Theokepasti chapel which has been carved out of the rock. **Evdilos:** Just west of Evdilos is the beach village of Kampos, or Kabos, once the ancient capital of Ikaria when the Island was called Oino. There are ruins nearby of a Roman Odeon and the Archaeological Museum on the hilltop of Agia Irini and is well worth a visit. The beach is long and sandy. Bamboo grows right to the water's edge fed by the fresh water river that crosses the plain at the back of the beach forming small pools. A snack-bar opens in the summer and a popular bar and club lies behind the sands. **Messakti:** On the coast road west of Evdilos lie a string of good beaches with some of the best sands to be found on Ikaria. The village of Gialiskaris is home to a huge white sand beach called Messakti where the water is as clear and blue as the Caribbean. Two small rivers form fresh water lagoons at the back of the wide and long Messakti that is mostly pure sand. Shallow water makes it ideal for families but there are strong currents offshore. At the eastern end of the beach, a traditional white and blue chapel sits at the end of an outcrop of rock. **Livadi:** The far end of Messakti beach is Livadi. The attractive setting is enhanced by a freshwater lagoon that adds lush vegetation to the shoreline scene. Sunbeds line the sands in front of a beach cantina. Over the headland to the west and below the road as it snakes along the cliff is the tiny cove of Ammoudaki. The beach is sand and shingle and the seawater is sparkling and clear…

The Island of Ikaria:

Armenistis: The small fishing village of Armenistis is one of the more popular tourist resorts on Ikaria, thanks mainly to the necklace of nearby beaches. The village consists of clusters of newly restored old houses that climb up the hillside overlooking the fishing boats in the harbour and a small patch of beach about 13 kilometres west of Evdilos. The traditional old Greek village only has about 70 permanent residents and it has a bakery, mini-market, tavernas and bars. **Christos Raches:** The beautiful inland village of Christos Raches or Christos Rachiou, is about five kilometres from Armenistis and buried deep in mountain pine and oak woods and surrounded by vineyards. The village has a school, police station and health centre as well as a number of small shops, tavernas and cafes around the central square. **Nas:** About five kilometres west of Armenistis is another of the more popular Ikaria beaches, known as Nas, which can be reached by a very attractive coastal walk. The river Chalaris flows into the beautiful deep inlet creating a deep freshwater beach pool. The small bay of pebble and sand is enclosed by outcrops of rock but the water is prone to heavy swells and a rope is strung out for swimmers to grab if waves get too big. Several tavernas offer outstanding views over the sea, particularly good at sunset. **Seychelles:** The only other beach of note on Ikaria is on the south coast below the dramatic white cliffs of Seychelles, or Seichelle in one of Ikaria's most memorable settings. Found on the south-west coast about 25 kilometers from Agios Kirikos, the pretty village of Manganitis is entered through a tunnel cut into the granite bluff. The beach is down a very steep path that follows the river bed from the village to a shore of brilliant white stones huddled in a picturesque cove. This is so beautiful a spot so do not forget to take your camera…

The Greek Island of Ios

Ios is in the southern part of the central Cyclades group of Islands, just south of the Greek Islands of Naxos and Paros. The closest airport is found on the Island of Santorini. This airport gets very busy in summer and receives many domestic as well as international flights. Many visitors arrive by plane in Athens or Santorini and then continue by ferry to Ios. Once considered the party capital of the Med, the glory days of Ios have faded as the Island lost out to more nakedly aggressive beach party resorts of Faliraki, on Rhodes, and Ayia Napa, on Cyprus. Nevertheless, Ios remains a major hedonist outpost where sun, sex and sin await youngsters from all over the world. Once it was neck-and-neck with Faliraki for the Greek Islands' top party Island title, Ios is now considerably tamer today than it once was. Long-suffering Islanders have worked hard to cast off the Island's poor reputation. Locals, annoyed at the booze-sodden behaviour of young visitors, imposed a 3 am weekday shutdown on clubs. The clubs, bars and discos are totally confined to the Island capital port, Chora village on the hill above it and Mylopotas beach beyond. Outside the capital there lies a classic Greek Island with some simply wonderful beaches and timeless villages easily reached on the well-paved Island roads. Head north or east for peace and tranquillity on some of the best Greek Island beaches you will ever come across. In addition to the notorious nightlife, Ios can boast beaches that are the envy of many other Islands. The Island regularly picks up 'best in Europe' awards amongst its 75 kilometers of sandy shore. Mylopotas is the busiest and the noisiest; a party beach crammed with music bars and fast food outlets. Beyond Mylopotas, it is a different story where beautiful, un-spoilt beaches are the norm. Many beaches are remote and very relaxed…

The Island of Ios:

Chora: Chora is the only large settlement on Ios. By day, a dormant village of white cube houses blue domed churches stacked up the hillside and capped by a dozen decaying windmills. By night, it is a frenzy of drinking and partying with discos competing to out-decibel each other with techno-pop, heavy metal, punk, rock and even jazz. The centre is a rash of bars and clubs wrapped around the main square, all very small but together number more than 100. The narrow streets keep Chora free of cars and there is plenty to enjoy by day. Windmills, a dozen of them and the ruins of a medieval castle crown the hill along with the chapel of Agios Nikolaos and just beneath is Panagia Gremiotissa (Our Lady of the Cliffs), built by Turkish occupiers. The Archaeological Museum is housed in a yellow neoclassical mansion and has displays of ceramics, Roman artifacts, prehistoric tools and Cycladic figurines. **Ormos Yialos:** Below the Chora is the port area of Ormos Yialos, or Gialos, one of the biggest natural harbours in the Aegean and the first glimpse most visitors get of the Island. The central plaza is packed with shops and the promenade thick with tavernas, cafes and gift shops with a small quay beyond the marina where fishing nets are laid out to dry. The long sandy beach is to the west of the port, has yet more restaurants and bars and is a popular alternative to the crowded party beach of Mylopotas on the other side of Chora. **Koubara:** On the headland south of Yialos lies Koumbara, or Koubara, an area of small coves and sandy beaches. The main beach is long at about 300 metres and sandy with tavernas. Koumbara's main attraction is the clutch of small coves dotted all around the headland. The odd rock outcrop makes it great for snorkelling and the secluded coves make it popular with naturists. Koumbara is within walking distance from Yialos, it takes about 30 minutes, but a regular local bus service leaves Ormos Yialos on the hour…

The Island of Ios:

Mylopotas: Mylopotas is the main beach for Chora and has a one kilometre crescent of wide, golden sand that will rival any in the Mediterranean. In season, non-stop beach music is broadcast continuously all day as young revelers warm up for a frantic night's drinking at the infamous all-night beach parties. The bay is awash with cafes and bars with watersports galore to keep the young entertained. Local buses leave Chora every 15 minutes or so to go to the beach.
North Coast Beaches: The north coast has a number of attractive beaches but they are widely separated. Many more coves can be found in sheltered bays but are remote and without facilities so they tend to be very quiet. The most beautiful beach of them all is Manganari. **Plakatos:** The first beach of any note north of Yialos is at Plakatos, about 13 kilometres away on the northern tip of the Island beneath Pano Kambos, the reputed site of Homer's Tomb. **Agia Theodoti:** The huge sandy beach at Agia Theodoti is about 12 kilometres from Yialos, set in a sheltered bay facing east for breathtaking sunrises over the islet of Ikaklia in the bay. The local tavernas serve basic, but delicious, food. The beach is overlooked by the ruins of the 15th century Venetian fortress of Paliokastro, built in 1400 where the remains of the old Venetian town can still be seen inside. **Psathi:** The coarse sand beach at Psathi, is the domain of egg-laying loggerhead turtles and of windsurfers. The flat wide sand is backed by a line of tamarisks providing shade. A taverna just above the long beach puts out sunbeds in the summer. More tavernas are found in the nearby village. The sand is sharp underfoot and shelves steeply in places. The north-facing beach can get very windy at times and this can bring out the windsurfers…

The Island of Ios:

Kalamos: The long sand and pebble beach at Kalamos on the eastern coast, about 16 kilometres from Yialos, is a good alternative to the increasingly popular Manganari beach to the south. The local area is a nature reserve and, being relatively remote and well off the tour bus route, remains a peaceful and tranquil haven that attracts only a few visitors every summer. The clear seawater and some outlying rocks offer bathers some very good snorkelling. Even more remote coves lie both north and south of Kalamos, all are within easy walking distance.

Manganari: One of the most romantic areas of Ios, Manganari sits on the south-east coast about 23 kilometres from Yialos. Manganari has four white-sand beaches along a coast of crystal clear seawater. The beach has become a popular day out for trippers on regular bus excursions. The beach has the usual cluster of tavernas, bars, cafes and watersports. Despite the number of daily visitors, Manganari beach is big enough to accommodate those seeking peace and quiet and prepared to do a spot of walking to achieve it. Secluded bays make this an attractive spot for unofficial naturists. Excursion boats also offer day trips from Ormos Yialos but the boat trip is long, slow and can be expensive…

The Greek Island of Ithaka

The Island of Ithaka, also spelt Ithaca or Ithaki, is one of the Ionian group of Islands and the tiny Island lies just four kilometres off Kefalonia's eastern coast. To get to the Island you need to fly into Kefalonia and get a ferry over to the Island. Ithaka has mostly escaped the notice of package tour holiday firms but it is still a favourite destination of independent travellers and day trippers. Ithaka is a sleepy little Island and the ancient port was dismissed by Homer as only 'good for goats'. It is a place where time, when not standing still, often appears to be wandering about rather aimlessly. Apart from the visiting yachts and ferries full of day trippers there is little to disturb the gentle, relaxed Ithakan atmosphere. The Island is small, about 120 sq km, and it's almost split in two by a narrow hill ridge at Aetos, with peninsulas to the north and south. The north has the better beaches and the more interesting walks while the south has the relatively busy capital port of Vathi. The west coast of Ithaka is rough and ragged with only a couple of decent beaches while the east is typified by rolling hills and farmland. Many houses on Ithaka were destroyed in the earthquake of 1953. Ithaka is reputed to have an olive tree that is more than 1,500 years old. Ithaka is neatly divided north and south by the wasp-waist ridge at Aetos. The north of Ithaka has the better resorts, the biggest villages and the more interesting walks. The north-west side coastline is rough and ragged with only a couple of decent beaches while the north-east has rolling hills and fertile farmland. South Ithaka is mostly barren rock and scrub with the south-west virtually inaccessible. The south of the Island is identified with sites mentioned in Homer's classic Odyssey…

The Island of Ithaka:

Vathy Port: The south of the Island is empty but for a few Homeric sites and the main port of Vathy or Vathi. The port has one of the most idyllic seafront settings in Greece, nestled at the end of a long, deep bay and embraced on three sides by steep hills. The wooded islet of Lazaretto sits in the bay where a hospital was built in 1668, used as a prison in 1864 then demolished by an earthquake in 1953. Despite the lovely setting Vathi itself has a utilitarian quayside lined with functionally bland buildings that owe little to the pre-quake Venetian architecture. Vathy is where most of the Islands amenities are found like the post office, bank, cash machine, bakery, mini markets and so on. Ferries leave the port for mainland Greece, Kefalonia, Corfu and Italy while excursion boats offer round-Island trips, a good bet given the poor state of many roads. **Piso Aetos Port:** The narrow mountain ridge at Aetos is a favourite place for walkers with views to the sea on either side and with the ruins of an 8th century citadel abandoned in Roman times. On the opposite side of the ridge from Aetos, and facing west with views across the strait to Kefalonia, is the small port of Piso Aetos. More of a ferry port than a beach resort, the tiny harbour has been enlarged to take bigger ferries which usually avoid the long sail around to Vathy on the other side of the Island. **Dexa:** The road north out of Vathy follows the bay to a narrow beach of coarse sand, pebbles and stone at Dexa, the beach upon which Odysseus is reputed to have landed on his return home. Dexa is about two kilometres from Vathy so it's a popular spot for those staying in the Island capital. The very narrow strand of pebble is backed by a low wall and there are clutches of tamarisk trees as well as olive trees where visitors can relax on shaded sunbeds. A small cantina opens in the summer. Car parking can be a problem on the narrow road and a desalination plant nearby can, if the wind is right, produce an irritating hum…

The Island of Ithaka:

Skinos: On the headland east of Dexa is the long and narrow beach of Skinos, set in very attractive woodland dotted with very exclusive Ithaka villa properties. The pebble and stone beach seems to attract a good share of tidal rubbish that, being in such an isolated spot, rarely gets a clean-up. The beach is very narrow and backed by a low stone wall and offers good snorkelling along the rocky shore. A pleasant place to hide away Skinos has shade from tall cypress trees but has no facilities. **Filiatro:** Filiatro is a very pretty east-facing beach set in a medium-sized bay and serviced by a summer cantina. The water is shallow but footwear is recommended as the beach of pebble and stone has no sand under the water. Chairs and tables are set out under shady trees. Car access is good from the road east out of Vathy. Olive trees and tamarisk provide good shade. **Sarakiniko:** The Sarakiniko bay gives it name to a couple of small shingle beaches separated by a rock outcrop into the sea. One of the Sarakiniko beaches is not very nice but the other beach is a quiet, attractive beach in a sheltered bay. Olives and cypress provide shade but there are no facilities there. The steep bank of pebbles can be uncomfortable to lie on but nearby sandstone slabs provide a good alternative. **Perachori:** The large mountain village called Perachori sits above Vathy in an area where most of Ithaka Island wine is produced. Small tavernas open in summer although Perachori is very much a working, not a tourist, village. The ruins of fortified houses show this was once used by the residents of Vathia to escape passing pirates. Terraces tumble down hillsides planted with neat rows of vines and small citrus orchards or vegetable plots…

The Island of Ithaka:

Agios Ioannis: The beach at Agios Ioannis looks spectacular viewed from the cliffs above with a whitewashed chapel and an old windmill helping to complete the romantic scene. Visitors will find a long narrow strip of pebble and stone with fine views across the straits but no shade and no facilities. **Polis:** Polis is the only west coast resort on Ithaka. It has a bay of white limestone and shingle and a small harbour at the southern end with a taverna crouched beneath eucalyptus trees. Polis lies below the main town of Stavros and, with parking on the beach, a taverna and plenty of sunbeds, it can get crowded and there is no shade. A small harbour at the southern end has boat trips around Ithaka and to Fiscardo on Kefalonia. It was a ferry port before the expansion at Piso Aetos, just down the coast. **Stavros:** Inland from Polis, and overlooking the bay, is Stavros, the capital village of north Ithaka at the foot of Mount Neritos. Stavros, which means crossroads, also envelops the hamlets of Pilicata and Kalyvia and acted as a 'chora' in the 16th century to avoid pirate attacks. A stern and imposing bust of Odysseus stands in the shady central platia and the village has several traditional old houses that survived the 1953 Ithaka earthquake. Stavros has several good tavernas and cafes as well as a mini-market. **Exoghi:** Exoghi village, just north of the village of Stavros, is one of the oldest on Ithaka and it is picture postcard stuff for the tourists with panoramic views over the countryside. Many houses here may have fallen into disrepair but this is still a picturesque village in a picturesque spot with wonderful vistas down to Afales and over the sea. Exoghi is noted for its three small pyramids built in 1933. The eccentric builder and his mother are buried under two of them. The main village church of Agia Marina is well worth a visit and there is also a small cafe here…

The Island of Ithaka:

Afales: Dramatic white cliffs enclose the deep inlet at Afales which sits a few hundred feet below the village of Exoghi. Remote and relatively inaccessible it is rarely visited except in the high season. Those that venture here do so by boat as the descent on foot is suicidally dangerous. Visitors may be disappointed as this north-facing beach of stone and pebble tends to collect its fair share of detritus. There is no shade and there are no facilities here. **Frikes Port:** Frikes is a major holiday resort in the north of Ithaka, along with its neighbour Kioni which lies just around the headland. Frikes retains plenty of Greek charm with cafes and tavernas are strung around a dainty harbour and a sleepy village luxuriantly planted with bougainvillea. Streets are so narrow that a one system operates for traffic. Ferries from Lefkas arrive in the morning and Frikes is briefly busy with arrivals before settling back to its sleepy ways. This is a good base to explore the Island with splendid countryside walks along cleared coastal trails. The bay to the south offers a string of small coves and beaches, most of them easily accessible from the coast road. The beaches are all much the same, small pebble and stone coves with no facilities. One of the best, and nearest to Frikes, is Kourvoulia, a narrow scoop of shingle. **Kioni:** Kioni is the premier resort on Ithaka. It is a picture postcard idea of a Greek Island resort with smart houses and apartments climbing the hills around a secluded horseshoe bay. Holidaymakers parade around the harbour before moving into one of several waterside bars and tavernas. Cars are banned from Kioni village over the summer. Kioni is so cute it should be cheesy, but it somehow manages to marry authentic charm to the demands of tourism. Those who tire of tavernas can visit tiny coves at the mouth of the bay, windmills on the headland or walk donkey trails in the hills. The beach sits below the windmills, a steep, short and narrow bank of pebble and shingle with overhanging trees at one end. A beach cantina opens in the summer…

The Greek Island of Kalymnos

Kalymnos is one of the most northerly Islands of the Dodecanese group of Islands and is located about 100 kilometres north-west of the Greek Island of Rhodes. It lies near to the Turkish coast, with the Islands of Leros to the north and Kos to the south. The airport of Kalymnos works only in summer and receives flights only from Athens. Ferries depart from the Athens port of Piraeus 3-4 times per week. The busy port capital of Pothia is set in an amphitheatre around a large harbour. The lack of an international airport and a relatively low number of mostly poor beaches means tourism has not yet taken off in a big way here. The main tourist area on the Island is found at Massouri on a stretch of the west coast opposite the impressive Islet rock of Telendos. Most beaches on Kalymnos are shingle and stone but there is a splendid sand shoreline at Emborio, a charming resort at Vathi and several beach coves on the Islet of Telendos. Kalymnos largely consists of huge areas of barren, grey rock, a huge attraction to serious climbers who arrive in good numbers to tackle some of the most spectacular climbs in Europe. Despite its lack of old Greek charm, regular visitors who come to Kalymnos are fiercely positive about its charms. Good beaches are few and far between on Kalymnos. The main beach strip is in the west at Myrties and Massouri, opposite the islet of Telendos. Beaches here, however, are narrow steep strips of stone and shingle. The remaining resorts are flung far and wide. The best is at Emborios, to the north, with other sandy beaches at Vlychadia, to the west, and Akti in the east…

The Island of Kalymnos:

Pothia Port: The Island capital of Pothia is squeezed between steep grey mountain slopes in the south-east of the Island. The town is a colourful and lively amphitheatre built around the harbour with a complex of public buildings at the centre of the waterfront. The south end of the port is full of tourist shops, bars, hotels and yachts while the more interesting northern end has a market, traditional fish tavernas and shops. Wherever you are in Pothia expect lots of noise. This is a busy place, with a reputed 6,000 motorbikes and most of them whining along the sea front or growling down side streets. Pothia's streets are a narrow maze of bars, cafes, pool halls and bike shops. It's easy to get lost in back streets lined with crumbling neoclassical houses, many with extraordinary wrought iron balconies. An Archaeological and Folk Museum sits on the northern hillside and the Nautical Museum at the west end of the port with details about the lives of Pothia sponge divers of years gone by. A beach just beyond the museum is little more than a strip of rubble dotted with a few tamarisk trees. About a kilometre south are the warm water springs at Therma where a spa offers modern bathing facilities. Above Pothia are the ruins of a Byzantine castle.

Vlychadia Bay: West of Pothia is the village of Vothini and beyond that the inlet at Vlychadia which has two pleasant bays each side of the small harbour, one a gentle curve of shaded sand the other a small strip of clean pebbles. Both are backed by good tavernas. The main Vlychadia beach is a pleasant crescent of coarse sand and shingle with a line of tamarisk trees providing good shade. The water is shallow, though a little stony underfoot. Clearly marked behind the beach is the extraordinary Museum of Submarine Finds, open most days. Regular boat excursions leave here for the cave at Kefala just along the coast to the south-west. It's a 30 minute walk off the boat but visitors are rewarded with vividly colourful rock formations and a particularly imposing stalagmite in the largest of the six chambers…

The Island of Kalymnos:

Rina Port: The coast road heading east out of Pothia winds along the coast before heading up into the hills where the views are dramatic. About 10 kilometres out of Pothia, the short, fertile valley of Vathi snakes down to the sea covered in groves of olive, tangerine and lemon. On the shore lies the pretty port of Rina where a clutch of tavernas feed the visiting tourists and where boats line the long narrow inlet that has hills rising sharply on each side of the port. Boat excursions leave here for the stalagmite encrusted Dhaskilio cave, set in the cliff along the gorge and there are tiny beaches at Almyres and Dhrasonda that are only accessible by boat. **North West Beaches:** Vlychadia is pretty well the only beach resort in the south west while the south-east has the port of Rina. The main Island beach strip lies north-west of Pothia and is reached along the road that runs along the valley towards the islet of Telendos. Almost all tourist development is concentrated along the coast that lies opposite the islet of Telendos. **Linaria:** The beach at Linaria where the sand is a coarse grey gravel and grit that tends to collect rubbish; it's thin and narrow with a few overhanging trees to provide a little shade in the mornings. Two tavernas edge the road above Linaria with fine views over the bay. **Platis Gialos:** Platis Gialos beach is one of the best beaches on the Island with access down a steep road or steps leading down from a taverna high up that also serves excellent food. The long swathe of shingle beach is clean with interesting rocky coves at both ends. A few sunbeds are set outside a basic, but excellent, taverna that has been built into the cliff at the back of the beach to provide food, drink and toilets at beach level…

The Island of Kalymnos:

Myrties: North of Panormos lies Kalymnos Island's main tourist strip which starts at Myrties, although it is very much low key. The road snakes down a steep hillside with impressive views of Telendos islet offshore. A line of tourist shops and a mini-market edge the main road through Myrties with a couple of bars. Side streets lead down to a ferry jetty flanked by tavernas and a narrow stone and shingle beach. Stone and shingle continue underwater so bathers will need footwear. Sunbeds appear in the high season and tamarisks add some natural shade. The jetty is where visitors to Telendos catch the hourly ferries. **Massouri:** Massouri is packed with hotels, souvenir shops and English breakfast bars. The main street of Massouri runs straight through the resort and the seashore. It's a very impressive stretch of coast with steep hills behind, lush vegetation along the coastal strip and the spectacular sight of Telendos soaring out of the sea across the narrow bay. The beaches are narrow and of grey sand, stone and shingle which dips quite sharply into the sea. Shade comes from a line of tamarisk trees and sunbeds are on the beach in high season. Ferries leave regularly for day trips to Telendos. The best beach areas are at the southern end, notably at neighbouring Melitcahas, well signposted off the main road, with a couple of lines of sunbeds and some tavernas. **Telendos Islet:** The Islet of Telendos soars out of the sea opposite Myrties like a giant volcanic plug. It was actually formed by an earthquake in 500 AD that split it off from the mainland, destroying the ancient capital of the Island as it did so. Today Telendos is one of the best reasons for visiting Kalymnos, with a smart quayside packed with good tavernas and tiny beaches dotted about in the islet's many coves. There are no roads on Telendos and no traffic. The wide quayside is paved and a dozen or so tavernas place tables along the shore. It's a romantic setting and a favourite of couples enjoying evening views across the water to the twinkling lights of Myrties and Massouri…

The Island of Kalymnos:

Climbing in Kastelli: The Kastelli area is a huge draw for climbers eager to tackle the rugged limestone crags for which Kalymnos is renowned while the coast is laced with rocky coves. There is also a picturesque white chapel by the seashore nearby and, although steps have been laid down the cliff, the climb is a difficult one and should only be attempted by those who are fit. **Arginondas:** Past the coastal hamlet of Karavostavi are some spectacular views over the sea, now dotted with fish farms is the sheltered inlet of Arginondas. It has a small pebble beach backed by olives, pines and with a couple of tavernas. The village is also the start of a good inland walking trail between the mountains to the port of Vathi on the other side of the Island. Arginondas is also another jumping off point for many climbers tackling the many sheer cliffs and challenging rock faces found on this part of the coast. **Emborios:** The road north ends at the sheltered, peaceful and south-facing the beach of Emporios, otherwise called Emborio, and considered one of the best on the Island. A coarse sand beach is backed by tamarisk trees and a string of tavernas. It shelves steeply into a sea of large stones and banks of seaweed so it's not good for children but the views to the offshore Islets are delightful. A couple of shoreline tavernas put out sunbeds in the high season and there is a caique to Massouri that leaves in the afternoon for those who do not fancy the local bus. A steep climb at the western end of Emborios leads over a small hill to Rachi, for even more secluded sands, shaded by trees and with a summer beach cantina. Emborio is the end of the road for the daily bus and only hardy hikers will venture into the hills from here…

The Greek Island of Kefalonia

Kefalonia is one of the larger Greek Islands in the Ionian chain that runs down the west coast of Greece with Corfu and Lefkas to the north and Zante (Zakynthos) in the south. Kefalonia has an international airport. Popularised by the hit Hollywood movie 'Captain Corelli's Mandolin', the Island has long been a favourite of the British. The main holiday resorts stretch along the south-west coast where the best of the beaches are to be found. Most of the beaches on the Island are big and sandy with shallow water and the usual tourist facilities. The forest-carpeted mountains offer spectacular views over the Island, although drivers face long drives over mountain roads to reach the more remote northern and eastern resorts. Car hire on the Island of Kefalonia is a must for those aiming to explore the Island's attractive, but remote, beaches or planning to visit the Pali peninsula opposite the main port of Argostoli. Kefalonia is a big Island and public transport is relatively infrequent. Consequently most tourists, without cars, are confined to the south coast with organised day trips to attractions in the north by coaches or boats. As well as magnificent scenery and excellent beaches, Kefalonia also boasts some unusual attractions such as the spectacular caves at Melisani and Drogorati that attract thousands of visitors every year. Kefalonia is a large and mountainous Island and the beaches are widely spread out. The main resorts are at Lassi, Lourdas and Skala which are all widely spread along the south-west coast. Other beaches such as Myrtos and Antisamos are relatively remote and often difficult to reach. The Pali peninsula grows more popular each year but again, it's relatively isolated…

The Island of Kefalonia:

Argostoli Port: The capital once bursting with stylish Venetian mansions and elegant bell towers are no more thanks to the bombs that were dropped by the Luftwaffe in World War II and a 1953 earthquake that reduced much of Argostoli to rubble. Cement was used extensively to rebuild the City and the result is a mish-mash of sober cubes that might be termed 'utilitarian' by the more generous. Paved mosaics on the harbour promenade emulate waves in a spirited attempt to brighten up a vista of seaside cement and a large grey-flagged square provides the city a central focus. Around the edges of the square are outdoor cafes and tavernas with food of a high standard. The traffic-free shopping street of Lithostroto is mostly department stores and shoe shops. In the afternoon siestas Argostoli turns into a ghost town. A British-built stone causeway across the lagoon connects Argostoli to the rest of the Island. **The Beaches of South West Kefalonia:** The south-west coast is the main beach strip of Kefalonia with sandy bays stretching from Fanari, in the north, to Skala on the south-east tip. The main resorts are at Lassi, Lourdas Bay and Skala with many small coves between. A good road links them all but other resorts demand long and tiring drives over the central mountains. **Fanari:** Fanari is the coast road, also called the 'Romantic Road', that skirts the headland from Argostoli to Lassi and it has several beach coves to explore. First out of Argostoli is Maistrato beach, a tiny shingle bay with a small taverna. On the headland is Katovrethes where a restored watermill fronts the famous swallow holes where the sea disappears underground to resurface on the other side of Kefalonia. Nearby, the picturesque Fanari lighthouse turns out to be only a replica of a rotunda built by the British here in the 1820's. There are several shingle coves along the shoreline. Near Lassi is a sandy cove at Kalamia, named after the bamboo that surrounds it. Just before Lassi are small coves of pink sand, sea caves and large rock formations located at Grandakia…

The Island of Kefalonia:

Lassi: Lassi is a ribbon of modern tourist development with a string of fine sandy beaches nearby. There is no village, just a narrow road flanked by tavernas, tourist shops and the odd mini-market. The inventively named Makrys Yialos (Long Beach) and Platys Yialos (Wide Beach) have fine soft sand and gently sloping shorelines making them great for families with children. There are the usual watersports to entertain and a few rocks to add interest. The tiny hamlet of Minies has a mini-market, taverna and a good beach, although it's too near the airport runway to be very popular. Next door are the pink sands of Spasmata, separated from Minies by a rocky outcrop. **Svoronata:** Just south of the Island airport is the peaceful village of Svoronata, rather spread out but with a few good tavernas, a mini-market and a garage. The main attraction is a clutch of small beaches and the popular tourist strip at nearby Lassi. The beach at Ammes is small, narrow and sandy, rarely crowded and with a small cantina. South beyond the cape is Al Helis, is a pleasant secluded bay with pinkish sand, a beach bar and sunbeds at the bottom of steep stone steps. Around the headland is a narrow sandy strip at Megalipetra, where huge rocks lie offshore, and beyond that Avithos, the furthest and the best, with a long south-facing beach of soft sand, clear shallow seas and a taverna set in the cliff. The beach is well protected by sloping sandstone cliffs. Gently shelving, it offers safe swimming for families while the offshore islet of Dias is topped with a tiny white chapel. **Lourdas Bay:** The long bay of Lourdas accommodates several beaches. The small harbour at Spartia has sandy coves each side of the small quay, one of which has rocks encrusted with fossilised shells which makes for some interesting snorkeling. Pessada is the port for the Zakynthos ferry and next to the harbour is a small cove of flat rocks and a small sandy strip below some steep steps. Ferries to Skinari, on Zante, run twice daily in the summer months…

The Island of Kefalonia:

Trapezaki: Trapezaki is much favoured alternative to Lourdas beach and it is reached down a steep road from the village of Moussata. The road is so narrow that a one-way traffic system operates in the summer. It has two sandy beaches split by a small marina, where a beach bar opens in the high season. Both beaches are narrow but there is plenty of shade from trees along the shoreline. The waters are shallow and the sands long enough to ensure they never get crowded. Sheltered by the mountain behind, Trapezaki can feel almost tropical and, being a little off the beaten track and very relaxed and peaceful. **Lourdas:** Also called Lourdata, the village square has tavernas and shops set around a huge plane tree and here the road drops steeply to the sea. The beach is downhill from the village and is a beach of white, sandy grit and is combined with the neighbouring Trapezaki to create a five kilometre swathe. At the Lourdas end the eye-glaring sand is edged with a grey cement sea wall topped by a dirt track and a handful of tavernas. **Katelios:** Katelios, also known as Agia Varvara, has a series of good sand beaches. A small fishing harbour sits at the western end of the main beach, about 200 metres long and backed by eucalyptus and pine with tavernas serving fresh fish. To the east is Potomakia beach where the loggerhead turtles nest. Guided tours of the sands are offered and a trail of blue ribbon leads visitors past the nest sites to the next beach at Kaminia, a pleasant spot with good sands, shallow water and a cantina. Several beach coves here are collectively called Mounda that end at a cape and even more turtle nesting grounds. Shallow waters make coves along this part of the coast ideal for families, although they are encouraged to stay near the shoreline and away from the turtle nesting sites. To help protect the nests visitors are asked to leave the beaches before dusk…

The Island of Kefalonia:

Skala: The huge sandy beach at Skala is long and deep, sweeping around the headland for about four kilometres. Sharp sand and a steep shoreline shelf make it less than ideal for children but the deep golden sand more than offset this. Skala resort has grown fast in recent years and it's now one of Kefalonia's most popular beach resorts. Around 30 tavernas and a scattering of music bars and souvenir shops meet the demands of rising numbers of visitors. Most of the bars and shops are found in the main street or just off it. For the more culturally minded there are well-preserved mosaics at a Roman villa. **East and North Coast Beaches:** Just a smattering of resorts lie along Kefalonia's east coast, from Poros in the south to Fiskardo on the northern tip. Sami Bay is more a port than resort. This part of Kefalonia enjoys splendid scenery with the Island of Ithaka just offshore. The north has mountain trails but little else, apart from the entrancing hamlet of Assos and the jewel of a beach at Myrtos. **Poros:** The coast road north from Skala goes to beaches around Poros where the ferry docks from mainland Kilini. Poros has a fine marina, a narrow beach of pebble and sand and a good selection of tavernas. It's a good base for exploring this side of Kefalonia away from the tourist crowds. The town beach, called Aragia, is a 600 metre stretch of shingle and sand, with a wide, promenade behind. Sunbeds are for hire but the steeply banked beach makes it a poor choice for children. Another pebble beach lies across a short river bridge offering more sunbeds, some motor boats for hire and several pleasant tavernas. A motor boat is needed to reach the few pebble-dashed coves north of Poros. The best of these are at Makria Petra (Greek for long stones) and at Koutsoupia, both of them backed by thick woods of pine…

The Island of Kefalonia:

Antisamos: Once a tranquil, rustic hideaway just south of Sami, the photogenic beach at Antisamos was once backed by small fields of grazing goats and attracted the few visitors prepared to attempt the scary descent down a rough track. But a new road was carved out of the hillside to accommodate movie crews and equipment for shooting scenes for Captain Corelli's Mandolin and now the beach has become a major Island attraction. A large taverna and car park has been built at the back of the beach and cars now make a relatively easy hairpin descent to the dramatic horseshoe bay with its steep bank of brilliant white pebbles. The beach is a sweeping crescent of white stones dropping sharply along an ultramarine shore and framed by tree-carpeted slopes. **Sami Port:** North of Antisamos, a dirt path off the coast road drops to the picturesque pebble bay at Paliouras where a narrow ribbon of pebble and rock is found. The main road leads on to the ferry port of Sami, the former capital of Kefalonia. The resort is a good holiday base, close to the spectacular Antisamos beach and near the Island's famous caves at Drogarati and Mellisani. Narrow and bare strips of shingle and sand line the shore at either end of a promenade. **Agia Efimia Port:** The pretty little fishing port of Agia Efimia (aka Efemia, Effimia or Evfimia) is sited a few kilometres north of Sami. The harbour is one of the departure points for boats to Ithaca and to the mainland port of Astakos. Agia Efimia is also a popular staging post for yachting flotillas and tavernas will often howl to the exploits of holiday sailors. A small selection of tavernas, mostly lined along the harbour wall, serves good food. Agia Efimia suffers from a lack of beaches; just three tiny coves around the resort and a few more scattered further along the coast…

The Island of Kefalonia:

Fiskardo: Fiskardo's building were almost the only ones on Kefalonia to escape the 1953 earthquake, lending a Venetian authenticity to the village not found elsewhere on the Island. A favourite on the day trip circuit Fiscardo heaves with visitors at most times of the year, but July and August are a swarms of visitor and expensive boats tossing about in the harbour. **Assos:** The north-west coast of Kefalonia is a rugged wilderness but for the single coastal resort of Assos where an almost unreal beauty stops visitors in their tracks. There is no beach to speak of, just a few small tavernas perched on the quayside overlooking a small, circular bay but this Greek hamlet oozes a perfectly placid charm. A spectacularly steep and winding road snakes down into a village tucked neatly inside the narrow neck of a peninsula. The huge rock outcrop is topped with the ruins of a Venetian castle. The 1953 earthquake reduced the original Assos to rubble. A narrow pebble and sand strip lines the village square but more attractive and deserted coves lie each side of the peninsula, although a boat is needed to reach them. Astonishingly, Assos was the capital of northern Kefalonia in 1593 when the castle was built. Today, the fortress is in a state of disrepair but worth a visit for the spectacular views it gives. Assos is also notorious for the German slaying of 1,500 Italian soldiers after Italy surrendered to the Allies in 1943. The beauty of this village is amazing and a must see for holidaymakers. **Myrtos:** It's the beach all the brochures boast about; Kefalonia's postcard pin-up of Myrtos Beach. It is a long ribbon of white stones curtained with pale yellow, almost vertical cliffs. Myrtos has won many awards including best beach in Europe. But the scene from the hill above is just as memorable. On the beach the white pebbles drop sharply into the sea and on windy days the waves can be rough. A basic cafe and sunbeds arrive on the bleached stones in high summer. South of Myrtos, near the village of Agonas and the start of the Pali peninsula, is the long and little frequented beach of Agia Kyriaki. It's mostly pebble with some sand. There is a small marina with boats for hire, a fish taverna and a summer beach cantina…

The Island of Kefalonia:

Paliki Peninsula: The Pali or Paliki peninsula lies on the north side of Argostoli Bay, almost another Island. Large and remote its resorts are much less visited. Regular ferries run from Argostoli to Lixouri while the road route loops in a long arc north, then south through tiny villages. Beaches on the south coast of Pali are mostly sandy, pleasant and without the crowds. **Xi:** Just east of Vatsa Bay is the popular and singularly named Xi or Ksi, a flat beach of shingled sand backed by high white cliffs. It is both very long, at four kilometres, and quiet. Underwater rocks litter the shallow seashore. The coast here benefits from an annual clean-up by volunteers. Hotels and apartments line the shore and water taxis visit nearby Vardiani islet. To the east of Xi, down a turn-off before the village of Soullari, is a huge stretch of red sand called Megas Lakkos. A snack bar opens and sunbeds appear in high season. Lepada beach adds some welcome colour to nearby Lixouri. Golden to reddish sand in a sheltered cove bound by attractive rocky sea outcrops that will appeal to snorkelers. There is a beach bar, sunbeds and boats for hire. Along the beach is a cave and the abandoned monastery of Aghia Paraskevi.
Lixouri Port: The second largest town on Kefalonia, Lixouri lies on a peninsula across the water from the City of Argostoli and is best reached by using one of the regular ferries. Lixouri was virtually destroyed in the 1953 earthquake. Lixouri was rebuilt and its shops have genuine local products on sale and the Lakovatos Mansion is a rare example of how elegant Lixouri once was, being one of the few Venetian houses to survive the earthquake. A few nondescript beaches lie to the north although they offer splendid views of the coastline opposite and the Agios Dinati Mountains above. Risata is just a narrow strip of stone while a thin stretch of sand and shingle at Andronikikos runs parallel to the road. At Livadi is another pinched strip of beach with fine views out over the bay…

The Greek Island of Kos

Kos Island, Greece, sits bang in the middle of the Dodecanese chain of Greek Islands that hug the Turkish coastline between Rhodes in the south, and the Island of Patmos, in the north. Holidays on the Island of Kos are hugely popular with the British. There are international flights to Kos, as well as ferries to Kos from Athens. Kos is one of the best Islands in Greece when it comes to a typical beach holiday. It was among the first to go for mass-market tourism in a big way with many Kos hotels built on the long, sandy coastline to the east and the south of the Island. Kos is long and thin, about 45 by 11 kilometres and, unlike many other Greek Islands, it's mostly flat and low-lying, especially in the north and west of the Island. As a result, much of the scenery on Kos is not outstanding by Greek standards, although it does get more mountainous in the south and east. The lack of hills has helped to make cycling a very popular Kos holiday activity and there are no end of bicycle rental outlets and even dedicated cycling lanes on the Island. As well as the nightlife of Kos Town and the plethora of beach resorts, the Island also boasts some of the best archaeological sites to be found in the Mediterranean. For many though, it's the long, sandy beaches that make a holiday to Kos so appealing with day trips by boat to nearby Turkey a very popular holiday excursion. The Island of Kos airport is one of the busiest in the Greek Islands and attracts international charters from all over the world. It lies to the west of the Island some 26 kilometres from Kos Town. It may be a long way for east coast holidaymakers but it is very handy for the main south-west beach resorts of Kamari and Kardamena. Daily local bus services run from Kos Airport to the east coast passing through north coast resorts such as Mamaris, Tingaki and Mastichari. A few ferries dock at Mastichari, the main ferry port is in Kos Town. Ferries also run daily to other Island and local tour companies run regular day trips to Turkey…

The Island of Kos:

Beaches of Kos: Kos has been a popular beach holiday destination for years and the influence of package holiday companies is felt mostly on the east coast, around Kos Town, where the big hotel complexes dominate. Apart from a string of pleasant beach resorts along the north Kos coast, the main holiday areas are to the south-west around Kamari Bay. **Kos Town:** Kos Town is a heady blend of beach resort and historic site where ancient Greek columns and Roman street mosaics are pitted against music-thumping tourist bars and the neon blink of open-air nightclubs. It was an earthquake in 1933 that unearthed many of Kos Town's ancient ruins, subsequently excavated and restored by the Italians. It was the Italians too that laid out Kos Town's 'garden suburb' grid of streets, punctuated by the Ottoman and Italianate buildings. The Town has a one-way traffic system, protection for monuments, a traffic-free main square and a smart new marina. Kos Town is at night is noisy but in the daytime it is very different and a lovely place to wander around. Kos is a pleasant town of neatly arrayed streets, wide, tree-lined and converging on attractive squares profuse with flowers and trees. The main Eleftherias Square is traffic-free and has a restored Defterdar Mosque and the Archaeological Museum with a small but excellent collection of Roman sculptures. The square also has a lively market and taverna tables galore. Nearby are the ancient Agora, a sunken bowl filled with a confusing jumble of ruins, and one of the oldest trees in Europe, said to have shaded Hippocrates himself. There is also a Venetian Castle of the Knights, built in the 14th century, is approached over a bridge that spans a former moat. An impressive 16th century gateway opens into a large compound liberally littered with crumbled statues and pillars. The Western excavation has impressive ruins that include a Roman nymphaeum, the House of Europa with a floor mosaic depicts a bull carrying off Europa, a 3rd century Roman villa with courtyards, bathing pools, and mosaic floors and the Roman Odeon. Kos Town beach marks the start of a long trail of sand that leads south to the cape at Agios Fokas. Nearer to town the beach is narrow and can be noisy with edge-to-edge sunbeds…

The Island of Kos:

Platani: Inland from Kos town is the village of Platani, the last refuge for the Island's dwindling Turkish community. In the 1960's there were around 3,000 Turks in Platani but as the enmity between the two countries has grown so the population has declined to a few hundred. **Asfendiou:** A group of hamlets lie clustered on the slopes of Mount Dikeos, or Dikaion, known collectively as the Asfendiou district. Lost in the greenery of thick forests, Asfendiou is about as traditional Greek as it gets on Kos these days. At Pilaiopoli a ruined castle perched proudly on a pinnacle of rock offering wonderful views over hills and sea. Asomati has the most picturesque of the whitewashed houses on the Island while Evangelistra boasts some of its best tavernas. At west-facing Zia tour buses unload scores of visitors every evening to enjoy dramatic sunsets and 'Greek Night' parties. The friendly locals never seem to tire of the visiting hordes. Zia claims to have the oldest windmill on the Island and many local shops sell the locally-produced thyme flavoured honey and olive oil. **East Coast Beaches:** A coast road runs from Lambi in the north to Agios Fokas in the south with back-to-back hotels, hemmed in by a service road and cycle track. **Psalidi:** South of Kos town, and really just an extension of it, is the holiday beach area of Psalidi which has little more than a sprinkling of tavernas, a few supermarkets and lots of large hotels. Psalidi beach is pebbles and shingle with a little sand now and then with access down paths from the main coast road. The facilities on the beach are sunbeds, brollies, showers, toilets, beach bars and watersports. The best area is at Blue Beach which has grass on which to sunbathe. Local buses to town are frequent and cheap and there is a good cycle lane. It is possible to walk, but only by dodging the cycles that career along the path both day and night…

The Island of Kos:

Embros Thermi: Popular with windsurfers, Agios Fokas has hot thermal springs and a beach of grey sand and grit. The hot springs lie beyond the headland on a south coast strip of grey volcanic sand backed by brooding rocks and dominated by a huge rock outcrop that towers above. A regular bus service to Kos Town and the novelty of a warm sea makes the resort a popular target for day trippers. The hot water flows into the sea over a pebble beach so it's ideal for swimming. **North Coast Beaches:** North Kos is flat and featureless, giving easy access to beach resorts but offering little scenic interest except out to sea where Pserimos, Kalymnos and Turkey are all visible. Seawater in the north are warmer but it is also breezier. Cycling and horse riding are popular and the beaches tend to be quieter. **Lampi:** The beach at Lampi, or Lambi, lies to the north-west of Kos Town within bus, cycling or even walking distance. The fine, long, straight one kilometre stretch of gently shelving white sand is considered by many the best family beach on the Island and very safe for children. With a regular and frequent bus service Lampi attract daily visitors from Kos Town, with evening traffic in the opposite direction as Lampi holidaymakers check out the night-life in Town. Sunbeds and brollies litter the shore and watersports on offer include parasailing. Like all northern beaches, it can get rather windy at times and the waves can come crashing in. **Tingaki:** Tingaki, or Tigaki, is a busy and often crowded beach resort that has become very popular with British and German holiday makers. The resort is a single street of bars, cafes and tourist shops in a flat and featureless landscape. Facing north, the long and sandy beach is mainly good white sand backed by low dunes and, although it drops sharply at the water's edge, is shallow for some way beyond. The sand improves to the west until they reach the salt pans where it turns hard and flat. The salt pan marsh which can stay wet well into June is an ideal stopping off point for migratory birds, tame terrapins and **zillions of mosquitoes**…

The Island of Kos:

Marmari: East of the large salt pans of Tigaki is the beach resort of Marmari where the white sands broaden and bank up into low-lying dunes. Marmari is about 15 kilometres from Kos Town and enjoys quieter seas than Tingaki with the sand sloping even more gently into the sea, although swells can get pretty heavy in windy weather. Several tavernas and small shops sell basic foodstuffs as well as the usual tourist souvenirs. **Pyli:** Inland from the beach resort at Marmari is the area known as Pyli, the joint name for the three neighbouring hamlets of Armaniou, Agios Giorgios and Agios Nikolaos. Set in lush countryside, the villages are a maze of cobbled streets and whitewashed homes with the odd taverna and coffee shop. **Mastichari Beach and Port:** Mastichari, or Mastihari, has an attractive beach of flat white sand with by clutches of shady tamarisk trees with a long line of tavernas behind. Beyond the tavernas is are shopping streets lined with tourist shops, cafes and a few small bars. The resort has several seashore restaurants and bars, half a dozen mini-markets and a handful of gift shops. The beach is good, with sharp white sand, although it suffers from seaweed which collects in long banks along the shore, a problem that locals try to combat with regular clean-up operations. At the east end of the beach is a harbour wall where ferries sail daily for the nearby Islands of Pserimos and Kalymnos. **Antimakia:** Around five kilometres inland from Mastichari is one of the most photographed windmills on Kos. Antimakia is a well preserved working mill and museum that's a popular picnic spot. Pretty impressive it can look too, standing on the main street with its dozen sails unfurled. Antimakia is a picturesque hamlet of whitewashed houses that are covered with flowers. Nearby, a large 14th century fortress built by the Knights of St John dominates the central plain. It has an imposing gateway and parapets beyond that offer great views. Little is left of the buildings that were within except a couple of churches…

The Island of Kos:

South Coast Beaches: The south coast is the most popular area of the Island for beach holidays with endless stretches of sand and a scenic landscape. Seas in the south are usually much calmer than the north, but can feel colder too. Mountains provide scenic interest and, in the far west, the countryside gets very wild indeed. **Kefalos:** The Island of Kos narrows to just two kilometres before widening again at the rugged, volcanic area of Kefalos to the west. Kefalos village sits high on the hillside, with the old town above and the sprawling bay and beach resort of Kamari below. The old streets are awash with white houses and colourful doors and windows. Views from the hill fort at Kefalos are impressive. Even higher up are the twin peaks of Mount Zini and Mount Latia, both spiked with radio masts and Zini is also scarred by a large quarry. Kefalos is the end of the line for local buses and is an outpost for adventurous hikes into the western wilderness that ends at the rugged peninsula of Cape Kikello. Regular tours leave Kefalos for the ruins of the ancient Astypalia amphitheatre and to a cave at Aspi Petra, said to be inhabited in Neolithic times. To the north is Limnionas that has twin beaches each side of a peninsula and a small harbour. **Kamari:** Kamari Bay is the beach resort of Kefalos with a five kilometre stretch of shingle and sand reaching almost to Agios Stefanos. The resort is packed with restaurants and bars aimed squarely at the British tourist market with its all-day breakfast, chips with everything, happy hours, giant TV screens and plenty of karaoke. Kamari is a relatively sedate beach resort for the middle-aged UK package tour holidaymaker. The shingle shoreline of sand turns to large stones under the sea and dips sharply and there are plenty of sunbeds and watersports on offer. The offshore islet rock of Kastri is within swimming distance but reaching it is not easy given the volume of passing boats, windsurfers and other water traffic. The seawater is crystal clear but it's said to be the coldest on Kos…

The Island of Kos:

Agios Stefanos: The Kamari beach stretches five kilometres to Agios Stefanos, a once pretty village now it is overshadowed by a Club Med complex which has also nabbed the best sand. At this point Kos is only two kilometres wide and even south facing beaches like this have little protection from the strong northern 'meltemi' summer winds. A nearby headland has the ruins of a couple of triple-aisled 6th century basilicas with some excellent bird mosaic floors.
Paradise Beaches: Opposite the resort at Kamari sits a succession of sandy Kos beaches that attracts holidaymakers from all over the Island. A single stretch of sand runs for several kilometres, sheltered by a cliff backdrop. Camel beach is in a small, pretty bay, has fine golden sand and dramatic wind-sculpted cliffs behind. Rock formations out in the clear water add interest, especially for snorkelers. A beach cantina sits behind on a beach which tends to be less popular as access from the large car park above is very steep. Camel beach is a favourite with nudists. Paradise beach is also known as Bubble beach on account of underwater volcanic vents which warm the water here a degree or two. It is immensely popular, gets very crowded all along its considerable length. Sheltering cliffs, good clean sand and shallow water make it ideal for families with children. There are several cantinas on hand in the high summer and this is a popular day out destination for those staying in Kefalos and Kamari across the bay. To see the bubbles bather must wade out to sea. Banana beach is probably the cleanest beach of the lot and the most picturesque, with junipers straddling the low sand dunes behind. Sunny beach which is long and narrow and backed by low scrub carpeted rocks. There are sunbeds and cantinas but it tends to be much less crowded. Magic beach, also called Poleni, is the longest, broadest and least tamed of them all. It is also the least populated. The far western end of this strip of beaches is called either Xerokambos or Exotic beach depending on whether visitors can pronounce Greek. But it can be quite dangerous as it is backed by an army tank and artillery range so venture there with caution…

The Island of Kos:

Kardamena: Kardamena beach resort is a heaving tourist resort of discos and burger bars that wouldn't look out of place on the Costa Brava but is in fact located just five kilometres south of Kos airport. This once picturesque Greek fishing village, was once charming, friendly and famous for its fine ceramics, but it has been changed due to commercial interests and is now aimed mainly at the youth holiday market. A beachfront of concrete frontage closely follows the coasts contours and has rows of noisy bars and cafes opening out onto the wide sandy beach that runs for two kilometres each side of the resort. During the day youngsters are flayed by the sun and then get puddled with alcohol at bars called Slammers, Bonkers and Crackers by night. Kardamena bars must turn off the music at midnight but clubs still stay open until 3.30 am during the week and until 6 am at the weekend. The bars hold foam parties and karaoke nights and the visiting youngsters love it to bits. The persistent may find moussaka on a menu somewhere but most will settle for chips, baked beans and lots of lager. There are boat excursions to the volcanic islet of Nisyros and in summer, during the White Bait Festival, even the locals let their hair down with street parties. At the eastern end of the beach is the self-contained package resort of Tolari, a 1,000-bed hotel complex where a village used to stand. All in all this resort is not for the faint hearted or for those looking for a relaxing holiday in the sun…

The Greek Island of Lefkas

Lefkas, or Lefkada as it can be called, is one of the Ionian chain of Islands that lie just off the west coast of mainland Greece. Corinthians cut a canal through sandbanks connecting it to the mainland in 600 BC and Lefkas still only just qualifies as an Island. Holiday interest grew in the Island with the opening of Preveza airport on the Greek mainland coast and an improved road connection that paved the way for tourism. The large, sheltered bays on the east and south coast of Lefkas make both Nidri and Sivota a favourite haunt for yachts as are the heavily indented bays of the offshore Islets such as Meganissi. On the much less populated west coast, rugged cliffs, rocky shores and exposed beaches are a magnet for the more adventurous while Vassiliki, in the south, is a world class windsurfing centre. Those seeking modern facilities in a traditional Greek setting will find the Island of Lefkas an attractive beach holiday destination. Parts of Lefkas are quite astonishingly beautiful, notably inland where flower strewn hill villages nestle in lush, green pine forests. Like most of the Ionian chain of Islands the best Lefkas beaches are found on the gently sloping east side of the Island. The west coast of Lefkas is mostly sheer cliff although there are notable beaches on the south-west at Porto Katsiki and a clutch to the north-west around Agios Nikolaos. The main Lefkas beach resorts are at Nidri on the east coast and the noted windsurfing beach at Vassiliki to the south. The waters on the eastern shoreline are very sheltered and the deep bays are a popular stop for yacht flotillas. Increasingly popular are the Islets that lie off the southern coast of Lefkas such as Meganissi…

The Island of Lefkas:

Lefkas Town: The capital Lefkas Town, at the north-east tip of Lefkas, has suffered three major earthquakes since 1948 and today's town is an odd, architectural mix of brightly painted houses, many of them topped with wood and corrugated iron to mitigate any future damage from seismic shocks. Narrow streets help give Lefkas Town a village atmosphere, although the richly decorated Venetian churches, packed with works of art, add a cosmopolitan touch. The main square is an attractive and splits the traffic-free shopping street in two. Cafes and tavernas surround the square which can become lively at night as the street sellers set up their stalls. Other bars and tavernas can be found at the harbour that have views across to mainland Greece. Lefkas Town lies alongside a huge lagoon where the 650-berth marina is well worth a stroll around. A series of fortresses along the causeway approach testify to the Island's strategic importance in the past. The 13th century fortress at Santa Mavra has been damaged by earthquakes and an explosion in 1888 reduced many of its buildings to rubble. Lefkas Town has four museums, the oddest being the Lefkas Phonograph Museum's collection of old gramophones. Other sights include the 17th century Faneromeni Monastery set in pine woods on the hills above. The Town holds a wide variety of cultural events and festivals; it even has its own philharmonic orchestra. The town has no beach, but a four kilometre stretch of sand and pebble lies across the lagoon at Yra, also spelt Gyra. Daily local buses leave the Town for all the main Island resorts. **East Coast Beaches:** The fine beaches, good roads and attractive offshore Islets of the east coast Lefkas has lured the package tour operators, with the area around Nidri the main target for tourist development. Despite an idyllic setting, Nidri has bowed to the demands of cut-price tourism with fast food outlets and neon-lit music bars the order of the day. Many east coast resorts lie in sheltered bays and, as a result, are favourite stopover ports for the yacht flotillas…

The Island of Lefkas:

Lygia: The port resort of Lygia, or Ligia, lies about five kilometres south of Lefkas Town on the main coast road. This busy main road runs through the middle of the village and skirts the waterfront where tavernas and bars are found. The Lygia beaches are just small patches of shingle but they are sheltered and quiet, with good views across to the mainland and to Agios Giorgios castle. **Karya:** Inland from Lygia and about 15 kilometres south-west of Lefkas Town is the mountain village of Karya, with a central square full of taverna tables laid out beneath a huge, shady plane tree. Karya is worth a visit to see the local Karysaniki embroidery, once a vital part of the Island national dress. **Lazarata:** The traditional hill village of Lazarata is north-east of Karya and surrounded by craggy cliffs, olive groves, towering cypress and lush mountain scenery. Like Karya, the village has a traditional shady square with tavernas and cafes. Lazarata is a good area for walking and every turn seems to offer a stirring view of red-roofed houses, neat vineyards, olive groves, citrus plantations and lush woodland. Lazarata is an ideal spot to see the traditional rural Greek life. **Nikiana:** South of Lygia and about nine kilometres from Lefkas Town is the tiny fishing village of Nikiana spreading along the coast road with densely wooded hills rising behind. A string of sand and pebble beaches lies beyond the small harbour. The waterfront tavernas serve good food. Nikiana has a mini-market and a few shops. There are many good walks in the surrounding hills. Regular local buses head north and south, although they can be crowded with tourists travelling between Nidri and Lefkas Town. Excursion boats also leave daily to offshore islets such as Meganissi. Just off the main road to the north is the small shingle beach at Episkos where there are a few villas and a beach cantina…

The Island of Lefkas:

Nidri: Nidri is 17 kilometres south of Lefkas Town and it is now the Island's biggest holiday resort and is in a handsome setting at the mouth of the long Vlycho Bay. Once the playground preserve of billionaire Aristotle Onassis, Nidri remained undeveloped until his death in 1975 after which the locals made up for lost time. Now noisy tavernas line the Nidri seafront, part of the former beach was used to build a new quay and hotels have sprung up all over the flat, marshy ground behind. Delightful corners still exist in the village centre but the resort is now mostly geared to cut-price tourism with a plethora of cafes and music bars as well as a couple of nightclubs. Beaches are found to the north. Great settings and knockout views must be offset by long, narrow, crowded pebble beaches artificially enhanced by lorry loads of imported sand. Nidri is a major yacht and boat centre with the annual Ionian Regatta, in late September, one of the highlights of the Mediterranean year. Excursion boats leave daily for local islets and the many secluded coastal bays of Lefkas. There are also ferries leaving the port for Ithaca and Kefalonia. Inland from Nidri, the countryside is fairly flat so cycling is popular and good walking trails etch the hills beyond. **Dessimi:** The seaside village of Vlicho, or Vlycho, lends its name to the large bay that has Nidri on its north bank and the heavily wooded Geni peninsula curving around to the south. Vlycho has a pleasant string of shops and tavernas and is handy for the pebble beach at Dessimi, found down a dirt track from the village. There are tavernas, bars and a mini-market near the beach and Lefkas cruise boats often include Dessimi on their round the Island tours. **Geni:** The Geni peninsula overlooks the pretty Vlycho Bay. The village at Geni gives its name to the peninsula and it is a friendly traditional fishing village with several good waterfront tavernas…

The Island of Lefkas:

South Coast Beaches: The south coast of Lefkas is a jigsaw of inlets nestling beneath pine cloaked hills. To the east is Sivota, a favourite of the yachting flotillas, and, in the west is Vassiliki which hosts the world windsurfing championships. Beyond Vassiliki is the wild, windswept peninsula that ends at Cape Lefkas. A good road gives easy access to many of the beaches. **Poros:** The village of Poros is full of narrow alleys and beautiful traditional houses built on the steep wooded slopes and overlooking the attractive Rouda Bay, with the islet of Arkoudi offshore. About 25 kilometres south of Lefkas Town, Poros has a population of just 300. **Mikros Gialos:** The once hide-away sands of Mikros Gialos, sometimes spelt Mikros Yialos, lie below the hillside village of Poros. Tucked away at the end of Rouda Bay, the beach now has a restaurant-cum-beach bar complex that now packs in the summer visitors by the hundred. Strings of duckboards cross-cross a sand and pebble beach that's chock-a-block with sunbeds while music blares out from the beach bars. It's a beach to enjoy if you don't mind the crowds. **Sivota:** At the head of the next deep inlet lies the sheltered anchorage of Sivota, a firm favourite with the boating set. The resort boasts a bevy of fish tavernas to satisfy the yachting crowds, most of them lining the long quayside on the west side of the bay. Nestled in a picturesque wooded valley about 33 kilometres south of Lefkas Town, Sivota has a small pebble beach at the end of its harbour. It is much quieter by day than it is at night when the sailing set comes off their boats and out to play. The tavernas that overlook the harbour, take full advantage of the fine views across the bay, with olive groves and wooded hills behind…

The Island of Lefkas:

Vassiliki: The Island's highest peak at Mount Stavrotas has been eaten away by quarry firms and now looks badly scarred, and below is Vassiliki, or Vassilikos, about 38 kilometres from Lefkas Town and the Island's main water-sport resort. Huge numbers of windsurfers take to the water at Vassiliki Bay in high summer where the local geography ensures the bay is often calm in the mornings and breezy in the afternoons. The long beach is gently shelving, but stony and rough, while the bay is ideal for surfers, with the water thigh deep for many metres out. In July and August the bay is often packed and surfing clubs and rental outfits abound with boats and catamarans for hire. Vassiliki has a pleasant harbour with a ring of quayside tavernas serving good food and even a disco for the surfing youngsters. A campsite sits nearby and beachfront hotels cater mainly for younger visitors. Daily cruises leave the port for Ithaca and Kefalonia and boats offer day trips to Lefkas beaches and local islets. Vassiliki is on the east side of the bay, while the west side is known as Ponti. Pleasant walking trails follow the coast and cycling is popular in the surrounding flat countryside. A short walk south along a coastal path reveals a small and attractive beach at Agiofili which has no facilities but is a regular port of call for day trip boats. **West Coast Beaches:** Wild and windy, the west coast of Lefkas has the Island's best beaches although many require a steep climb down the cliffs to reach them. Tamer in the north-west, they get progressively wilder as you head south. The reward for those that tackle the narrow hairpins are staggering views from the cliffs and sensational beaches that must rank among some of the best locations in the Ionian Sea…

The Island of Lefkas:

Agios Nikitas: The road west out of Lefkas Town threads through Tsoukalades, a pleasant village with a small beach at Kaminia, before reaching Agios Nikitas, one the most attractive resorts on the north-west coast. The beach of sharp white sand and pebble is about 12 kilometres from Lefkas Town. It's flanked by hotels and tavernas and is quite small so it soon gets busy, especially in high summer. The beach road is traffic-free so visitors must park at the top of the hill where spaces can be in short supply on busy summer weekends. It is quite a long walk to the beach, past all the cars parked at the side of the village road. Surrounding hills are covered in olive groves and pine forest. Boats leave Agios Nikitas daily for surrounding beaches throughout the summer, notably to neighbouring Milos Beach. A little further north still is Pefkoulia, a long wide strip of coarse sand backed by shady pine trees. There is a beach bar and taverna and it can also be called, confusingly, Agios Nikitas. **Milos:** Just over the hill south of Agios Nikitas is the coarse sand and pebble beach of Milos, one of a trio along with Agios Nikitas and Kathisma which form one of the finest stretches of sandy beaches on Lefkas. Above the beach is a stone windmill, built in 1741, that has been converted into a cafe and bar. The cliff top offers spectacular views over the bay while the beach below is a long and deep stretch of coarse sand and pebble. It slopes quite steeply and the sea can get quite choppy if there is an offshore breeze. At the southern end of the beach there are some good caves. **Kathisma:** The sand at Kathisma is among the best on Lefkas, wide with pebbles and sand along the shore and a sandy seabed. It has interesting rock promontories and caves to explore and a couple of large rocks in the sea at the southern end of the beach. Kathisma often makes it into the top ten of the Med's most beautiful beaches and it's easy to see why with its long, deep, flat sands and attractive rock formations. The sand can be steeply shelving though, so children must be watched. In Kathisma many visitors stay to enjoy the sunsets from the west-facing tavernas. There are plenty of sunbeds on the beach and regular local buses run from Lefkas Town to the resort…

The Island of Lefkas:

Kalamitsi: Several beaches can be reached by walking south along the shore from Kathisma. All of them are relatively remote and without facilities but it makes a nice route for walkers. There are tiny coves at Giadoros and Theotokos, a mix of sand and shingle shaded by pine trees, and at Stous Pilos where several beach coves are strung out along the shore. The highlight of this stretch of coast is the village of Kalamitsi where attractive stone houses nestle among almond and olive groves. There are 13 old stone windmills nearby and as many chapels in the hills. Close by is a small and attractive beach that lies at the end of a three kilometre dirt track. It has large rocks along the shoreline and a cantina and a few sunbeds are put out in the summer. **Gialos:** The west coast of Lefkas is mostly rock and cliffs until you reach Gialos, or Yialos, beach near the village of Athani. The road drops from the village down a steep and narrow road with several death-defying hairpin bends to reach a car park and a couple of seasonal cantinas. The long beach of Gialos, or Yialos, is of pebble and shingle stretching south. There are sunbeds near the cantinas. Gialos beach stays in shadow until noon and the pebbles, like many beaches along the west coast, dip very sharply into the sea. **Egremni:** A three kilometre dirt track road south of Athani that snakes down to a small car park at the beach of Egremni. Then it is down a long wooden staircase (300 steps) that starts at the cliff top taverna and ends up on the long and deep beach. There are sunbeds at the bottom of the staircase and a cantina in the summer. Egremni beach is never crowded but even more secluded spots can be found both north and south, although the southern end has the greater number of coves. Egremni is not recommended for children because of the steps but also because the sea gets deep very quickly and currents can be very strong here. The seawater at Egremni beach also tends to be a little cloudy, so it is not all that great for snorkeling…

The Island of Lefkas:

Porto Katsiki: The spectacular white beach at Porto Katsiki is an astonishingly beautiful sight and one of the most attractive on the Island of Lefkas. The asphalted road takes you to the top of the cliff where there is a large car park. It is 40 kilometres from Lefkas Town and in summer traffic jams are not unknown on the narrow road. There are also excursion boats to the beach from Nidri and Vassiliki. To get to the beach a narrow staircase of around 100 wooden steps has been built into the white limestone cliff. These lead to the narrow strip of white pebbles and sand, shaded by overhanging rocks in the morning, and the sea so clear that the shadows of anchored boats darken the sea bed. Porto Katsiki beach is also a heat trap in the afternoon, with virtually no shade and no toilet facilities. There are other small coves along this stretch of coast but they are un-signposted, difficult to reach on foot and have no facilities. A landslide in 1999 caused a section of the soft limestone cliff to collapse onto the beach, but it is now been made safe. The beach has become very popular and very crowded in the high summer in recent years. **Cape Ducato:** At the southern tip of Lefkas Island is the remote and barren Cape Ducato, or Cape Lefkas, where the white cliffs drop abruptly for 70 metres into the sea. It was from here that the poet Sappho is said to have leapt in despair over unrequited love that makes this cliff top the original Lover's Leap! It is said that lunatics and criminals were once thrown from these cliffs as a cure for their afflictions and that followers of local cults have also made sea plunges from this very spot. A lighthouse is perched at the end of the cliffs and from this headland visitors can see all the way over to the Island of Kefalonia on a clear day…

The Greek Island of Leros

The Island of Leros was an Italian naval base for 30 years and once home to a notorious mental asylum, later a penal colony, the Island of Leros Greece has been a late arrival on the Greek Island holiday scene. Leros has been quickly making up for lost time and the Island is now one of the more sought after destinations among the Greek Islands, and growing in popularity, with visitor numbers rising every year. The Island of Leros is located among the north Dodecanese group of Islands, just off the Turkish coast between the Greek Islands of Kos and Samos. Ferry connections are good but the Island airport can currently only take small domestic flights. Leros has a long coastline with lots of deeply indented bays. The bays do not have any memorable beaches but they do offer that tranquil, picturesque charm that has unfortunately vanished from many of the other Greek Islands. On the Island cappuccino may have largely replaced Greek coffee in the pavement cafes but craft shops and bakeries still prevail over trinket stalls and fast food takeaways in the narrow streets of the villages. Leros has a lack of good beaches and with the stiff competition from better known neighbours has kept it largely off the tourist trail but the Island is now getting well known as a more 'traditional' Greek Island for discerning travellers. Although scares good beaches can be found, the Island landscape is as delightful as any of the other Island in the Dodecanese and its position on a major ferry route makes it easy to reach and a good base for Greek Island hopping. The growth may be low key on the Island but Leros is beginning to make its mark…

The Island of Leros:

Agia Marina Port: The port of Agia Marina is one of two large harbours on Leros (the other is at Lakki) and the main tourist centre and the port of call for most ferries and excursion boats. Cafes line the quayside which eventually leads to a narrow shingle beach, a thin strip of sharp sand and backed by a bare concrete wall. There is compensation in the sweeping views across the bay and a picturesque windmill perched on a causeway at the northern end of the beach. The warren of whitewashed back streets somewhat marred by the steady stream of traffic that squeezes through alleyways and makes crossing the roads a head spinning pain. Cafes have soft cushioned settees and internet access with cappuccinos and ciabattas on their menus. The brightly painted boats bobbing at the quayside and fishing nets sprawled to dry on the quay all add to the charm of the port. The whitewashed homes of Agia Marina sprawl up the hillside to merge with Platanos, while the impressive Byzantine castle stand aloof on the treeless skyline of Apityki, visible from virtually everywhere on the Island of Leros.
The Geography of the Island: Leros is a jigsaw of an Island that divides neatly into north and south at the capital port of Agia Marina/Platanos. The south is slightly more mountainous with a large bay gouged out at Lakki. Both parts of the Island are thinly populated. In the south the coastline both east is barren cliff and rock with little or no road access. Large quarry works on the eastern hillside at Vathia Lagadia are plainly visible. **Platanos:** The village of Platanos spreading south up the hill from Agia Marina, and now almost indistinguishable from it, is the Island's commercial and political capital. Attractive houses line the main road and the narrow alleys that branch off left and right. Platanos houses the Leros Island council and library and there are many shops, cafes and supermarkets. At the top of the hill is the main square which holds one of the biggest markets on Leros. On top of the hill the Venetian castle dominates and gives extensive views of Leros. There is a good archeological museum on the main road, housed in the renovated Astiki Sholi built in 1882 which is well worth a visit…

The Island of Leros:

Panteli: To the south, down the hillside from Platanos is the small seaside resort of Panteli or Pandeli. The road drops steeply down to the beach where there is limited parking. Cafes and tavernas embrace an attractive strip of sand and shingle in the deep bay with a couple of tavernas on the shoreline. The sea is shallow here with a few stones that give way to a sandy seabed further out so this is a good beach for families with children. Tamarisk trees behind provide natural shade while the small harbour is usually packed with fishing boats and yachts. Overlooking Panteli on a ridge below the ruins of the Venetian castle is a line of six ancient windmills. **Vromolithos:** Around the headland from Panteli is the beach at Vromolithos. The beach is shingle and coarse sand and has a couple of tavernas and some sunbeds. The coarse sand turns to shingle and stone in the middle with dense vegetation all around and some trees at the back of the beach to provide shade. The straight beach runs the length of a large open bay. The biggest problem is the slabs of rock just under the surface of the sea along the length of the beach. The slabs are large, flat and extend well offshore, many with deep crevices and a slippery seaweed coating on top. The slabs are extensive enough to make swimming a problem unless bathers are prepared to venture some way offshore. There are shops, mini-markets and cafes within easy walking distance of the beach. **Lakki Bay:** The large bay at Lakki is one of the deepest natural harbours in the Mediterranean. The Italians created the grandiose town of Portolago, now Lakki, and erected wide, boulevard streets, impressive parks and buildings in an Art Deco style. A long promenade runs the length of the shore and has eucalyptus trees and ornate lampposts, ending in a large yacht marina. A couple of small beaches lie around the bay at Koulouki and at Merikies. They are mostly of stone and have no facilities, although they are popular with the locals. A couple of cantinas provide the basics. Also near Lakki is the temple of Agios Iiannis Theologos, which dates from 1000 AD that has some astonishingly good 11th century mosaics that are well worth seeing…

The Island of Leros:

Xirokampos: Located in the extreme south of the Island Xirokampos or Xirokambos is an old seaside village at the end of a small inlet. The village is only four kilometres from Lakki. The village, although tiny, has an impressive football stadium among the olive groves, with almond and cypress trees spread along the valley. Above the village is an ancient castle, Paliokastro, built on the site of an even older Acropolis, thought to date from around 2,500 BC. The village beach is coarse sand with a few trees and bisected by a small jetty from which local schoolchildren like to dive into the sea. Shady tavernas are behind the beach and out to sea sits the tiny islets of Glironisa and beyond them the very northernmost tip of the Island of Kalymnos. **North Coast Beaches:** The road heads north from the capital port at Agia Marina to the main tourist beach strip of Leros at Alinda past the Island's small airstrip and on to the north coast at Partheni, with a military training ground to the west and mountains to the east. The long coast road has a number of beaches that are well worth a visit. **Alinda:** The main beach strip of Leros lies just north around the bay from Agia Marina at Alinda, or Alinta. The beach is a long and narrow string of shingle and sand that peters out at a rocky area where wooden jetties stick finger-like out from the shore. Taverna tables dot the shoreline offering a romantic setting with waves lapping nearby and views over the bay to Agia Marina. A line of tamarisk trees give plenty of natural shade. Cars park along the main road, separated from the sands by a low wall. To the north is a small crescent of sand on a sharp bend in the road at Krituoni. It has a small roadside cafe and there are even quieter sand and rock coves just a short walk away. Inland is the Beleni Tower, a renovated mansion house that is home to the Island's Folklore and History Museum. In August, its large courtyard hosts several cultural events…

The Island of Leros:

Panagia: Tavernas sit above the coarse sandy beach at Panagia. This is a very pleasant spot with a swathe of fine sand and clear, shallow waters, rock outcrops and low cliffs. The sands are known locally as Dio Liskaria and it is only a short climb up some steps off the beach to enjoy a taverna meal overlooking the sea. The sand here is among the best on Leros with fine views of Agia Marina, nestling between mountains across the bay. Another small beach can be found at Krifos further round the headland. There are no facilities there. **Gourna and Drymonas Beaches:** Set in a large bay on the west coast of Leros is the small resort of Gourna. The wide bay is home to two beaches, at Gourna and a little way south at Drymonas, both with long stretches of grey sand. Gourna has a wide swathe of dark sand with a clutch of tamarisks trees at the far end of the beach. Banks of dry seaweed line the shore and rocks litter the sands to the south. This is a very rural part of Leros with rolling fields behind. The beach at Drimonas is similar to Gourna but much narrower and the southern end is marred by mounds of seaweed that bank along the narrow stretch of sand with stunted tamarisks along the roadside that runs immediately behind the beach. On the north side of the bay, and approached through the inland village of Kamara, is a tiny shingle beach at Agios Isodora with a tiny white chapel spectacularly perched on an offshore rock and connected to the shore by a stone causeway…

The Island of Leros:

Partheni Bay: The coastal fishing port of Partheni, set in a long, deep bay and with the islet of Archangelos at its mouth. There are just small scraps of sand in the coves that dot the shore west of the village. A large boat repair company and various semi-industrial sites complete the scene along with the nearby airport runway and a military base. From the port tracks lead west into the hills for walking in the mountains of Kasteli, Markelos and Tourloti, although the coastal path unfortunately leads to a military area that have warning signs to keep out. Tracks to the south of the village port lead to a small, stony beach at Lia with the 10th century church of Agios Georgios built nearby that was built with stone taken from an ancient temple to Artemis. The area around Partheni is notorious with the locals for the mental asylum that was once sited here which closed in 1999, where seriously ill patients were kept in shocking conditions. To the north of the port is Agios Kioura where the church has wall paintings done by political prisoners locked up in the same asylum from 1967 to 1974. **Plefouti:** A jewel in the crown of Leros beaches, Plefouti lies to the east of Partheni over the headland in a long and peaceful bay fringed by a beach of coarse sand. At the western end several small jetties provide anchorage for fishing boats and yachts with a pleasant taverna set back among the trees. Tamarisks trees are every few yards and provide the beach with natural shade. The seabed is stone for a few metres off shore before giving way to sand. The sea is shallow and crystal clear and the beach has views out to the uninhabited islets of Strogili and Tripyti. Low hills behind the beach have fields of wheat, olive, citrus orchards and a small white chapel with the odd home here and there. A long road down the back of the beach leads to rocky coves, one of which contains an old a machine gun post from World War Two. The road turns into a rough track before curving along the coast for several kilometres until it reaches a small and remote cove of stone and pebble at Vagia…

The Greek Island of Lesvos

The Island of Lesvos or Lesbos lies among the north-eastern Aegean Islands and close to the Turkish mainland. Also called by its capital town of Mytilini, It's relatively isolated with the nearest Islands of note being Chios to the south and Limnos to the north, both some distance away. Big and beautiful, Lesvos is the third largest of the Greek Islands and although it has stretched its arms wide to embrace the tourist market it still exudes a traditional small Greek Island atmosphere. The Island has its own international airport that can take regular holiday charter flights so Lesvos doesn't have to rely on ferries to bring in the business. Where holiday tourism is evident on Lesvos, it does not dominate. The production of exceptional olive oil and the Greek trademark ouzo are still two of the Island's most important industries. Lesvos Islanders have a proud identity marked by long established cultural traditions. The beaches may not be as many, or the landscape as lovely as some of the other Greek Islands but this is still an impressive destination for discerning holidaymakers. The main attractions of the Island is its traditional Greek way of life, the varied landscape, the quaint hill villages and a sprinkling of splendid beaches. The Bay of Kalonis almost splits the Island of Lesvos in two. North of the Gulf is the main tourist area with popular resorts on the north coast. To the east is the capital Mytilini and the low-key resorts of the Gulf of Thera and west the wild and rugged mountains with few roads and even fewer people…

The Island of Lesvos:

Mytilini Port: The Island capital at Mytilini, or Mitylene, is a big, noisy port of some 30,000 people (a third of the Island's population). Mytilini has an industrial area dominated by the chimneys of olive oil refineries, but also has the waterfront and an attractive double harbour split by a castle-topped headland. Mytilini's main attractions are its castle and a wealth of good museums. The castle, founded in the 6th century and rebuilt in the late 14th, has fine Roman sculptures and mosaics plus a nice display of jewellery. Museums are plentiful and impressive. On the waterfront, the old harbour-master's house is now the Museum of Traditional Arts and Crafts while the Theophilos Museum is as delightful as it is unexpected, stuffed with paintings by local artists. To the south of Town is the Teriade Library and a Museum of Modern Art that boasts illustrations by artists such as Picasso, Matisse, Chagal and Miro while a very fine collection of icons can be seen in the Byzantine Museum beneath the impressive dome of Agios Therapon. A mock up of a 19th century Lesvos village house and a museum of costume and embroidery complete the cultural feast. The Mytilini waterfront is a hectic mix of shops and stalls. Full of surprises, the city even has its own 'Statue of Liberty' erected by one of the Island's emigrating sons. Mytilini tavernas are noted for fine dishes especially sardines. Fine Mytilini public gardens can be found near the small artificial beach at Tsamakia and, to the north-east is the Hellenistic Theatre, reputed to have held 10,000 in its heyday. **North Coast Beaches:** North of the Gulf of Kalonis, the main tourist area has several popular resorts from the bigger beach resorts of Petra and Anaxos in the west to the small coves of Mandamos and Aspropotamus in the east…

The Island of Lesvos:

Molivos Resort: Molivos, sometimes spelt Molyvos, is the main holiday resort on the Island and is a spectacularly beautiful one. Solid stone houses are topped with red-tiled roofs and many old timbered buildings have been meticulously restored to there former glory. The steep, cobbled and traffic-free streets thread their way up the hill to an imposing Genoese fortress, romantically illuminated at night. Below the central market is a narrow, cobbled main street, overhung with vines and stuffed with craft shops and art galleries while tavernas offer impressive sea views. The very pretty Molyvos fishing harbour is also lined with tavernas with a long, narrow, stony beach nearby with the best sand being at the southern end. Other attractions include a small museum, an open air cinema and a big midsummer festival of music and theatre. Excursion boats and tour buses offer daily around the Island trips. **Eftalou:** Along the coast road east of Molyvos is the small resort of Eftalou, or Eftalos, with a pebble and sand beach. The beach is set below a cliff and fringed with trees. The beach is of mostly round pebbles with a few patches of sand here and there. It also has a taverna and a bath house for dipping into the local thermal springs. Visitors can swim along the Eftalou shore where hot mineral water seeps through the rocks into the sea to create warm pools. **Skala Sikaminias Fishing Harbour:** The road east of Molyvos ends up at the charming village of Sikaminia with its attendant north coast fishing hamlet of Skala Sikaminias which is even more charming. The road drops down the steep hill to a picturesque harbour enclosed by a concrete jetty that's tipped by the tiny chapel of Panagia Gorgona (Mermaid Madonna) set into the rock. Taverna tables line the harbour beneath huge plane trees and a more romantic setting would be hard to find with splendid sunsets adding to the atmosphere. Tourist boats arrive regularly from Molivos. Beaches are in short supply, although there is a pebble one at Kaid and, further east down a six kilometre dirt track, a long swathe of pink volcanic stones at Tsonia with a taverna set back in the trees. Tsonia is a regular stop on the round-Island boat trips. An even more remote beach sits on the southern side of the bay at Limani…

The Island of Lesvos:

Aspropotamus: The road turns inland from Skala Sikaminias to the hill village of Mantmados, noted for its cheeses and fine pottery and beyond to the north-east coastal resort of Aspropotamus with its long stony beach. At the nearby hamlet of Kapi is the start of a marked hiking trail that takes in some of the finest scenery on Lesvos. **Petra:** South of Molyvos is a string of resorts that have attracted package holidaymakers in recent years. First is the resort of Petra where a wide sweep of fine, grey sand is overseen by a sheer rock outcrop. In Petra village are charming old houses, many with wooden balconies, are set in narrow winding alleys. Tavernas abound in the winding streets and a women's co-operative runs its own taverna offering more authentic local crafts. Just off the road south is the sprawling mountain village of Stipsi whose huge tavernas are candidates for popular tourist 'Greek Nights'. There is noted hill walking here along old donkey trails, with sparkling views over the sea. **Anaxos:** West of Petra lies the holiday resort of Anaxos and a three kilometre stretch of coarse sand. Anaxos is a resort with character. Sunbeds clutter the smartly kept beach where sand pitches sharply into the sea. Beach tavernas with good food and snack bars sit nearby. Anaxos offers all the usual beach facilities and watersports. West-facing Anaxos enjoys splendid sunsets over a trio of offshore islets. A few kilometres west is Avlaki where a tiny, sand beach boast a couple of excellent tavernas. Other coves along this stretch of coastline offer opportunities to escape the crowds…

The Island of Lesvos:

Skalochori: From Anaxos the road turns inland and heads over the mountains to the west coast and through the lovely mountain village of Skalochori. A secluded beach lies nearby with a pretty church above it and a taverna nearby. Small and beautiful, but lonely, beach coves lie all around the headland. To the west is the long beach at Campo Antissa where a couple of tavernas offer views right across to Turkey. **Gavathas:** The remote fishing hamlet at Gavathas is built on a peninsula. Nearby is the long, narrow and sandy Gavathas beach which has a couple of tavernas. A small harbour sits at one end of a beach backed by a few trees. The headland shelters the main Gavathas beach with several pebble and rock coves nearby. **South Coast Beaches:** The south-east is dominated by the mountain of Profitis Ilias and flanked east and west by the gulfs of Kallonis and Geras. Olive groves and pine forest dominate. This is one of the most beautiful parts of Lesvos, with pretty villages flung around the rolling hillsides. The Bay of Yeras is almost an inland sea and it has some of the most important wetlands of Greece. **Moria:** At the village of Moria a Roman viaduct still stands, surviving from the late 2nd century AD. It is well worth a visit. The viaduct towers are remarkably intact given its great age. The preserved section is around 170 metres long and includes seventeen arches that soar above the trees. The pillars are of local marble. It once carried water from the many springs in the Agiassos region to the ancient port at Mytilini, a total distance of 26 kilometres. The viaduct was shorn up in 1995 but, apart from that, has had little done to it and it remains an impressive sight…

The Island of Lesvos:

Therma Baths: The iron-rich thermal springs at Therma are worth a visit. The ancient public baths are closed to the public but behind is a new public bath house. A Turkish tower standing next to Therma baths is impressive and there are restaurants and a small beach near the harbour. **Agios Ermogenis:** At the mouth of the Gulf of Geras, is the charming beach of Agios Ermogenis with its idyllic double beaches slung either side of a chapel-topped rocky promontory with a taverna tucked into the pine clad hillside. **Tarti:** South of the Gulf of Gera is the small sheltered bay of Tarti. The beach at Tarti is a big favourite of the locals. Set in a pretty bay, the beach of coarse sand and pebble has sunbeds and tavernas. Boats often tie up to the small quay as the beach is easier to reach by boat than it is overland. The underwater caves off the nearby islet of Fara are a popular target of scuba divers. **Agiassos:** Inland from Tarti are a number of very pretty villages on the slopes of Mount Olympos. The lovely village of Agiassos sits high on the slopes in a forest of pine. The maze of narrow streets and pleasant houses is about 26 kilometres from Mytilini. Leafy tavernas and tourist shops line the cobbled Agiassos streets beneath a medieval castle. Many of the village homes have upper floors with projecting wooden balconies often bedecked with beautiful flowers. Agiassos is known for its quality crafts too, with local pottery and weaving sold everywhere on Lesvos. **Megalohori:** Located on the south side of the Olympus Mountain range are the very attractive villages of Skopelos and Palaiokipos and what many claim to be the prettiest hill village on the Island. Megalohori village shelters in a remote wooded valley about 10 kilometres north of the port resort of Plomari. The central 12th century church, with its beautiful flower filled courtyard, is in a central square lined with coffee houses, tavernas and yogurt shops. On weekend afternoons music plays as Megalochori locals dance in the streets and its August 15th celebrations are some of the liveliest (and most inebriate) in the whole of Greece…

The Island of Lesvos:

Plomari Port: Plomari is the only settlement of any size on the south-east coast of the Island of Lesvos. It is a charming town, it's the second largest on the Island and home to around 10,000 people mostly working in the local ouzo distilleries. Despite its lack of beaches Plomari has no shortage of visitors, attracted to the luxuriant surroundings, the charm of a lively port and some of the best ouzo in Greece. Many houses have timbered, overhanging galleries and Ottoman architecture is very evident. Tavernas line the palm fringed harbour but the stony beach in the Amoudhelli suburbs is small. A longer and better beach lies to the east where the road turns inland but an even better pebble beach sits six kilometres out of town at Melinda next to some remarkable rock formations. The best beach of all is further east still. Agios Isodorus which boasts a good long stretch of coarse sand. The shallows here are ideal for snorkeling and the rocks teem with sea-life.
Vatera: The longest beach on Lesvos lies west of Plomari at Vatera, a huge and magnificent bank of sand and shingle beach backed by wooded hills and about 50 kilometres from Mytilini. The beach is ideal for those seeking wild solitude. Several good walking trails can be found east of Vatera. The nearest village is four kilometres inland at Vrissa, where walls remain of an ancient Trojan town destroyed in 1180 BC. Vrissa has a good museum with a mastodon fossil and various other treasures. At the west end of Vatera beach are views of the cape at Agios Fokas and the ruins of a temple to Dionysos beneath a Christian basilica. The chapel of Agios Fokas marks the spot where an ancient port lay and paved slabs can still be seen under the water. Today, it is a small fishing port with a coffee house and some good fish tavernas. **Skala Polichnitos:** The small resort at Skala Polichnitos is noted for its many tavernas and its salt pans which stay wet even in high summer and can attract as many bird-watchers. There are three mineral springs in use near Polichnitos. The main bathhouse is close to the river bank above the seashore and has two pools (male and female). There is another spa at nearby Lisvori where the seawater is red stained by iron and has a small but excellent, taverna…

The Island of Lesvos:

West Coast Beaches: The western half of Lesvos is much less developed than the north and east and dominated by impressive mountains with the coastal areas backed by large, fertile plains and gentle roiling hills. The only two beach resorts of note are Skala Kaloni in the Kaloni Gulf and Skala Eressos in the south-east. To the far west of the Island is the world's second largest Petrified Forest of Sequoia trees. **Skala Kalloni :** On the Gulf coast, about three kilometres south of Kalloni, is the beach resort of Skala Kalloni, now a major package holiday resort thanks to a long beach of coarse sand backed by tamarisk trees. The resort can get overcrowded and busy, especially in the high season. The sands are long and deep and the waters generally calm and shallow, making it an ideal place for children. Sardines from the sheltered Gulf are prized throughout Greece and tavernas in the harbour serve up the freshest catch of the day. The Skala Kaloni Sardine Festival in August centres on the village square with free ouzo and sardines accompany the music and dancing. There is no shortage of tavernas, both in the harbour and along the beach, with several shops and a bakery. The resort's other attraction is birds. Thousands descend on the salt pans, reed beds and other wetland spots for the spring nesting while flamingos flock to the shallow waters edging the Gulf. **Agia Paraskevi:** North-east of Kalloni is the charming village of Agia Paraskevi, full of crumbling old mansions. The village is noted for its Bull Festival, celebrated for more than 200 years. Near the village are the ruins of ancient temples dating from the 3rd century BC and traces of a temple to Aphrodite are found at nearby Messa, although only the 11th century BC foundations and a few pillars are left alongside the ruins of a 14th century basilica. There is a small museum here that is stuffed with a cornucopia of treasures, from ancient copper trays to stuffed birds. The road north-west winds through the attractive hill villages of Filia and Skoutaris…

The Island of Lesvos:

Skala Eressos: The main resort in the west of Lesvos is Skala Eressos, a magnet for lesbians thanks to the ancient Greek lyric poet Sappho, who penned her verses and ran a school for girls here around 580BC. The locals are relaxed about the connection and these days Skala Eressos is as popular with typical families and a firm favourite of honeymooning couples. The reasons are pretty obvious. A long, sandy and beautiful beach lines the shore with tamarisk shaded tavernas fringing the sands, many built on bamboo decking and specialising in fish dishes. The Gulf being famed throughout Greece for its sardines. Behind the beach, the village is modern but well laid out with car-free streets and a cheerful charm with an attractive central square. A small harbour with its own sheltered beach sits nearby while a spring-fed lake is full of wildlife including storks and tame turtles that take food by hand, always with the risk of an occasional nip. Several beaches lie to the east. Chrousos has a fine crescent of golden sand at the mouth of the Mallonta River while the sand and shingle at Tavari is shaded by tamarisks and has beach tavernas and a small harbour. Further east, the hamlet of Podaras has a deep swathe of sand at the end of a fertile river valley carpeted in olive and citrus groves. **Eressos:** Inland from the beach resort, through lush and fertile farmland, lies Eressos village which at the end of a wild and grand mountain gorge. With its old houses, tiny shops and exceptional tavernas some consider this the most authentically old-Greek village on Lesvos. A nice sandy beach with shallow waters is found at Tavari, south of Mesotopos, with a couple of cantinas and a small harbour. **Sigri:** On the far west coast of Lesvos, the remote seaside village of Sigri. The quiet fishing harbour is overlooked by a small Turkish fortress, built in 1757, and a narrow sheltered crescent of sand and pebble shelves gently into the sea. The seawater is shallow and the usual offshore breezes keep sunbathers cool. Sigri harbour has a traditional feel and the village is so quiet that some liken it to a ghost village but the end-of-the-world feel suits those looking for a really relaxing holiday away from it all…

The Greek Island of Lipsi

Lipsi is found at the northern end of the Dodecanese chain that runs up the west coast of Turkey. The closest airport is located on the nearby island of Leros. Only domestic flights from Athens arrive in Leros. From Leros, visitors can take the ferry to Lipsi. It lies between the larger Greek Islands of Kalymnos and Samos and benefits greatly from having a very large and deep natural harbour and also from being on a main ferry route. The large harbour accommodates the many visiting summer yacht flotillas that make the Island of Lipsi a must-visit stopover on any Greek boating holiday route. Visitors can walk to virtually any of the beaches and back for a day's sunbathing and it is crossed with a network of roads and walking trails. The beaches are mainly shingle and sand and all are no more than a narrow waterside strip. Lipsi has all the charm and backwater atmosphere that many Greek holiday visitors want from the smaller, out-of-the-way Greek Island. If it is peace and tranquillity you are after then Lipsi is an ideal destination. The tiny Greek Island of Lipsi lies just south of Samos and has just one resort in Lipsi Town and a few beaches. A large harbour puts Lipsi on the main ferry route and makes it a popular port of call for yacht flotillas. Good roads make access to most beaches very easy, with a taxi service from the port. All beaches can however, be reached on foot although the going can sometimes be tricky. The Island of Lipsi will suit those looking for a place to have a peaceful time sunbathing, swimming and a relaxing holiday away from the crowds…

The Island of Lipsi:

Lipsi Town: The Island of Lipsi is just the place to laze away a Greek Island holiday. The only access to the Island is by boat and visitors are greeted by a vast harbour in a very large lagoon. Lipsi has some visual charm that is mainly down to use of white paint, some lively splashes of colour and a string of shady tavernas around the long quay. Villagers keep the place spick and span and colourful boats are always moored up in the port, their nets spread out to dry on the quayside. Lipsi is a favourite port of call for the yachting set so it's not always quiet but the crowds are easily avoided. A mini market near the central square sells just about everything and up the steps from the children's playground is an excellent bakery. Taxis, if required, will get you to most of the Island beaches or you can just simply walk to them. Boats nearby offer day trips to nearby local Islands. The blue domed church of Agios Ioannis dominates the hill above the Town and it is worth a climb up the steps for the views over the harbour and to visit the shops and cafes that are at almost every turn in the narrow alleyways up the steps. The Town is charming, peaceful and unhurried and for peace and quiet Lipsi Town is pretty hard to beat. **Liendou:** Liendou is the Lipsi Town beach and it's found over the brow of a small hill at the western end of the harbour just before the ferry jetty. Set in a narrow bay, the coarse sand and pebble shelves gently into the sea with some roadside tamarisk trees behind for shade. It is usually quiet, but can get noisy with children when school closes in the afternoon. The sea bed is stony at first but sandy further out and the seawater is shallow for some distance so it's safe for children. There are no facilities here but tavernas in the harbour are only just a short walk away…

The Island of Lipsi:

Kambos: Kambos beach is remarkably similar to Liendou beach, with a few patches of sand on the narrow shingle shoreline, the Kambos sand is gritty and not as pleasant as at Liendou. Some shade is provided by a row of tamarisks trees that edge the low stone wall. The seawater is clear, good for snorkeling, but stony underfoot. Goats often graze in the fields behind to an endless clonking of goat bells. **Elena:** Further along the coast from Kambos is a solitary whitewashed chapel (easily visible from Lipsi Town) and, beyond that, the stone and rock beach of Elena, or Helena. The beach is little more than a shower of rocks spilling into the sea and shade is hard to come by so Elena beach is only for the adventurous. **Kimisi:** It's a two hour walk to the tiny, but pretty, bay of shingle and rock at Kimisi, once the home of an octogenarian hermit and a sacred place for Lipsi Islanders. The beach is also home a pretty 16th century chapel. **Platys Yialos:** The beach at Platys Yialos or Platis Gialos, has the best sand on the Island although there's not a great deal of it. A narrow strip of sand edges the end of a deep bay, south facing and with no shade. The bay is long, shallow and sandy underfoot making it ideal for families and children. A shady taverna on the hill above offers good food. **East Coast Beaches:** Beaches east of Lipsi Town are a little more difficult to reach than those in the west as progress is mainly along unmarked paths and goat tracks. Beaches are mainly stone and shingle with little or no shade, but they do have dramatic settings and the stark, isolated beauty that many visitors crave. **Kamaris:** Kamaris, or Kamares, The main beach is 100 metres of pebble and large stones with fir trees at the southern end before ending at a headland with a rocky inlet. To the north are a couple of small coves. Beyond a quarry and an isolated chapel is a left fork along the path that keeps Aspronissi (White Island) directly ahead on the horizon. The track turns into a goat trail before dropping down to the stony beach so good shoes are a must…

The Island of Lipsi:

Monodendri: The name Monodendri means single tree and that's what the visitor gets. One lonesome pine growing out of the flat sloping rocks on the end of a pebble spit. There are in fact three beaches here. The most northerly has the single tree, the central one is just a small bay of large stones and the south beach has a small stretch of stone. There is no shade but the seawater is crystal clear and ideal for snorkeling. **Tourkomnima:** The beach at Tourkomnima lies north of the headland, back to back with Kserokambos and is usually deserted. The main beach is north facing and mainly stone with patches of sand. There is decent snorkeling on both sides of the bay and some trees for shade. A pretty chapel sits on the headland. **Kserokambos:** South east facing, with Islands offshore, Kserokambos has more sand than its neighbour Tourkomnima but not much. There are smaller coves further south along the shore and some splendid snorkeling to be had around the offshore rocks. **Kohklakoura:** There is a fine wide beach of white pebbles at Kohklakoura but it suffers from the lack of shade. Beware it can get very hot here on the sizzling stones. **Katsadia:** Katsadia bay and the neighbouring cove at Panpandria make a very popular anchorage for yachts and a largish taverna has sprung up to serve the yachting set. It is a beautiful wide bay with a very narrow shingle and sand beach and the islet of Limni offshore. The water is shallow and sandy offshore with the occasional large stone. A broken sea wall provides seating beneath the shady trees along the back of the beach and the eastern end has a good taverna overlooking the sand with tables set among shady palms and has car parking nearby…

The Greek Island of Meganissi

Located south of the Greek holiday Island of Lefkas, Meganissi is considered by many to be the best, as well as the biggest and most interesting of the offshore islets in this area of the Ionian Sea. There is no airport on Meganisi. The closest airport is located in Aktion/Preveza, which works only in summer and receives charters and low cost flights from Europe. The airport of Aktion/Preveza is 1 hour drive from Nydri, the small port town of Lefkada where the ferry to Meganisi Island departs from. Meganissi lies about six kilometres south-east of the Lefkas port of Nidri and so attracts plenty of day trippers from it is much larger neighbour. Meganissi is one of a cluster of islets that sit between Lefkas and the Greece west coast mainland. Meganissi means 'large Island' in Greek but it measures only 20 sq km while the Island's population of around 1,200 mostly live in the three Island hamlets of Katomeri, Vathi and Spartohori. The Island has an enticing lacework-like coastline, with many deep and long, fjord-like inlets especially on its northern shores and on its rocky and rugged west coast. A network of dirt tracks and walking paths make most of the beaches walk-able from the main ports although many of them are small and isolated. Meganissi is a balmy Greek Island with plenty of character and charm. Carpeted in pines and dotted with olive groves, what Meganissi lacks in sandy beaches is more than compensated for by the relaxed atmosphere and the serene and tranquil landscape. The resort trio of Vathi, Spartohori and Katomeri make up most of Island life which is soporific and secluded. The beaches are mostly pebble and few of them have any facilities such as cantinas or even sunbeds…

The Island of Meganissi:

Vathi: Vathi may the largest settlement on the Island but it is still very small. Vathi, or Vathy, lies on the north-east coast at the head of a long, narrow and sheltered inlet, with views to the islet of Skorpios, formerly owned by the Onassis family. Pastel-painted houses cluster around a picturesque bay with a green curtain of heavily wooded hills behind the resort and pines cascading down to the shore. A few tavernas and a couple of chapels line the harbour, often full of summer yachts from the neighbouring Island of Lefkas or just laying up for a few hours on the flotilla route. The busy looking bay, often crammed with every sort of boat, belies the resort itself which seems very much immune to any kind of activity. Peaceful contemplation or simply snoozing over a cold beer seem to be the principal pursuits. Day trippers from Lefkas can give Vathi a bit of a buzz, but when the visitors leave in the late afternoon the atmosphere turns calmer until the evening tavernas start to fill. In and around the harbour, a few small shops provide the basic provisions. Several small pebble beaches are within walking distance of Vathi, the most notable being the beaches of Pasoumaki and Abelaki. **Pasoumaki:** Pasoumaki is a small pebble cove backed by plenty of greenery so, although there are no sunbeds, plenty of natural shade is available right down to the shore. The pebbles drop steeply into the sea and it is stony underfoot for some way out so bathers should wear some protective footwear. The seawater is very clear and the nearby rocks appear free of sea urchins making Pasoumaki a good place to swim and snorkel. There are no tourist facilities on the beach, not even a summer cantina, but it's only a short walk to the tavernas and cafes of Vathi. **Ampelaki Bay:** Ampelaki, or Abelaki, is found to the north-east of Vathi. A small strand of pebble edge the bay and there is no denying the beauty of Ampelaki Bay. It is usually dotted with yachts at anchor offshore in the sheltered horseshoe bay and has low pine-covered hills and trees that tumble right down to the shoreline. Olive groves, hemmed in by low stone walls, have been carved out of some of the less steeply inclined hillside slopes…

The Island of Meganissi:

Fanari: Fanari beach is one of the most popular beaches on Meganissi and is noted for its picturesque setting. It is located north-east of Vathi on the east side of the neighbouring inlet to Ampelaki. Fanari is set in a small sheltered, north-east facing bay and backed by pine-clad hills. The beach is mainly pebble and some fine grit. There are enough visitors here in the high summer to warrant a beach cantina. The seawater is very shallow. **Spartohori:** The village of Spartohori or Spartochora, perches high on the hills overlooking Spilia Bay. A long and deep inlet located to the west of the main port of Vathi. The hilltop village has impressive views over the bay and also overlooks one of the best beaches on Meganissi, as well as the small ferry port of Spilia. Attractive houses are scattered all over the hillside interwoven with whitewashed alleyways and bright bougainvillea. There are a couple of mini-markets, a few small shops and a peppering of tiny pavement tavernas. **Spilia:** Spilia beach, also known as Agios Ioannis, is located at the far end of Spilia Bay about one kilometre from the harbour and directly below the hilltop village of Spartohori. It has one of the best, and prettiest beaches on Meganissi. Spilia beach has a long deep, stretch of white pebble and shingle with a waterfront taverna at the far end. The seawater is crystal clear but the stones are steeply banked and it is a very sharp drop into the sea, so this is not a beach for unsupervised children. Sunbeds are set out in the summer season and a line of tamarisks trees along the middle of the beach provide some natural shade. **Herniades:** Beyond the port at Spilia, a track follows the coast to a small north-facing beach on the headland of the inlet at Herniades. A narrow beach of shingle lines the shore for about 50 metres. Narrow goat tracks drop down to the beach from the dirt track behind and pine trees come right down to the sea here, so there is plenty of natural shade. It is a very picturesque spot but there are no facilities here and it is rather isolated so most visitors to Herniades arrive by boat bringing plenty of provisions for the day with them…

The Island of Meganissi:

Agios Ioannis: The beach of Agios Ioannis is a long pebble beach on the western coast and some distance from the resort village of Spartochori. It takes its name from the tiny chapel located near the beach. There is a small jetty to tie the boat up but little else, with no cantina or sunbeds so visitors must take their own supplies. Views across to Lefkas help make this a very attractive spot. Trees sweep right down to the waters edge in places. **Katomeri:** Katomeri is an attractive hill village about one kilometre south of the main Meganissi port at Vathi. This traditional, flower-decked, Greek Island village has a popular taverna, a bakery, a shop and even a tiny petrol station. The village is the Island's nominal capital but its permanent residents barely number 500. The locals are famously friendly and treat each visitor like long-lost family. **Limonari:** The nearest decent beaches to Katomeri are the twin beaches of Megalo Limonari and Mikro Limonari. The names mean 'large' and 'small' although size is only relative here. Mikro Limonari is about half the length of Megalo and separated from it by a small rock outcrop. South-east facing, the narrow strips get plenty of sunshine and the sea here is a notable blue/green thanks to the reflective white stones along the shore. Pines drop right down to the shore so there is good shade. The beach at nearby Elia is no more than a narrow strip of stone and shingle at the edge of a deep inlet on the Island's east coast. The small bay swarms with visiting yachts in the summer. **Atherinos Port:** Atherinos is the port for Katomeri and lies to the north-east of the village at the end of a long sheltered inlet. It is a pleasant enough place to visit with colourful fishing boats tied up to the long promenade and fishing nets spread out to dry along the quayside. **Barbarezou:** Barbarezou is a long cove on the eastern coast of Meganissi, about five kilometres north-east of Katomeri. It is also known as Cape Akoni and it is one of the least frequented beaches in Meganissi, perfect therefore for the visitor to enjoy some privacy…

The Greek Island of Mykonos

Mykonos, or Myconos, lies at the heart of the central Cyclades Islands and was once a byword for trendy and chic Greek Island holidays. There are ferries to Mykonos from Piraeus and Rafina, the two largest ports of Athens. These ferries also connect Mykonos with other islands, such as Santorini, Naxos, Paros, Crete and more. Flights to Mykonos are daily from Athens, while many charter and direct flights from abroad arrive in summer season. Some have dubbed Mykonos the archetypal Greek Island, a treeless granite rock dotted with sugar cube houses and blue-domed churches and all bathed in a dazzling light. Mykonos, in recent years has focused more on families and young couples who now marry and spend their honeymoon on the Island. The glamour and glitter may have faded, but the Mykonos magic still sparkles brightly. The rich and famous can still be seen on the succession of sandy beaches that run along the south coast of the Island. Mykonos is still the place to see and be seen amid some of the most attractive scenery to be found anywhere in the Greek Islands. Mykonos is a cosmopolitan Island. It can be seen by some as being expensive and few venture here for a cheap and cheerful holiday. The main attractions of the Island is the beautiful main port, a succession of sandy beaches, all-night clubs and beach parties with the added bonus of having the sacred Island of Delos nearby…

The Island of Mykonos:

Mykonos Town: Once seriously stylish and exclusive, Mykonos Town has lost its edge of late. The chic bistros and designer bars are still here, but fewer clients top the celebrity charts. It still attracts a well-heeled clientele. It has to: meals cost double the average, drinks even more while menus are more Mexican, Thai or vegetarian than they are Greek. Diners mostly gravitate to Little Venice, a clutch of tavernas perched over the sea where they ooze charm and squeeze wallets. Other holidaymakers head for the main drag where cafe tables overlook the long quayside. Unlike most Island ports, Mykonos Town is not on a hillside but spread out over a flat plain. The harbour area is split between the fishing quay where small boats are beached on the sand, and the main ferry port. Most traffic is banned from the waterfront and new building is confined to the outskirts of Town so the centre invites exploration on foot with the chance to get lost in a maze of narrow streets. The trademark quartet of windmills are perched on the hilltop while the remarkable chapel of Panagia Paraportiani poses for pictures, the cluster of chapels fused into what has been called 'an organic masterpiece of accidental architecture'. The town mascot, Petros, was resident for 30 years before being replaced by a couple of streetwise Great White pelicans that now court the cameras. Mykonos Town has a folklore museum and a Maritime Museum with some beautiful models of ships. The House of Helena is decked out with 19th century furniture and an Archaeological Museum which is a disappointment, given the proximity of the Island of Delos. The Tagoo area, just one kilometre north has a string of hotels offering sunset views over Tourlos Bay with regular buses to nearby Tourlos and to Agios Stefanos. Tourlos has a new marina, a sandy beach and plenty of watersports. The chapel at Giorgis Spilianos is built inside a rock. At the nearby lovely church of Agia Sofia there are great views over the whole area…

The Island of Mykonos:

Agios Stefanos: Just two kilometres north of the Island capital of Mykonos Town is the popular family beach of Agios Stefanos which takes most of the overspill from its better known neighbour. This is very much a family resort with a good sandy beach and plenty of tavernas and cafes both on the beach and also inland. There are plenty of sunbeds and lots of organised beach sports such as volleyball. Watersports include windsurfing and water skiing. Mykonos Town can be seen to the south and on the horizon is the islet of Delos. Agios Stefanos also has good sunset views from the west-facing shoreline tavernas. **Megali Ammos:** Megali Ammos is so near to Mykonos Town it is often referred to as the town beach. The sands are a 10 minute walk south of Town. It is a pleasant spot with a narrow strip of sand and shallow water. There are large flat rocks at one end and a sea wall at the other. A triple row of sunbeds cover most of the beach and there are the usual watersports and facilities with views across to Agios Ioannis. It also has fine sunsets. **Ornos:** The tiny fishing port at Ornos sits on the southern side of a narrow neck of land and has a flat beach that is crammed with pricey sunbeds. The Ornos sands are ideal for families though, with a gently sloping beach and lots of watersports. Tavernas and cafes run the length of the beach and there are even more to be found inland. Boat trips to other beaches are also plentiful and many visitors use Ornos as a base for exploring the rest of the Island. **Agios Ioannis:** Well known for many location shots during the shooting of the 1989 feature film Shirley Valentine, Agios Ioannis is thought by many to be one of the most picturesque places on Mykonos. It's located about five kilometres west of Mykonos Town on an 'ear-shaped' headland, a little isolated from other Mykonos beaches. The small west-facing beach is set in the captivating bay with views across to the Island of Delos. The pebble and sand beach is well protected and has sunbeds and watersports as well as tavernas and cafes. The beach is split in two by a large, rocky area. The seawater here is shallow and the nearby coves add interest…

The Island of Mykonos:

South East Coast Beaches: The south-east coast is Mykonos Island's main beach strip with a succession of sandy bays linked by a long coastal path. Beaches here tend to be long, straight swathes of caramel coloured sand. **Psarou:** Psarou is a more select version of its popular neighbour Platys Yialos. A 150 metre strip of white sand is backed by a line of tavernas and the occasional tamarisk tree. Psarou lies at the head of a long gulf that offers good protection for the yachts and boats which regularly anchor in Psarou Bay. The beach is of good fine sand and the seawater reasonably shallow, so it is good for families with children. **Platys Yialos:** Platys Yialos has a long sandy beach and is the biggest and longest established resort on Mykonos. Platis Yialos is now more cosmopolitan than Greek with its sights firmly set on the international holiday market. The long crescent of sand is backed by low hills and terraced tavernas. The beach has a large number of tavernas, beach bars, a mini-market and shops. Platis Yialos is also the main starting point for small taxi boats taking visitors to other south coast beaches such as Psarou and Paranga as well to the surrounding Islands, Delos in particular. **Agia Anna:** Agia Anna is a quiet shingle beach that lies south of Platys Yialos just across the headland from Paraga beach. Agia Anna is a small, west-facing beach of sharp sand. It has a long sea wall that provides a backdrop to a narrow stretch of sand with shallow seas. Surrounding stretches of the coastline here are very scenic and were used for lots of location filming on the Shirley Valentine movie. There are a couple of good tavernas and a footpath that leads over the headland west to Platis Yialos with fine offshore views. **Paraga:** South of Platis Yialos is the small, picturesque south-facing beach of Paraga, or Paranga, good enough to attract both locals and tourists. Paraga consists of two sandy strips split by a headland. Both beaches are long and flat with rocks offshore in the shallow sea. A deep horseshoe bay makes the resort well sheltered and away from northerly winds and a line of tamarisk trees provides natural shade…

The Island of Mykonos:

Paradise: Paradise is also the Island's premier party beach where tavernas and music bars pump out party music and visitors are never far away from a burger. Once a favourite of the 70's hippy generation, Paradise is better known these days for its big outdoor discos, international DJs and special events such as full moon beach parties. Paradise beach parties usually start around 5 pm and last well into the night, while the closing beach party in early September is now an Island institution. **Super Paradise:** East of Paradise beach but with no direct easy access route is the beach called Super Paradise instead of its proper Greek name of Plyndiri. It has a magnificent strip with crystal clear blue seawater, Super Paradise is not ideal for families as the water runs deep and nudity is still common at the rocky end of the beach. This is also a big party beach, one of the most visited on Mykonos, and with loud music belting out from the beach bars day and night. **Agrari:** Agrari beach is in a hidden cove west of Super Paradise and to the east of Elia beach that has somehow managed to avoid the massive exploitation of its neighbours. Those looking to escape the Mykonos crowds may find Agrari beach just the ticket as it rarely gets crowded. It has just a single beach cantina and one restaurant. Small and rather exposed, Agrari has a small stream running across it. **Elia:** Regarded by some as the best beach on Mykonos, Elia is a long, broad swathe of coarse sand backed by a steep circle of hills and split by a rocky headland. The sand quickly turns to sharp pebbles under the sea. It is a cosmopolitan beach with sunbeds, showers and plenty of watersports. It has some very attractive tavernas and is often the last port of call for water taxis that frequent the southern shore. The seawater is shallow and the beach clean and well kept. Access is from the pleasant inland village of Ano Mera, just two kilometres away or it's a 45-minute boat trip from Platys Yialos. However, you get there it is well worth the effort…

The Island of Mykonos:

Ano Mera: The only inland village of note on Mykonos is Ano Mera and it's one of the few places on the Island where visitors can find something resembling traditional Greek village life. The main square has a kafenion and a taverna while the 16th century red-roofed monastery of Panagia Tourliani has a fine collection of icons and an unusual baptismal font of marble. Just north of Ano Mera is the 12th century Paleokastro monastery in a magnificent oasis setting on a barren hillside. **Kalo Livadi:** The long sandy beach at Kalo Livadi is the last port of call for some taxi boats that serve the south coast beaches. A rustic setting on the road out of Ano Mera adds to the charm of a pleasant beach with loungers, watersports, restaurants and bars. The valley behind is particularly scenic and scattered with farmhouses. The two kilometre stretch of sharp sand is good for those who prefer to avoid big crowds and, although not exactly quiet, Kalo Livadi is very much a family beach. Yachts are usually anchored out in Kalo Livadi bay. **Agia Anna:** Agia Anna is a small, quiet shingle beach that is well sheltered from the northerly winds. It shouldn't be confused with the more developed beach of the same name that lies to the west. This Agia Anna is near Kalafatis and makes for a pleasant area to stay with a beautiful landscape and fine views from the hills. Small beaches, mainly shingle and stone, lie on either side of an isthmus and there are a few sunbeds in front of a bamboo fence that runs the length of the beach to provide protection from wind. On the other side of the isthmus lies Kalafatis which runs into the beach at Tsarna, a long stretch of coarse sand with a taverna and water sports. **Kalafatis:** North of Agia Anna is the long beach known as Kalafatis. The large sandy beach has a beach restaurant, bar and hotels. Nearby, on the main road, is a mini market, a large taverna and a pizza restaurant. Kalafatis is well known for its watersports such as windsurfing and parasailing as well as a diving school. Boats leave here for Dragonisi, an islet off the east coast that has many caves some populated by the rare protected Mediterranean Monk Seal…

The Island of Mykonos:

Lia Ammoudia: Lia Ammoudia marks the end of the main south coast tourist beaches and this is the last to be reached by road and is about 14km from Mykonos Town. Once a hideaway beach for Greek celebrities, Lia Ammoudia has become much more popular recently and ranks of sunbeds now line the shore and a taverna behind serves good food. Bamboo windbreaks provide shelter and there are some excellent fish tavernas here. A footpath to the east goes over the headland and leads to a tiny sand bay at Tsangari. **Tsangari and Frangia:** There are several beaches and coves beyond Lia Ammoudia but they are remote and will only appeal to the more intrepid holidaymaker. They are popular however with boat parties who often use them for beach barbecue trips and cruises. The most notable are Tsangari and Frangia. All of them are dominated by the Island peak of Profitis Illias. **North Coast Beaches:** Far wilder than the soft south, the northern coastline is for those who prefer a little wild adventure on their holidays. Large beaches are few, are exposed to the northerly winds, are more difficult to get to and have fewer facilities. But visitors can enjoy wild windswept scenery and there are numerous small coves and tiny bays for those with their own transport. **Fokos:** Fokos is a superb sandy north-facing beach, newly discovered by tourists but still far enough away to remain peaceful. The beach is large and deep with dramatic rock formations on the headland. Fokos is surrounded by wild and beautiful scenery and has a small summer taverna to serve the growing numbers that venture away from the usual tourist haunts to delight in the deep sands of the bay. The northerly winds can get very strong and the waves choppy. As a result Fokos is more popular with surfers than sunbathers. **Ftelia:** The huge Panormos Bay in north-east Mykonos has three main beaches. The first, at the southern end of the bay and nearest the capital, is the increasingly popular beach of Ftelia. North-facing and exposed to the strong winds that whip around the bay, this beach is another big favourite with surfers. It has fine sand, a beach cantina and a few sunbeds…

The Island of Mykonos:

Panormos: The main Panormos Bay beach is called Panormos and lies just north of Ftelia on the west side of the bay. Facing east, it enjoys a little more shelter from the winds although the seawater can get very choppy when the wind does get up. Panormos has a fine long stretch of white sand that has become increasingly popular in recent years. The beach has a couple of tavernas at the northern end which open in the summer to provide the basics where the bamboo and tamarisks trees offer some shade. There is little natural shade and the sand banks quite sharply into the sea. Naturists favour the southern end of the beach where the low dunes offer more privacy. There are some good walks to be found in the surrounding countryside although, with no trees it can feel a little exposed up there. There is no local bus service to this part of the Island of Mykonos so visitors need to have their own transport. **Agios Sostis:** Agios Sostis is a small, wild and windswept beach at the northern mouth of Panormos Bay and another big favourite with surfers. Rollers crash in on a sand beach in July and August when the meltemi winds are at their strongest. In such an exposed spot the long beach is prone to picking up litter and seaweed. That said, the beach is an excellent one with a long swathe of golden sand, shallow seawater along the shoreline and with scrub and low dunes behind and small outcrops of rock at one end. There is no public transport and parking is limited so many park on the hill above and walk down along a rough track. A couple of good beach tavernas open in the summer season to provide the visitor with good food and much needed cold drinks…

The Greek Island of Naxos

Naxos Greece sits at the heart of the central Cyclades group of Greek Islands and is one of the groups most mountainous. There are daily flights and ferries to Naxos from Athens, while there is also good ferry connection with nearby Islands such as Santorini, Mykonos, Paros and Amorgos. Naxos is a big Island but most tourism is confined to the south-west coast where resorts are peppered along a huge blonde swathe of sand. Unfortunately, much of the sand is gritty and coarse and many of the beaches are backed by large, desolate salt pans. Naxos Town port has a large harbour with the noted Portaras gate sitting proud on the offshore islet of Palatia and the walled kastro towering above a tangled web of narrow whitewashed streets. Inland are some very impressive mountain scenery, particularly around Mount Zas where abundant springs and rich soil help create lush green valleys of citrus orchards and olive groves. Rich farming mean the Islanders have little need to attract tourism so Naxos maintains a strong Greek identity, particularly in its many un-spoilt traditional hill villages. The Island of Naxos is a good beach holiday Island without the crowds, beautiful inland hillside villages and gorgeous mountain scenery to add interest with easy Island hopping on the many ferries can put Naxos high on any Greek Island wish list. Noted for a string of majestic sandy beaches on the south-west coast of the Island of Naxos and for its good ferry connections Naxos makes a good choice for a holiday off the beaten track. Some beaches may seems too big for comfort but small family beaches can be found on the Island. Visitors will mainly find beaches with huge swathes of sand backed by low dunes, scrub or even desolate salt marshes…

The Island of Naxos:

Naxos Town: The capital town of the Island of Naxos claims to be the gateway to the Cyclades group of Greek Islands and has the doorway to prove it. The gigantic marble door frame of Portara stands 21 ft high on the tiny Palatia Islet which is linked to Naxos Town by a short causeway. The frame is all that remains of a 6th century BC temple which was never completed. The giant doorway to nowhere is all that is left standing. North of the causeway is the Grotta area of Town where an old settlement lies sunken beneath the waves. To the south is the main Town, a happy mix of tavernas, bars, car rentals and tourist shops. The web of whitewashed back streets are packed with craft and curio shops. These historic narrow alleys wind uphill to the Venetian kastro. Further south still is a suburban of hotels and studios that backs onto the long Town beach of Agios Giorgios. The waterfront is a promenaders' paradise with an extensive and attractive sea wall, dozens of street tavernas and shops. The cobbled whitewashed alleys up to the 13th century kastro are places to get lost among arched porticoes, crumbling mansions, flowerpot gardens and street tavernas. The kastro is topped with a Catholic Cathedral and a good museum whose exhibits include early Cycladic goddesses with prominent breasts and bellies and some stunning views of the Town, Island and out to sea from the balcony. Naxos Town may have its tourist glitz but it's essentially Greek in character and few will be surprised that visitors stay longer in Naxos Town than any other Greek Island resort. **South West Coast Beaches:** The whole of the Naxos south-west coast is one line of beaches, many blending into each other with only the names of the nearest village to separate them. Some are huge swathes of sand backed by dunes and bamboo, others are narrow slivers of sand that shelve steeply into the warm inviting seawater…

The Island of Naxos:

Agios Giorgios: Agios Giorgios, or St George's, has solid ranks of sunbeds and surfboards but it's less commercialised than first appearances might suggest. There may be hotels by the score, and a broken line of bars and cafes backing the beach, but the atmosphere is still family friendly and the taverna food is mainly Greek. The sand is soft, deep and gently shelving into the shallow sea and has a boarded walkway that runs the length of the tree-shaded crescent fronting the beach tavernas and bars. The closer to Naxos Town the more hectic the pace. Further south the sand turns gritty but there is the compensation of greater tranquillity. Around the headland is a small inlet and bay at Mandari that houses a windsurfing school and beyond that a dyke, built at some cost to the local wildlife, to prevent periodic flooding of the Islands airport. **Agios Prokopios:** Agios Prokopios at the southern end of this long, deep beach is good but it is less so at the northern end of the beach. Tamarisks trees shade the soft sand southern end of the beach where hotels, studios, cafes and tavernas provides the backdrop however, the north end of the beach, towards Naxos Town, is a desolate, flat salt marsh and a long, flat stretch gritty hard sand and ends in almost Saharan desolation. Great slabs of rock along much of the northern shoreline don't add to the appeal. **Agia Anna:** The small harbour at Agia Anna is the first destination of caiques out of Town. North of the small jetty is a fine beach of soft, golden sand. A few scattered rocks appear where the beach gives way to the coarser grains of Agia Prokopios but the lovely setting and shallow sea make this a splendid beach. It is relatively short at around 300 metres, the beach can get quickly full when the caiques and local buses arrive, so an early visit is needed to bag the best spots on the beach. Agia Anna beach is well placed for exploring the Island's more remote beaches whilst staying in touch with lively Naxos Town seven kilometres away…

The Island of Naxos:

Maragas: Around the headland south from Agia Anna and past a tiny church, the coast opens up into a huge vista of flat, sparkling white sand. The huge beach area is known as Plaka. The most northerly section is known as Maragas is lined with shady tavernas, bars, apartments and shops. A few straggly trees on the beach give shade to taverna chairs and tables. **Plaka:** Plaka beach is almost impossibly huge, with deep golden banks of sharp sand for several kilometres backed by low dunes and rolling farmland. It is just sand, sand and more sand, very exposed and with little shade. Low dunes lie behind and the uninhabited islet of Aspronisi lies offshore. **Orkos:** About 18km from Naxos Town the sands of Plaka eventually gives to small, pebble coves surrounded by cedar trees in an area that is known as Orkos beach. This pleasant spot has pebble and sand coves extending for more than a kilometre backed by red coloured fields. **Mikri Vigla Headland:** Mikri Vigla beach is on a large promontory around 19 kilometres from Naxos Town. There are beaches both north and south of the large headland. Parthenos is an exposed stretch of sand where onshore winds make it a popular haunt for windsurfers. The sand is a white coarse grit and the islet of Panagia lies offshore. To the south is the long straight swathe of Sahara beach. A four kilometres of coarse white grit that disappears into the flat desolate distance. **Kastraki Coves:** Kastraki is a succession of small coves running for about three kilometres. Kastraki means 'little castle' in Greek and the small Venetian fortress of Pyrgos Oskelos sits about two kilometres east. The main beach is long and sandy, backed by dunes, scrub pine and prickly pear and some impressive rock formations can be found between the various coves to add interest while trees here and there provide some natural shade. A few seafront tavernas open in summer and sunbeds go out on the most popular parts of the sand. It is 20 km from Naxos Town. The southern end of the beach is known as Glyfada which has two small lakes behind the beach and some very good seafront tavernas…

The Island of Naxos:

Alyko Headland: Alyko headland is one of the most beautiful headland spots on the Island of Naxos that has several narrow beach coves tucked between wild rocky outcrops with near vertical cliffs covered in deep green scrub pine and cedar trees. Alyko is 21 kilometres from Naxos Town. The scenery from the top of the cliff tops is exquisite. The north side of the headland has a string of sandy coves and a small port, while on the south side is a splendid cedar forest and a long beach of white gritty sand. This end of the Island can be windy and waves can get very choppy. **Pyrgaki:** The beach of Pyrgaki, about 23 km from Naxos Town and the last stop on the local coastal bus route. It has a shortish, sand and shingle beach that marks the end of the coastal swathe of sandy beaches for which the Island of Naxos is famous for. The beach is very deep and exposed with no shade unless you retreat to where the cedars or to the nearby beach taverna. The beach is sandy and well protected from the wind, although there are rocks along the shore. Often deserted, this is one of the most beautifully peaceful beaches on Naxos. **Agiassos:** The road south out of Pyrgaki hugs the coast to the remote sandy beach of Agiassos. A few scattered houses make up the hamlet about 24 km from Naxos Town. The large beach is a mix of sand and shingle with a gentle slope into the sea. The taverna above the beach has great views. There are no sunbeds and little shade except at the northern end where a large clump of trees is set back from the shoreline. **Beaches on the North East Coast:** Draw a line from Pyrgaki, in the south-west, to Moutsouna, in the north-east, and it will mark the boundary for all decent roads on Naxos. With a few exceptions this is donkey track territory with beaches that are less attractive…

The Island of Naxos:

Kalandos: The south-facing beach of sand and shingle at Kalandos sits about 42 kilometres from Naxos Town at the head of a small sheltered inlet in the far south of the Island. The remote cove is well protected from northerly winds, has no facilities and is difficult to get to. Kalandos beach is visited by some excursion boat tours from Naxos Town but the sea journey is a long one. **Panormos:** Panormos is an attractive but remote south-facing sand and shingle beach on the south-east coast, about 45km from Naxos Town. Shade is provided by a line of tamarisk trees at the eastern end of the beach. **Psili Ammos:** The east-facing beach at Psili Ammos is a long scimitar of rolling sand that banks up in drifts to the cedar trees behind. It is 42 kilometres from Naxos Town. A couple of kilometres south is the even more remote Kleidos, a beach area of three inlets split by rocky outcrops and one of the prettiest places on Naxos. Rock overhangs provide shade on two of the stone and shingle beaches and walled hillside terraces reach down almost to the seashore. **Moutsouna:** Once the main port for shipping out the emery mined in and around the villages of Apiranthos and Koronos, Moutsouna is now the gateway to the remote east coast beaches of Naxos. Moutsouna is a pretty port and one of the few genuine fishing harbours left on Naxos. It is 45 km from Naxos Town. Pleasant fish tavernas overlook the small east-facing sandy beach and the port where the old derricks still stand that once swung emery onto the waiting boats. A little to the north, over the headland, is Axala beach, known for its fine and varied pebbles. To the south are many pretty coves that extend all the way to Psili Ammos. **Lionas:** The scenic seaside village of Lionas, another of the old emery ports of Naxos. At about 40 kilometres from Naxos Town. Lionas beach is stone and shingle with no facilities, apart from some very pleasant seafront fish tavernas. The asphalt road goes right down to Lionas beach but drivers should take great care on the narrow, twisting bends. Lionas is a beach for escaping the holiday crowds...

The Island of Naxos:

The Apollonas Statue: A colossal stone statue, or 'kouros', abandoned on the hillside around the 6th century BC has turned the remote north-east seaside village of Apollonas into a tourist draw. Once an emery exporting port, tourism is now the main money spinner with tour buses arriving at the village daily from Naxos Town, which lies about 54 kilometres away. The beach is very public, overlooked by dozens of taverna tables (one taverna is named Baywatch) but it has soft sand with some shingle. The kouros lies just outside the village on a well marked route. The statue is more than 10 metres from top to toe and some cement steps have been built around it to provide easy access. Also worth seeing are the old marble quarries at Empoli. **Beaches on the North West Coast:** The north-west coast of is noted for its beautiful countryside, particularly around the Engares region but the coast is mostly inaccessible cliffs for much of its length. There are only a couple of beaches of note, although these are exceptionally beautiful. **Abram:** The windswept Abram beach, also called Abrami, is a lovely shingle beach overlooked by a huge head carved into the rock by the Greek sculptor Rokkos. A taverna overlooks the beach offering great views of the bay. Rarely crowded this is an ideal spot for a quiet holiday. The beach is shingle with some sand with views across to the Greek Islands of Paros and Mykonos. Abram is about 20 kilometres from Naxos Town. **Amyti:** The beach at Amyti, or Amytis, lies below two reservoirs that supply drinking water to Naxos Town. The beach is an idyllic spot with fine, soft sand, it offers the best bathing on this part of the coast, though the meltemi winds can bring the waves crashing in. Amyti is close enough to Naxos Town to make it a popular target for day trippers and the beautiful Engares region provides walkers with lovely scenery. Close to the beach is the fortified monastery of Ypsilos…

The Greek Island of Paros

The Greek holiday Island of Paros, along with its much larger neighbour Naxos, forms the hub of the central group of Greek Islands known as the Cyclades. It is very easy to travel to Paros from Athens by ferry or plane. There are also many ferry connections between Paros and other nearby islands, while in the summer season Paros receives many direct flights from abroad. They are the epitome of the Greek Islands, with scenic mountains, rich fertile valleys, white sugar cube houses and long sandy beaches. The lack of a large airport means that Paros largely caters for the more independent traveller and, with its good ferry connections, the Island is a favourite with campers and backpackers. The capital port of Parikia, lies in a huge bay with the old Venetian Kastro, several splendid churches and a signature picturesque windmill on the long waterfront. The Island has many good beaches. The much photographed port at Naoussa is one of the most picturesque in the Cyclades with sugar cube houses dotted around harbour and several pleasant beaches lining the large bay. The Island of Paros will suit those looking for a quiet destination with a good tourist infrastructure. Its central Cycladic location and good ferry connections make this an ideal base for Greek Island hopping. Paros is a large Island that combines mountains, rolling hillsides and sandy beaches. The best beaches are on the east coast; a succession of sandy strips with the famous windsurf centre at Chris Akti the mid point. The bays of Naoussa and Parikia have their share of good beaches while neighbouring Antiparos, though less well endowed with good sandy beaches, is a step back in time…

The Island of Paros:

Parikia Town: Parikia, sometimes spelt Paroikia, is the busy Paros Island capital of some 2,000 people. There are cafes, tavernas and shops concertina out in all directions away from the central harbour windmill, a popular meeting place and the main waterside focal point. The port handles around 30 ferries a day in high summer when it can appear to be bursting to the seams. To the east of the port is the main coast road which bottlenecks at the small, beach of Livadia, shaded by tamarisk trees with a clutch of tavernas before splitting into a warren of one-way streets. To the west of the port is a line of restaurants behind a sea wall that peters out at a small shingle beach and a few old windmills that are lost amongst the flourishing cafes. The atmosphere changes away from the waterfront. Signs to the Traditional Settlement reveal a wide paved square and small triangular park fronting the remarkable cathedral of Ekatontachoni. Behind that is the Archaeological Museum, then a labyrinth of alleys jammed with shops, galleries, cafes and houses, but strangely only a single supermarket. At the heart of Parikia are the walls of the Venetian Kastro, marked by terraces of stone draped with foliage and flowers and a 13th century Venetian castle surrounded by picturesque churchesfull of treasures to view. **The Beaches around Parikia:** There are beaches within easy walking distance of Parikia. Beach lovers in Parikia should opt for the eastern side of the bay where a number of good sandy resorts can be found. A good road runs right around the bay and out to the headland at Agios Fokas. **Livadia:** The first beach heading east from Parikia is at Livadia, only one kilometre from the port. Livadia has good fine sand and plenty of trees at the back of the beach to sit beneath as well as the usual sunbeds, umbrellas and watersports. Games of beach volley are popular here and the sands may fill quickly at lunchtime when the locals go for a quick midday dip. The sands naturally divide into several sections. It narrows towards Parikia and beyond a clump of trees is a small bank of sand that tends to be much quieter than the main beach. Even further is a tiny beach called Kalokanas down a very steep dirt track…

The Island of Paros:

Krios: Krios lies about two kilometres from Paroikia and has a snack bar, taverna and a campsite. It is a long beach of fine white sand and clean seawater and views over the bay to the port. A water taxis runs from Parikia for Krios and neighbouring Marcello beach every 15 minutes. Walkers can opt for a scenic coastal route. The beach has sunbeds and beach volleyball courts and, although the area has hotels, apartments and a campsite it rarely gets crowded. **Marchello:** Just north of Krios, and almost part of it, is one of the most popular beaches on this part of the coast. Marchello, also called Martsello, is about three kilometres from the port at Parikia. The long, sandy beach has shallow water, ideal for families with children. There are also rocky outcrops and small, sandy coves past the main beach. **Souvlia:** Further around the bay from Marchello, and blending into it, is the beach of Souvlia. South facing, and well protected from the northerly winds by the hills behind, this is a very pleasant beach of good sand. There is some good shade and the seawater is shallow. A small taverna at the back of the beach opens in the summer. Close by is a cave thought to have been the home of Archilohos, one of the most noted Greek poets of the archaic period. The large cave in the almost vertical rock face is where he is said to have hidden himself to seek inspiration for his poems. **Agios Fokas Chapel:** More sand coves are found north from Souvlia all the way to the tiny headland chapel of Agios Fokas. Most of the coves have local names but they rarely feature on Island maps. The main stretch of sand here is called Kaminia, almost an extension of neighbouring Souvlia and a long crescent of sand and shingle cut off by a rocky outcrop, about five kilometres from Parikia. Boat trips from Parikia visit the beach on trips around the bay and water taxis drop visitors off on the road behind. Shade comes from a stand of trees in the centre of the beach but otherwise it is very exposed. The twin-roofed chapel on the headland has impressive views over the bay. **North Coast Beaches:** The coast is mainly inhospitable. At the bay of Naoussa there are good beaches. The area is considered by many as the jewel in the Cyclades' crown...

The Island of Paros:

Naoussa: Naoussa village is one of the prettiest fishing ports in Greece and its picturesque reputation attracts camera clickers in their thousands. The port is cradled in a giant crab's claw of a bay and the network of quays is usually awash with gaily painted boats. It has countless restaurants, tavernas, ouzeries, bars, cafes and nightclubs. Many former fishing sheds are now trinket shops and boutiques selling everything from cheap souvenirs to designer beachwear. Taverna tables spill out onto the harbourside and on some days tourists are so thick on the ground they queue to stroll just around the harbour. The port is packed tight in August when the villagers celebrate an ancient pirate battle with a torch lit boat procession. The remains of a 14th century castle lie half submerged in the sea, providing a great backdrop for holiday photos as does the dainty chapel on an Islet In the middle of the bay. There is a good Byzantine museum here and a small beach called Piperi that is a pleasant crescent of sand with rocky outcrops at each side and fine views over the bay. The large bay of Naoussa has many good beaches both east and west. Those to the west are more popular and better known but there are a couple of good beaches to the east before the road strikes north-east coast to Santa Maria. **Kolymbithres:** The coast road west of Naoussa passes various pockets of sand before reaching Kolymbithres, one of the best known, if hardest to pronounce, beaches in the bay. Some three kilometres from the resort, wind and sea have sculpted rock into smooth, but bizarre shapes. Between the striking rocky outcrops lie sandy coves of shallow, lucid blue seawater. The coves are tiny and the popular spots fill up quickly with every available space used. Less overcrowded spots can be found for those prepared to hunt around among the rocks. Trees are plentiful and provide good shade while the shallow water makes this an ideal spot for families. Offshore is the Islet of Agia Kali, with the small chapel, which can be visited by boat. The coast road is lined with tavernas and bars where rough tracks lead off down to the beaches from impromptu car parking. Inland at Koukounaries are the ruins of a 1300BC Mycenaean acropolis enclosed by the so-called 'Cyclopean' walls…

The Island of Paros:

Monastiri: Beyond Kolimbrethes the road winds for two kilometres over the headland past a waterworld centre full of plastic water chutes to the small sandy bay at Monastiri. The beach has been taken over by a huge taverna complex built on the hill behind and the sands are covered with taverna-owned sunbeds. The seawater is very shallow for many metres out to sea, making Monastiri ideal for children and for the myriad watersports on offer. **Agios Anargyri:** Several good beaches also lie to the east of Naoussa. The first, beyond the resort beach of Piperi, is Agios Anargyri, or Anargyros, only about 200 metres along the east coast road. A fairly long stretch of good sand has plenty of trees behind with good natural shade. The soft sand shelves gently into the sea and facilities include tavernas and cafes while Naoussa is only a short walk away. **Langeri:** There is a splendid stretch of sand and dunes at Langeri, about four kilometres from Naoussa. There are dunes sweeping up to low shady trees behind a long bank of fine, golden sand that makes up the main beach. The beach has very fine views over the bay of Naoussa. There are currently no tavernas or bars here so visitors will need to take provisions. **East Coast Beaches:** The east coast of Paros, from Santa Maria in the north to the rocky outcrop at Cape Fanos on the southernmost tip, is awash with fine beaches. This is the main beach strip of Paros with the windsurfing mecca at the beach resort of Chrisi Akti and the east coast port resort of Piso Livadi. **Santa Maria:** A belt of soft sand sweeps right around the beautiful crescent bay at Santa Maria. Backed by shallow dunes and dense green scrub this is a lovely spot of open skies and wide vistas. Golden sand reaches out for several kilometres with sunbeds dotting the more popular spots and with thumping disco music from the beach bars. This is a popular windsurfing beach and the facilities appeal to younger and noisier tastes. The bedlam is easily avoided however with a walk along the sands to the headland and a traditional beach bar. The sand beyond becomes thinner and unfortunately banks of dry seaweed line the seashore…

The Island of Paros:

Ampelas Fishing Port: South of Santa Maria and just five kilometres from Naoussa is the charming fishing port and beach at Ampelas, often spelt Abelas. The short, sandy beach lies protected by a small quay and line of large boulders that curve around from the north. The beach is small and fairly deep but it can get crowded when the round-the Island caiques arrive with boatloads of visitors. A couple of tavernas near the harbour are famed for their fresh fish, while a beach taverna offers luxury loungers complete with towels and iced water on the beach. The harbour has good parking for cars and there is a campsite nearby. Nearby rough tracks lead to remote coves, notably at Aspros Gremos (White Cliff) which has a small bay of pebble and sand. **Glyfades:** South of Ampelas is the long and narrow strip of shingle and sand beach at Glyfades. Glyfades beach is very exposed, with no shade and no facilities. It is a perfect place to escape the crowds. **Molos:** Another fine swathe of pebble and sand is found at the beach of Molos. Isolated and exposed, it lies south of Glyfades between the hills of Kefalos and Antikefalos and Molos is also an ideal spot away from the crowds. There are views across to the Island of Naxos and a couple of tavernas. The long beach never gets crowded and occasional stands of trees provide good shade. At the northern end of Molos beach is a chapel to Agios Nikolaos Ftochos ('Poor' Nikolaos). Another chapel to the south devoted to Agios Nikolaos Plousios ('Rich' Nikolaos) near a small fishing port. **Marmara:** Inland from Kefalos Bay is the attractive hill village of Marmara. The name means marble and many houses here are built with great slabs of the stuff, giving the village a sparkling white air. Marmara is an attractive village with the houses bedecked in flowers and small gardens often edged with reeds of bamboo to protect them from the winds. Marmara is surrounded by rich farmland with, unusually for Greece, cattle breeding and dairy production are the main source of income. Ancient pottery workshops have been unearthed in excavations made in the north-east of the village…

The Island of Paros:

Marpissa: About a kilometre south of Marmara is another pretty inland village at Marpissa. About 18 km from Parikia, tourists often take in both Marpissa and Marmara when touring the area. Marpissa is a charming traditional Cycladic village of whitewashed 16th and 17th century houses, standing in narrow paved alleys. Built on a hill overlooking Kefalos Bay, the Cathedral of Metamorfosi dominates the white cube houses. The small village square has a folklore museum and four old windmills. It is from here that a path leads up the hill to the monastery of Agios Antonios which has extensive views and the ancient ruins of a 15th century fort nearby. **Piso Livadi Fishing Harbour:** Approached through pines and eucalyptus, Piso Livadi is a pretty seaside resort, about 19 km from Parikia. It has an attractive fishing harbour. The beach runs to the south of the resort and is a long swathe of soft sand that is ideal for families with a children's play area and tamarisk trees behind to provide plenty of natural shade. Tavernas dot the quayside at the pretty port to welcome boats that arrive from Naxos, Mykonos, Ios, Santorini and Amorgos. There are also local buses to Parikia, Naoussa and Alyki. A dirt track north leads to the small beach of Kalogiras where Imposing rock outcrop overlooks a shingle and sand beach. There are currently no facilities at Kalogiras, although a beach cantina may open up in the high summer. The mineral-rich cliff clay here is said to be very good for the skin. **Logaras:** The beach resort at Logaras, just south of Piso Livadi, is much the quieter of the two seaside villages. A long, pine fringed beach of sharp, gritty sand is the main attraction of this holiday resort. It has tavernas, beach cafes, car rentals and other tourist paraphernalia. But the scale is still small and so Logaras retains the air of a sedate and pleasant seaside resort. On the headland fishing boats are anchored to the rocks. It is just a short and easy walk from Piso Livadi and there are also regular local buses to Logaras from Parikia, Naoussa and Alyki…

The Island of Paros:

Pounda: Not to be confused with the ferry port on the west coast the beach resort of Pounda, or Pounta, is basically one huge noisy holiday club to which the sandy, crescent beach, 26 km from Parikia, very much plays second fiddle too. Pounda is beach disco land where the boy's parade pectorals and girls wiggle and giggle. It is a place for windsurfers to play after a hard day on the boards. The sandy beach resort caters almost exclusively to youngsters who want to dance, drink and have fun in the sun. **Chrysi Akti:** This is one of the Islands most famous beaches, Chrysi Akti (Golden Beach) is a flat sandy beach, about 22 km from Parikia, that is a magnet for windsurfers. The main beach has a good 700 metres of soft sand backed by a string of tavernas, small hotels and studios. Both long and wide, the beach is big enough to swallow up a large number of visitors. The wide open sands, shallow seawater and strong breezes attracts surfers by the hundred to test their skills offshore. A wide variety of windsurfing, water sport facilities is available including surfing schools, scuba diving, water skiing, wind and kite surfing and catamaran hire. The long, flat sands and shallow seawater make for ideal surfing conditions, although beginners are advised to practice on calm days as the swell and currents can get very strong when the wind blows. During the summer the thermal winds kick in around noon just about every day. The seawater is crystal clear and surfers can test themselves on waves up to four metres high when the winds are right. The beach has plenty of parking and there are showers and toilets as well as tavernas and cafes. A surf shop opens in the summer and there is a fully manned rescue centre nearby. A smaller beach to the north at Tsardakia has been dubbed Nea Chrysi Akti (New Golden Beach) to cash in on its better known neighbour. The Paros Surf club is based here and it hosts the Professional Windsurfers' World Cup every August…

The Island of Paros:

Glyfa: The small crescent of sand at Glyfa sits below the northern hook of Cape Pyrgos which shelters it from the northerly winds. The name means 'brackish', a reference to the sheltered water which stays calm even when other beaches are affected by choppy waves. It is about 18 km from Paroikia. This is a relatively remote beach and, although a cantina may open in summer, there are no other facilities. Glyfa beach is sand and pebble with good natural shade provided by a long line of tamarisk trees at the back of the beach. Rocky outcrops at either end add interest and the shoreline seawater is quite shallow. **Drios:** Drios is a small fishing village, about 23 kilometres from Parikia, is very pretty with an attractive duck pond and several good tavernas and bars that benefit from large shady trees. The beach is a long, steeply banked strip of sharp sand and stone, lined with shady trees along the whole shoreline. Watersports are popular here and, in the high season, Drios can get crowded. A row of excellent fish tavernas overlooks the attractive harbour and there are plenty of beach bars and restaurants. There are regular local buses to Parikia and Naoussa. Drios was a major port in ancient times as the local rock formations provided natural protection for ships. At the end of the beach are rock fissures that were once used as mooring piers. Offshore is the small, uninhabited Islet of Drionissi. **West Coast Beaches:** The west coast of Paros is littered with uninhabited Islets and the Island of Antiparos further offshore. There are fewer beaches along the east coast with Alyki, in the south, the only major resort. Nevertheless, gems can be found along the coastal path which has some very fine and scenic views…

The Island of Paros:

Alyki: The once lazy fishing village of Alyki, about 15 km from Parikia is a charming Greek village with its freshly painted house walls of stone, neat streets and good tavernas. The village overlooks some of the best beaches on the Island of Paros with clean beaches and shallow seawater with tamarisk trees behind for plenty of natural shade. As well as the beach and tavernas there are lots of village facilities including a children's playground, a football pitch, a basketball court and tennis courts. Several coves lie nearby with the best of them down a dirt track signposted Farangas which leads to a quiet, sandy beach with a beach bar. The village despite having a beautiful setting is rarely crowded. North out of Alyki, near the village of Voutakos and what used to be the Island airport until it was moved to Pounda is the Museum Scorpios which has animated handmade miniature figures depicting past life on the Island. **Voutakos:** The hills around the little fishing port of Voutakos has spectacular views to Antiparos and to other offshore Islets. It is said that ten 10 islets are visible from these hills. The south side of the port is mainly rocks but the north has a good sandy beach well sheltered from the wind. The Island airport is inland from here, with regular flights to and from Athens and local buses to link the airport with many of the Islands resorts. **Pounta Port:** Pounta is the main ferry port to Antiparos. It is about 9 km from Parikia. The port should not be mistaken for the east coast clubbing resort of the same name. Most visitors to the port are taking the ferry to Antiparos or heading for the beaches to the south. The port is however, noted for its kitesurfing and has several beach surfing centres each year on the long, flat sands. The channel between Paros and Antiparos helps to funnel the wind and along with the shallow shoreline all makes Pounta almost as popular as Chrysi Akti for serious windsurfers but few other tourists stay here…

The Island of Paros:

Agia Irini: On the headland north of Pounta and opposite the Islets to the north of Antiparos, is the tiny resort of Agia Irini. It has a very pretty, sandy beach that lies at the end of a well sheltered bay that is noted for the many palm trees that line the beach which gives the beach an exotic feel. The two sandy coves are split by marble slabs, palm trees and a waterside church. The palms descend right down to the sea and there are rock pools to add interest although bathers must be aware of the many underwater rocks and stones. The good taverna next to a farm and a shady olive grove has a good menu of Greek dishes. **Parasporos:** Parasporos is the first substantial beach south of Parikia. A track drops from the main road then rises sharply to a rough car park on the exposed headland. An extensive wooden-built beach bar overlooks the best of Parasporos sandy beach which turns to stones as it sweeps around the bay although a pleasant grove of trees gives the beach some shade. Be aware that swimming is a very pleasant activity in the shallow bay, but only after a large bank of underwater stones have been safely negotiated. Parasporos beach has become very popular with youngsters and disco music can be a problem for those who just want peace and quite. A campsite at the southern end of the beach runs its own bus service while public local buses stop on the main road nearby. A coastal path leads to a small bay to the north called Souvlia. This can be somewhat confusing to the visitor as a long, sandy beach on the other side of the bay appears to have the same name. This one has only a small sandy beach with a few trees at the back of the beach for shade and is surrounded by recently built villas and apartments so it can become somewhat crowded…

The Greek Island of Patmos

The tiny Island of Patmos is located in the Aegean Sea just south of the Island of Samos and north of Leros, close to the Turkish coast. One of the most northerly of the Dodecanese Islands it might almost be classed, like neighbouring Samos, as one of the Aegean group. The closest airports are located in Leros and Kos. The airport of Leros receives domestic flights from Athens, while the airport of Kos is busier and receives daily flights from Athens and international flights in the summer. From either Islands, visitors can take the ferry to Leros. Patmos is small enough to allow the visitor to stand in the Island's central hilltop Chora and see almost all of its many indented bays. St John was exiled here in a cave where he reputedly wrote the Book of Revelations. The cave is now a popular pilgrimage site. The Island has plenty of attractive scenery as well as several good beaches and all but a few are reached relatively easily. The main port at Skala, with the Chora above, neatly splits the Island north and south. The combination of a deep seawater port at Skala and the religious attractions of the hillside Chora make Patmos a favourite place to stop for cruise ships. The main Island of Patmos beaches are found on the eastern shore, both north and south from Skala, and most are set in deeply indented bays with Islets offshore. The Island of Patmos is off the main tourist routes. It is a small, beautiful Island with a good road network, a scenic port and several fine sandy beaches. It has deep, sheltered coves that create a jigsaw shaped Island where an exiled St John wrote the Bible's Book of Revelations. Lots of summer cruise ships moor in the deep harbour at Skala and visitors stream to the hilltop monastery and the cave where the saint once lived. Those who holiday on the Island can enjoy sheltered sandy bays, fine walks and easy Island hopping…

The Island of Patmos:

Skala Port: The main Patmos port at Skala has a deep inlet that can easily accommodate the biggest cruise liners as well as catamarans, ferries and fishing boats. Ferries tie up opposite the main Skala square which is laid out with cafe tables and caged birds twittering beneath large white parasols. Beyond the square, narrow streets fan out in all directions, lined with small shops selling tourist trinkets up to designer goods all aimed at the cruise ship passengers on their way to the Chora and the holy cave of St John. Racks of clothes, sunglasses and craft work join cafe chairs as if by magic whenever a cruise liner docks; the empty white alleys turn into bustling shopping arcades in just moments. A short walk inland reveals a modest maze of whitewashed houses spreading up the hill. A narrow stretch of sharp sand lines the shore to the north of the port enlivened by cafe tables set out beneath shady tamarisks trees but the small beach is backed by a busy and noisy main road. Far better beaches lie close by. **Chora:** The Chora is a maze of twisting medieval alleyways circling the imposing fortified monastery of St John which sits above Skala and dominates the whole Island of Patmos. Strangely spooky thanks to an absence of colour, everywhere is whitewashed with doors painted grey or black and few trees, flowers or natural vegetation. The traffic-free alleys are narrow, often a little claustrophobic and wrap around the steep hill in a chaotic maze. Designed this way to confused pirate raiders of long ago and it is easy to get hopelessly lost today. Terrific panoramas of the whole Island are on offer from small cafes beneath the monastery walls while more romantic tavernas lie hidden away in small squares. The small, but impressive, monastery of St John the Divine tops the Chora and has very fine frescoes and icons. The trick is to avoid the cruise ships crowds when the place is crawling. Halfway up the long, steep and winding hill to the Chora is the Cave of Apocalypse where St John is believed to have written the Book of Revelation. Visitors can enter the cave where he is reputed to have received his religious revelations…

The Island of Patmos:

North Coast Beaches: The narrow waist of land at Skala neatly divides the Island north and south. Both have hilly interiors and a good selection of beaches. The best of the northern beaches are on the east coast, with a trio around the bay just north of Skala and some less visited, but delightful spots on the headland at Geranos. The less attractive beaches lie on the north and west coasts of the Island of Patmos. **Meloi:** The first good beach north out of Skala is a short walk over the headland to Meloi about 1.5 km from the port. The road to Meloi is at the eastern end of the port where the main road turns inland. This is an attractive beach of sharp sand curves around a small bay backed by a low stone wall and a distinctive line of tamarisk trees that offer good shade in the afternoon. The seawater is shallow at first but drops sharply a few metres out where stones and seaweed eventually give way to soft sand underfoot. Meloi beach is long enough to provide plenty of room, particularly at the northern end. Nestling among an attractive stand of trees is a pleasant taverna. There is a camping site 100 metres behind the beach and a small mini-market. A road branching south ends up at the small sand and pebble beach of Aspri, usually deserted, and a path over the headland passes even more solitary coves. **Agriolivadi:** Agriolivadi is signposted right off the road north out of Skala just past the petrol station. The beach is one of the best on the Island, with shallow seawater and good fine sand that sweeps right around the large open bay. A narrow line of tamarisks trees offers limited natural shade at the eastern end but the shallow seawater is sandy underfoot, making this an ideal beach for families. The uninhabited offshore Islet of Agia Thekla is planted picturesquely in the bay and a couple of tavernas sit under the trees and there is a cascade of vines at the back of the beach…

The Island of Patmos:

Kato Kampos: Kato Kampos, also called Kabos, is a large, deep beach of sharp white sand and is one of the most popular on Patmos. Set in a deep bay, as are many of the beaches on this jigsaw-shaped Island, the soft sand and shallow seawater make it a good family beach. Stands of tamarisk trees give lots of good shade while a couple of tavernas and a beach cafe open in summer months. The eastern end of the beach is far quieter and has a small jetty. The road behind leads up the hill to the village of Epano Kambos, the third largest on Patmos, with its square dominated by the church of Evangelismos and a taverna beneath a large plane tree. There are religious festivals here in March and August with plenty of feasting, music and dancing in the streets. **Yeranos Peninsula:** The Yeranos peninsula has several peaceful beach coves. The first is Vagnis, or Vagias, a clean sweep of white pebble and stone backed by tamarisk trees. This idyllic spot has views across the bay to the Islets of Agia Thekla and Agios Georgios. Next is Linginos, a flat stretch of stone, rather exposed and with no shade but superb views. Finally, at the end of the peninsula is Livadi Geranos, or Geranou, where a couple of sheltered sand and pebble beaches are backed by clumps of tamarisk trees. The south-west facing beach has views across to the offshore Islets of Agios Georgios and Kentronissi. Above the coves is the dazzling white chapel of Panagia Yeranos and a small taverna on the hill that opens in the summer. **Lampi:** There is a north-facing pebble beach at Lampi, or Labi as it is sometimes called. Lampi bay lies two kilometres north of Kampos and the long pebble beach has long been famed for its distinctive, strongly marked pebbles. They make ideal souvenirs and the biggest and best have long since been plundered to grace the homes of tourists. The sea can get choppy and the pebbles, though smooth, drop steeply into the water so this is not a great beach for children, but it makes for excellent snorkelling…

The Island of Patmos:

Avdelas: The small beach at Avdelas is below the chapel to Agios Nikolaos. Caiques often pull in here on their round the Island trips. Very peaceful it may be but there are no facilities or shade on the exposed beach. On the promontory is an 11th century chapel to Agios Avdelas. **South Coast Beaches:** The south of the Island below the main port of Skala is dominated by the Chora and the Monastery of Agios Ioannis (St. John) that sits above it. Slightly smaller that the north it has fewer beaches although they are just as good. **Grikos Fishing Port:** The picturesque fishing port at Grikos, or Groikos is a hugely attractive village which has a harbour at the eastern end, with tavernas lining the pleasant quayside. A long, sandy beach reaches out to the east, backed by a thick line of shady tamarisk trees. Offshore, almost blocking the approach to Grikos Bay, is the large uninhabited Islet of Tragonissi. The sheltered bay is usually crammed with yachts and fishing boats. Grikos beach is also one of the longest on Patmos and very sandy near the harbour, changing to sharp sand and pebble as it heads east. At the far end of the bay is the huge rock of Kalikatsou, also known as Petra (Greek for 'stone'). **Petra Rock:** A massive 10 metre high rock sits at the head of a barren stretch of mud flats at the southern end of Grikos bay. This is Petra is also known by locals as Kallikatsou which is Greek for the jackdaws that apparently used to nest there. Petra is a huge rock with an interesting shape and with many local myths linked to it, partly because it has been a refuge for many hermits down the centuries. Petra rock can be climbed quite easily but there are no safety features and visitors regularly slip and fall. Below the rock, Petra beach stretches out the south with sunbeds and a small beach cantina opening in the summer. The beach of sharp sand and stone that dips steeply into the sea…

The Island of Patmos:

Stavros, Diakoftu and Alykes: Just south of Petra is the narrowest point of the Island where beaches on both the east and west coast are only 200 metres apart. To the west is a pleasant sand and stone beach called Stavros while the twin beaches of Diakoftu and Alykes are found to the east. Both of the eastern beaches are a little more difficult to reach as there is no road but there are walking paths through the fields. Stavros has a small line of trees for shade but the other beaches are very exposed, with little in the way of shelter. Alykes is Greek for salt and there are a couple of small salt pans here. A beach taverna opens during the summer season. **Psili Ammos:** Considered by some to be one of the best beaches on the Island of Patmos, Psili Ammos is also one of the most difficult to reach overland, having no road access. Most arrive on the beach by boat from Skala while walkers have a difficult 30-minute scramble over a series of steep crags and deep gullies along the coast from the end of Stavros beach. Psili Ammos beach has a deep swathe of golden sand and many large trees that grow almost down to the water's edge, offering plenty of good natural shade. A small beach taverna opens in the summer. The beach is north-west facing so it is exposed to strong winds that creates heavy sea swells so it is worthwhile checking the local weather reports before setting out, especially out of season. High winds and heavy seas can even prevent a boat pick-up and visitors are then forced to walk back along the long coastal path which can pose some visitors difficulties…

The Greek Island of Paxos

The Greek Island of Paxos or Paxoi is located just south of the Greek Island of Corfu and, at just eight kilometres long by three kilometres wide, it's one of the smallest Islands in the Ionian chain of Islands that sit off the western coast of mainland Greece. Paxos is not just small in size, it can also feel very much like an Island in miniature with its dinky beaches, toy-town villages and dainty hills. The Island has just three small coastal resorts, at Gaios, Loggos and Lakka, Paxos and can sometimes feel a little crowded, especially in August. A ferry or other type of boat is the only way of getting to Paxos and, with a trio of large harbours, it is a big stopover favourite with yacht flotillas. The Island of Paxos is a much sought-after Greek Island holiday destination, especially for independent travellers. It is also a favourite with wealthy Greek and Italian families. Paxos is very pretty and its hillsides are carpeted in olive groves whose the ancient trees are renowned for producing the very highest quality oil. The beaches on the Island are stone and pebble and many are quite small. They can get crammed as the flotilla crews join the throngs of day trippers. The nearby Islet of Antipaxos has a couple of good beaches with the golden sands at Vrika particularly appealing. The Island of Paxos beaches may be pebble and stone but this is still one of the most popular Islands in the Ionian group and a favourite of the Italians. Sheer cliffs line the west coast and all of Paxos beaches are found on the gentler eastern shore, many set in idyllic bays backed by pine forest and most easily reached from the road that run the length of the Island. Those visitors who like the sand between their toes can sail to the nearby Islet of Antipaxos for two of the best sandy beaches in this part of the Mediterranean…

The Island of Paxos:

Gaios Port: Most ferries to Paxos arrive at the small port of Gaios, named after the saint who brought Christianity to the Island. Tiny, compact and very attractive, Gaios has a crescent quayside backed by a handsome Venetian square. Cafes and tavernas fringe the harbour and day trippers provide plenty of business for the locals. The streets may be too narrow for cars but it is not unknown for them to get packed and blocked by human traffic in the high season. A couple of outlying Islets, Agios Nikolaos and Panagia, provide natural protection to the harbour and pleasant views for the visitors even if only glimpsed through the myriad of masts of the perfusion of moored yachts. Whitewashed alleys lead off the main square, stuffed with souvenir shops, although the wares are more sophisticated than usual with good pottery and fine jewellery always available. Worth seeing are the castle of Agios Nikolaos, although a permit is needed from the local council and the monastery on Panagia Islet. The Church of Agios Apostoli behind the bus stop has many fine icons and there is an ancient cistern to the right of the church. **Beaches around Gaios:** The road south out of Gaios leads round the headland to a narrow strip of pebble at Plakes and a longer stone strand at Defteri. Around another headland is a pebble cove at Ballos near the tiny fishing port at Agia Marina which has the remains of an early Christian church at the end of the beach. At southern tip of Paxos at Mogonisi a new beach has been dynamited out of the cliff and filled with sand. Mogonisi is actually an Islet connected to Paxos by a causeway of stepping stones. There are some small coves found on this part of the coast which are great for swimming and for sunbathing on the slabs of rock that many contain. North of Gaios the road loops over the headland offering fine views across the bay to the small port of Geramonachus where ferries pull in from Corfu, Parga and Igoumenitsa. North takes the coast road past pebble strands at Kioni and Kamini before it reaches the beautiful sheltered beach at Kaki Laganda set in a very pretty bay where a beach cantina opens in the summer. There are more small beaches further north at Tripitis and Pigmeni…

The Island of Paxos:

Loggos Port: Loggos is the smallest of the ports on Paxos and even more photo-snappingly picturesque than Gaios with clusters of flower-decked houses overlooking the small fishing harbour. It has often doubled as a film set, especially the east-facing quayside which is an ideal spot for alfresco breakfast although early risers snap up the best tables at the waterside tavernas. Loggos also has three mini-markets, a bakery and a several tourist shops. The port of Loggos hosts the Paxos International Music Festival, usually in August or September, with events centred in the old school house. **Beaches around Loggos Port:** Just south of Loggos is a beautiful shingle beach at Levericho with has a beach taverna. Nearby are the beaches of Kipos and Marmari, the latter set in a very pretty bay with the advantage of shade from the olive trees that grow right down to the shoreline. There are many small coves in the area although many can only be reached by boat. Further still is the pebble and close by is the long pebble beach of Kipiadi, a favourite anchorage for yachts. **Lakka Port:** The port of Lakka sits in a lovely horseshoe bay flanked by silver green olive groves and stands of cypress. The village has a small square edged with Venetian buildings and a maze of narrow alleyways. There are plenty of shops and mini-markets as well as a fair number of tavernas and Italian restaurants. This is the best centre for Island walking. There are several good trails heading inland or along a coast with some spectacular cliff-side views. **Beaches around Lakka:** Two pebble beaches around the western edge of the bay at Lakka offer some sunbathing and there is sand underfoot at Harami once in the water, a rarity on Paxos. Harami also shelves gently into the sea so it's a popular spot for families and has scores of yachts and boats at anchor in the bay. At the head of the bay is a small pebble beach at Kanoni. There are beaches east of Lakka the first being Arkoudaki while nearby is a pebble strand at Orkos and another over the headland at Lakos. But the most popular beach on this stretch of coast is Monodendri (the name means single tree). There is another beach that lies further to the south at Glyfada...

The Greek Island of Rhodes

The Island of Rhodes, Greece, is the Crusader Isle, steeped in ancient history and boasting 300 days of blue skies a year. Rhodes lies at the southern end of the Dodecanese Island chain that skirts the Turkish coast and is one of the most sought after holiday destinations in the Mediterranean. Many of the beach resorts on Rhodes are now firmly devoted to package tourism and anyone expecting to see a Greek goatherd and his flock has definitely come to the wrong Island. The Island of Rhodes is well known for bargain holidays and there are plenty of quality Rhodes' hotels to choose from. To the west of Rhodes City are shingle beaches while, to the east lots of rows of holiday hotels are stacked along the coast like deck chairs. Only when you venture south of the popular resort of Lindos do the crowds thin out and only there you will find a more authentic glimpse of Greek Island life. Rhodes is one of the most visited of the Greek Islands with many thousands of holidaymakers flying into its international airport each year. The most popular beaches on the Island are found on the north and east coasts. North coast beaches are not very good but they are the closest to Rhodes Town and are also the home to very large hotel complexes. The east coast has the pick of the beach resort hotels with Faliraki the most notorious for lively entertainment. The crowds thin out in the south of the Island, with the hugely popular resort of Lindos marking the end of package holiday territory. The far south coast has fewer facilities but a more authentically Greek atmosphere than the noisier north…

The Island of Rhodes:

Rhodes Town: Renowned as being an archaeological treasure house, the city of Rhodes, or Rodos, sits on the northern tip of the Island with sea on three sides. Rhodes is really three cities in one. The first Rhodes Town is the modern city. The second Rhodes Town is the medieval walled city which is a national treasure granted World Heritage Status by UNESCO with a maze of cobblestone streets and beautiful sights. The third Rhodes Town is the seashore development that runs along the north and east coasts awash with luxury hotel complexes and overwhelmingly devoted to tourism. There are smart restaurants and some interesting shops and cafes. Rhodes Town beach is shingle and sand. The beach is usually very windy and the sea can get very rough and there is a steep drop into the sea, so it's unsuitable for children. **Modern Rhodes:** The 'new town' is dominated by blocks of hotels and throughout the summer it throbs to disco music and revving motorbikes. Mandraki Harbour, guarded by its twin bronze deer, is the hub and cafes banked up beneath the nearby arches are where to sit to watch the city go by. It oozes atmosphere with its street sellers, pavement artists and boat trips. The nearby aquarium is well worth a visit. Visitors can catch the scenic holiday train outside the town hall for a tour of the sites. **Medieval Rhodes:** To explore the old city, the wise visitor will get a map and a guide. A good place to start is Symi Square, near Mandraki harbour, for a tour of the Castello where the knights left their most enduring marks. For a different era in Rhodes' history find the Plane Tree Walk where the clock tower marks the wall that separated the knights' quarters from the rest of the city. The place is packed with shops, bars, cafes and restaurants. **North Coast Beaches:** The main road west out of Rhodes City follows the north coast to the airport at Leoforos Triandon. Resorts are strung along the road virtually without a break as this is the main tourist holiday strip for Rhodes. A series of narrow shingle beaches line the shore that have heavy swells and waves crashing in on them that are whipped up by the strong northerly winds…

The Island of Rhodes:

Ixia: Ixia beach is a deep and steep strip of shingle lining the busy airport road. Restaurants and shops edge the long esplanade which has a children's playground and a couple of watersport centres. The northerly wind can get very fresh on Ixia beach. A few tavernas do offer Greek food and music, but locals stay well away from the tourist traps and prefer the food delights of nearby villages such as Tris.
Trianda: Trianda beach is a long strip of shingle and sand backed by a busy road. There are all the usual watersports and the windy coast here is a big hit with windsurfers, especially in the afternoons when stiff breezes can sweep along the shore. Trianda is effectively the beach resort of the inland village of Ialyssos and it has a large and bustling village which retains some local Greek atmosphere. Regular local buses run into Rhodes Town and to other villages along the coast.
Ialyssos Plateau: On the hillside above of Trianda is one of the Island's most noted beauty spots at Ialyssos on the plateau of Filerimos. Studded with cypress and pines, this was once the site of one of three ancient city states that ruled Rhodes. The local monks sell their own liqueur, known as sette, made from seven local herbs. Memorable views and a riot of flowers make this a very popular area for photographers and nature lovers, especially in the spring. **Kremasti:** Kremasti has a wide pebble beach which is steeply banked pebble and stone, making it unsuitable for children. It sits at the end of the Rhodes airport runway and can get frenetic on transfer days. Kremasti village is famous for its Panayieri, or Festival of the Virgin Mary, on August 15. There is a giant street market, fiesta and funfair. The Panhellenic Craft Fair is held in Kremasti from August 14 – 22nd. The nearby village of Pastida is an oasis of calm, sheltering amid citrus and olive groves with a smattering of small shops and tavernas…

The Island of Rhodes:

Tholos: Further west along the coast road, and at the other end of the airport runway, is the village and coastal resort of Tholos or Theologos. The narrow strip of shingle and sand soon flattens out into a wide expanse, backed by scrub and low dunes. Tholos has a much more of a traditional Greek atmosphere than most north coast resorts with some typical Island architecture among the shops and tavernas. **Fanes:** One of the last resorts on the north coast is the village of Fanes with a picturesque harbour and a flat isolated beach dotted with stands of tamarisk trees. The flat beach, shallow seawater and strong breezes make for ideal conditions for windsurfing and kitesurfing and the sports are hugely popular here. **East Coast Beaches:** The main coastal highway snakes down to Lindos with every sand and shingle bay along its length a thriving tourist resort. The resorts vary from fun-filled holiday playpen of Faliraki to the upmarket kitsch of Therma Kalithea. **Koskinou and Kalithea:** Koskinou and Kalithea are small working villages about 10 kilometres out of Rhodes Town. Beaches here are mainly sharp sand and pebble, although patches of soft sand appear to the south towards the rock outcrop at Thermi Kalithea. There are no hidden coves or quiet bays on this part of the coast, just a long stretch of wide, flat beach. **Thermae Kalithea:** Thermae Kallithea, also variously spelled Thermi, Therma, and Kalithea or Kalithia was originally a health spa built in the Moorish style by the Italians in the 1930's. The dramatic setting and kitsch architectural with features, including domed pavilions and pink marble pillars, make it a favourite venue for fashion photographers. Palm trees offer shade on a small shingle beach while sun loungers are scattered around a small lido. The nearby coves have deep seawater so you will need to be a decent swimmer. In each cove there is usually a few sunbeds and a beach taverna that often gives the cove its name. The main road leads to Faliraki beach, a 20-minute walk away…

The Island of Rhodes:

Faliraki: Once a fishing village a visitor would be hard put to find a fisherman on the main beach at Faliraki these days. On the beach jet skiing, go-karting, bungy jumping are offered to the daily influx of frolicky young visitors whose idea of fun is getting smashed on lager and making a lot of noise. And noise there is, brain-addling at night as the bars and clubs wind up to full power. The din can be heard several kilometres away. Faliraki beach is a gritty flat sand and packed with bodies from dawn to well after dusk. Mosquitoes home in from the nearby lowland to gorge on the bare teenage white flesh. Faliraki waterpark is nearby, one of the largest in Europe, with water flumes and slides. There is a small harbour at the southern end of Faliraki beach where tavernas and shops abound. **Ladiko:** Just south of Faliraki is the small pebble-beached cove of Ladhiko, sometime spelt Ladiko, where many scenes were shot for the classic war film 'The Guns of Navarone'. Ladiko beach has huge and vertiginous cliffs behind with slabs of rock available for sunbathing on the beach. Underwater stones can be sharp so the beach is not ideal for children. Above Ladiko Bay is a small taverna and another small sandy bay down a nearby track. **Afandou:** Afandou beach has white stone and shingle that stretches out in one great seven kilometre swathe. The shingle dips steeply at the shoreline where large and slippery underwater rocks make even paddling difficult. The resort, about 20 kilometres from Rodos has an 18-hole golf course and a tourist train. Afandou village, the second largest on Rhodes, is a working village, although tourism is now well established. Dozens of tavernas and holiday bars line the main street of the village. All day music and karaoke blares out from busy bars around the village square. Just outside Afandou village, surrounded by pines, is the monastery of Agios Nektarios, with an immense pine tree and a drinking fountain fed by springs that tumble from the surrounding hills. Where people can wander around in peace and find an oasis away from the noisy village centre…

The Island of Rhodes:

Kolymbia: The approach to Kolymbia is dramatic, along an arrow-straight road lined with mature eucalyptus. Built as a model farm by the Italians, Kolimbia, Kolymbia or Kolympia, is remarkable for the local houses, noted for their over-large chimney stacks. The resort, about 25km from Rodos, is relatively small. It has a picturesque rocky cove with an attractive beach to the north, mostly shingle with watersports at each end. Some sandy coves to the south are a 10-minute walk. Kolymbia has an unhurried air about it. The resort has the useual tavernas and bars and there are boat trips and a local bus service to other resorts and to Rhodes city. **Tsambika:** Overlooked by a Gibraltar-like rocky outcrop topped by a monastery, the swathe of soft sand at Tsambika or Tsambiki, also spelt Tsampiki or Tsampkia, is reached down a precipitous, hairpin road. It has the usual the usual sunbeds, a beach taverna and several beach cantinas offering drinks, sandwiches and shady relief from the sun. According to local legend, barren women have only to climb barefoot to the tiny white Byzantine church of Panayia Tsambika above the beach to ensure pregnancy. As a result many of the Island's children are named Tsambikos or Tsambika, depending on their sex. The rock outcrop above overlooks both Kolimbia and Tsambika beaches with stupendous views along the coast. **Archangelos:** Archangelos is the largest village on the Island, outside Rhodes City, with around 6,000 people living there and lies on a plain circled by the mountains of Profitis Elias, Karavos and the hills of Kefaloti, Kastro and of Anagros. Home to a dwindling leather crafts industry which still makes carpets and traditional goatskin boots, Archangelos is now a firm favourite with the Germans. Many of the village houses are painted in rich colours and the centre is dominated by the Church of the Archangel Michael with its imposing bell tower. Tavernas and bars line the single main street and Archangelos also has the ruins of a 15th century Crusader castle, although little remains except the outer walls. The Archangelos area is full of citrus trees, olive groves and vineyards…

The Island of Rhodes:

Stegna: Archangelos' village beach is at Stegna, or Stengena, roughly two kilometres from the village and 33 kilometres from Rodos on a coast of sandy bays and rocky outcrops. Stegna beach is mainly sand with the odd patch of shingle, clusters of rocks with several small coves and rock pools to explore. Beachfront cantinas and bars open in summer and there is a tiny harbour at the end of the bay. There is only one local bus a day but four mini-markets offer the basics. **Agathi:** Deep, golden sand in a medium sized cove of clear seawater with a few underground rocks make Agathi beach one of the best beaches on the Island and is 36 kilometres from Rhodes town. There is no resort as such, just the 600 metre beach, a string of beach cantinas and a few rows of sunbeds. The sands at Agathi are golden and soft and the seawater is shallow making it an ideal spot for families with children. There are toilets and no natural shade. On the far side of Agathi beach is the tiny chapel of Ayia Agathi which is built into a cave. **Haraki:** Haraki is a quiet, small fishing port overlooked by the ruins of Feraklos castle which was one of the first castles to be held by the Crusaders. A promenade separates a row of chalets, shops and tavernas from the long and narrow crescent beach of shingle and stone. Haraki is noted for its good tavernas and the resort has a large number for its size, with plenty of variety on offer. Tavernas overlooking the bay are set in a very romantic setting. A small harbour at one end of Haraki beach is busy with fishing boats in the early morning and there is a steep path up the hillside to the Feraklos castle ruins above. Regular local buses leave for Rhodes City. **Kalathos:** The very long stone and shingle beach at Kalathos stretches along the shore for about four kilometres. The beach shelves rather steeply, making it a poor choice for children. A cantina, mini market and some tavernas sit on the road that runs behind the beach. The northern end of the beach is owned by the Greek military and access is restricted and photography is not advisable so be aware…

The Island of Rhodes:

Lindos: Lawrence Durrell once described Lindos as "of a scrupulous Aegean order, and perfect of its kind". Well, times have changed. Lindos has clearly inherited the perfect setting. The shimmering violet and emerald pool set in a horseshoe bay tinged with golden sand and sheltered by hills dotted with sugar-cube houses. The 'perfect order' however is now disturbed by the endless cars, coaches, bikes and boats that now blow into Lindos like a daily sandstorm. By 9 am the beach is already buzzing with holidaymakers as cars and bikes roar in, followed by an endless stream of Rhodes Island tour buses. In July and August, the packed amphitheatre of the beach can also turn terribly hot and airless. Temperatures can soar to 40° in high summer with little in the way of natural shade. The beach is fine soft sand, a sheltered bay of shallow seawater and watersports of all kinds; an ideal location for families with young children. Various steep paths that snake down from Lindos village where the narrow, traffic-free streets blare to music bars. **Pefkos:** Pefkos is about 56 km from Rodos and purpose-built for tourist visitors. The one-kilometre beach is narrow with sand and shingle and it lies parallel to the main road and approached through pine woods (Pefkos is Greek for 'pines'). Sun loungers hug most of the shore but, at the far end, the beach fans out into a flat area of small rocky bays with shallow water, making this an attractive spot for families with children. More small coves can be found by walking north or south. Pefkos has no village just a clutch of shops, restaurants and bars stretching out along the single main street. **Beaches on the South Coast:** Tourists tend to leave the southern beaches to themselves. Poor roads, fewer facilities and the distance from the capital keep the number of visitors down. **Lardos:** Lardos is set in a large bay, about 65 km from Rodos, is little more than a group of supermarkets, some tavernas, car hire firms and a few large hotels. The sand at Lardos is soft, if a little gritty, but the seawater is invitingly clean. The village has a proper Greek community feel and has bars, shops and good Greek food restaurants…

The Island of Rhodes:

Glystra: Glystra is a small cove with an inviting beach of good fine sand that lies to the south of Lardos. The sands at Glystra are quite deep and the beach makes a long sweep around an attractive bay. The seawater is shallow, so it is fine for families with young children. Snorkellers enjoy serching for the shell of a car dumped out in the middle of the bay. Glystra beach has a cantina, sunbeds but has little natural shade. **Kiotari:** Kiotari beach is large, at three kilometres and very sandy at one end, shingle at the other. There are some rock pools at one end of Kiotari beach but winds can bring occasional whiffs of the nearby sewage plant. There are several mini-markets, some souvenir shops and a handful of tavernas. **Gennadi:** Gennadi is a vast stone and shingle beach about 70 km south of Rodos. It is very long, at nearly six kilometres, and the stones drop sharply into the sea, although the seawater is clear and good for swimming. Gennadi village is above the beach over a main road where there are tavernas, small hotels and villas. **Plimiri:** Plimiri is a protected, sandy bay backed by low dunes and a peaceful spot with a marina in the old fishing harbour. A small roadside taverna near the harbour overlooks the long sandy crescent which backed by bamboo and scrub and lies about 85 km south of Rodos. There are miles of sand along this stretch of coast with beautiful, deserted bays, the most notable at Agios Giorgios. Inland from Plimiri is the farming village of Kattavia with fields of cereals and vegetables with scattered farmhouses, an old abandoned airport and some impressive cypress-lined roads. **Prassonissi:** At Prassonissi, a dramatic three kilometre spit of sand charges out to sea with the choppy Aegean on one side and the calm Mediterranean on the other. In winter the seas can link up and turn the spot into a genuine Island, about 80 km from Rhodes. Even in summer the strong winds can force sunbathers to seek shelter. Surfers find Prassonissi ideal, especially off the northern shore, and many professionals come here to train. On most days the sea is alive with sailboards. A lovely view indeed…

The Greek Island of Samos

The Island of Samos is one of the Dodecanese Islands sitting fairly close to the Turkish coast, a large and mountainous Island that was, in ancient times, one of Greece's richest ancient trading wealth. As well as ferries the Islands also gets domestic flights to and from Athens and Thessaloniki all year round. In the summer, it also has charter flights from abroad and there is also air connection with other Greek islands, such as Kos, Rhodes, Chios and Lesvos. Samos today is noted for its many architectural wonders of the ancient world, although unfortunately not all of them have been preserved for the present-day visitors to enjoy. The main Island resort of Pythagorion, in particular, has permanently paved over much of Samos Island's glorious ancient past. The Island of Samos has something for everyone, from rustic backwaters, miles of sand, towering mountains, lush forests and some singularly beautiful scenery. The hills inland are noted for wine growing, especially in the hillsides around Vourliotes, famed for its vintage muscat wine. Flamingos have been using the Island as a stopover for many years. Samos is a large Island and beaches are sited in three main clusters, north-west of Samos Town, in the south-west around Pythagorio and to the south-west at the resorts of Kampos and Votsalakia. Hidden gems lie along the east coast and in the wilder north while Kokkari and Pythagorio are two of the busiest resorts. In general, the beach resorts to the east of the Island are backed by gentle rolling hills while those in the west are dominated by big mountain ranges…

The Island of Samos:

Samos Town (Vathi): Noted for its beauty when approached from the sea, Samos Town which is also called Vathi sits at the head of a deep horseshoe bay. Pastel houses and weathered red tile roofs tier down the hillside to a long and deep sea waterfront promenade. A town of some 6,000 locals. The shops and tavernas of the waterfront is overlooked by a steep rise of streets up the hillside. In the middle of the waterfront is the main square, guarded by an imposing stone lion and edged with tree-shaded cafes. Further inland is a small, but attractive, municipal gardens. The town has a very good archaeological museum with exhibits spread between two buildings. A modern annexe houses the largest surviving 'kouros' statue at five metres tall and dating from 575 BC. The older building has displays of Egyptian, Turkish, Cypriot and Syrian artifacts testifying to Samos' ancient trading wealth. A Byzantine museum is located in the former Bishop's Palace it houses some icons, some 18th century silver bibles and the bizarre cast of St George's footprint. The road south heads to the hillside village of Ano Vathi, once a pirate refuge, where narrow streets thread between neo-classical houses and medieval churches. **Gagou:** The road north out of Samos Town leads almost immediately to the upmarket Kalami. The best beach area on this part of the coast is at Gagou or Gangou, which many regard as the town beach. A narrow strip of stone and shingle, only about 200 metres long and facing south-west, is backed by some restaurants. Gagou beach is relatively quiet. Sunbeds line the back of the beach which slopes fairly gently into the sea. A line of low trees gives good natural shade and sunbathers can watch the ferries sailing past to the harbour. A couple of tavernas sit at the northern end of the beach. **Agia Paraskevi:** The north-facing beach at Agia Paraskevi is 6 km from Samos Town. It has a very thin strand of sand and shingle with barely enough room to lie down in places. Although a pretty chapel and small attractive harbour graces the beach at the eastern end. The exposed beach has no shade or tavernas nearby. The local countryside is famous for its wide variety of butterflies...

The Island of Samos:

South Coast Beaches: The mountainous Bournias north-south ridge splits the south coast of Samos. To the east of this ridge is the Island's most popular holiday resort at Pythagorion. To the west lie the resorts of Marathokambos and Votsalakia. Between the two are many small coves. They are all difficult to reach except by boat. They are all just narrow strips of stone and rock. **Pythagorion:** Pythagorion is the main holiday resort of Samos, close to the Island airport, with a very long sandy beach and a number of notable ancient sites nearby. It was originally called Tingaki but renamed in 1955 to honour the Island's most famous native son, the ancient Greek philosopher and mathematician Pythagoras. The cobbled waterfront has an uninterrupted line of tavernas, bars and cafes overlooking the large harbour while the main street that heads inland is packed with tourist shops. Pythagorion has a relaxed and friendly atmosphere. The small sheltered pebble beach of Rematika, near the harbour, has shallow seawater and sunbeds with tavernas nearby but the main holiday beach lies to the west near the airport. The beach is shingle and sand and stretches for several kilometres to Potokaki. The Pythagorion area is noted for its archaeological treasures, although much has been lost or buried over time. The town museum has ancient statues, tombstone reliefs and Roman busts. A 19th century castle sits on a hill to the south-west, built mostly with stone pilfered from ancient temple sites and the Chora, to the north, was the Samos Islands capital until the 1850's. It is still a lively place today with plenty of good tavernas. Further north at Mytilini is a remarkable paleontology museum, housed in the village hall and boasting fossils of a 10 million-year-old giraffe-like creature and the skulls of prehistoric hippos and lions. **Potokaki:** The beach at the western edge of Pythagorion heads as far as the eye can see to merge with the beach at Potokaki. Potokaki beach is mostly shingle with some sand here and there. Potokaki beach is rarely uncrowded and rows of sunbeds cover the best sand. Visitors may prefer the hotel pool to the beach, which is unremittingly long, straight and without much in the way of character or shade…

The Island of Samos:

Ireon: Once a tiny fishing hamlet Ireon is now a minor resort with hotels and tavernas in a quiet spot that begins where the long sands of Potokaki eventually run out. The Ireon area is most noted for the huge Hera Temple archaeological site nearby. Ireon beach benefit from having several large trees that offer good shade. A couple of smaller coves can be found nearby, notably at Papa Beach which is a small crescent of shingle with a taverna above. **Tsopela Cove:** West of Ireon the road climbs towards Mount Bournias then drops south through a magnificent gorge to the scenic sand and shingle cove at Tsopela. A couple of beaches sit either side of a rock headland with a small Islet just offshore. Tsopela also attracts a lot of day trip boats from Pythagorio. Inland, the hillside villages here are worth a visit. The large village of Pagondas has astonishing views. This traditional village sits on the slopes of Mount Bournias and has an impressive pubic fountain in the main square, many narrow whitewashed alleys and some good cafes. The village of Myli, just north of Ireon, owes it is name to the watermills that once operated here. The mills have long gone, but the lemon groves and cool streams are still there to enjoy. **Ormos Koumeikon Region:** West of Tsopela the unmade road winds along the coast beneath the looming Mount Bournias around a number of small coves, most worth a visit with an occasional cantina or even taverna and some quiet, out-of-the-way shingle beaches. There are coves worth exploring at at Sikia, Pavlou, Avandi and Vergi before reaching the lovely shingle beach at Limnonaki. Beyond here the road climbs inland before dropping back to the shore at Kalogera, Kambos, yet another beach called Psili Amos, Kambos and then the long beach of shingle at Balos, or Valos. The coast around here is called Ormos Koumeikon and is relatively remote. **Ormos Marathokambos:** Ormos Marathokambos, more a working fishing village than a tourist haunt but busy and friendly, with a very good range of tavernas. The beach is stony but it has a relaxing little port and isolated coves can be found further along the coast…

The Island of Samos:

Votsolakia (Kambos): One of the Island's longest sandy beaches is found at Votsolakia, also known as Kambos. The beach is of fine, flat sand with a few stones and runs for about three kilometres. The straight road that follows the beach has tavernas and cafes with the glorious backdrop of Mount Kerkis behind. The beach is too big to get crowded and sunbeds cluster around the beach tavernas that spring up every now and then. A cluster of tavernas, bars and shops at the western end give the illusion of a village centre. **Psili Ammos:** Around the headland west of Votsalakia is a fine beach at Psili Ammos, not to be confused with its more popular namesake in the east and another narrow shingle strip near Kalogera. The eastern end of the beach is composed of large stones and pebbles but this soon gives way to a long, deep swathe of fine sand and sunbeds at the western end. The high cliffs behind offer shelter and the sea is quite shallow along the shore. **Limnionas Cove:** The road turns inland beyond Psili Ammos before arriving at the sheltered cove of Limnionas. A taverna lays out sunbeds on the stone and shingle beach which is a popular spot for day trip boats. Limnionas is a quiet and unassuming place where stones shelve gently to the shore and with good swimming beyond them. **East Coast Beaches:** South of Samos Town the road to Pythagorio neatly demarcates the east of Samos with the mountains of Katsarini to the north, Profitis Ilias in the east and Siharos in the south. Beneath the mountains along the eastern seaboard are several widely scattered seaside resorts. **Mourtia:** The fishing hamlet of Mourtia is seven kilometres from the capital. The small beach of steeply banked shingle is outstandingly beautiful with great views across the straits to the Turkish coast. Palm trees overhang the beach with the occasional stands of tamarisk trees provide shade. The bay and the tiny harbour always seems to be packed with small boats. The seawater is particularly clear on this part of the coast. There are quiet coves to be found to the south of Mourtia notably those at Mikri Laka and Megali Laka…

The Island of Samos:

Kerveli: The small seaside resort at Kerveli is very much a peaceful resort off the busy tourist track. The beach is in a strikingly pretty bay lies about eight kilometres from Samos Town. A line of large shady tamarisks trees line the narrow, shingle beach giving plenty of natural shade with a taverna and mini-market along the shore at the northern end. The village has some good tavernas and there are some fine walks to be had in the area with the mountains of Profitis Ilias to the north and Siharos to the south. **Posidonio:** South of Kerveli and about 10 kilometres from Samos Town is the tiny south-facing resort of Posidonio, sometimes spelt Posidhonio. It has panoramic views, wooded hills and the village set in a beautiful bay. There is more harbour than beach but the small stretch of shingle has a line of shady tamarisk trees at one end with a few sunbeds. Posidonio has several tavernas, some right on the water's edge, and the village is popular with boat trippers out on 'Greek Night' specials with boats mooring right alongside the restaurants. A number of tiny pebble coves dot the bay, the most notable being Sidera, just west over the headland; hardly a beach, just a small scar of pebble and rock but it is very peaceful. **Psili Ammos (East):** There are three beaches on Samos called Psili Ammos but this splendid sandy beach is by far the most popular with day trippers from Samos Town and Pythagorion. Sunbeds can be found at the western end of the beach but the east is free of them with clumps of tamarisk trees providing the shade. The shallow sea means visitors can wade out quite a distance, one reason why the beach is popular with families. There are tavernas along the shore and more at the back of the beach. Offshore is the Islet of Vareloudi and just a kilometre beyond it lies the Turkish coast. Notices warn of strong currents out in the straits should swimmers venture too far out. There are salt marsh and a lake to the west of Psili Ammos, both of which dry to salt pans in the summer. This is a good bird spotting area and flamingos will be plentiful early in the summer season…

The Island of Samos:

Mykali: West of Psili Amos is a three kilometre stretch of windswept sand and shingle at Mykali. The south-facing beach is a mix of stone and shingle, although it turns to sand beneath the shallow seawater. The large salt lake area to the east is a protected nature reserve where storks, herons and flamingos are frequent winter visitors. **North Coast Beaches:** Between the ports of Samos Town to the east and Karlovasi in the west is the Island's premier beach resort at Kokkari and some of the prettiest inland villages on Samos in the wine growing hillsides of the mountains at Lazarou, Ambelos and Aloni. A good road runs the length of the coastline, often close to the cliffs, with sea views to one side and mountain slopes to the other. **Kokkari:** Once a quaint fishing village Kokkari is now the third largest holiday resort on the Island after Samos Town and Pythagorio. The waterfront at Kokkari is lined with restaurants, cafes and bars and, although many of the traditional tavernas have been replaced by cocktail bars, the atmosphere still appeals more to families. A couple of picturesque rock outcrops at each side of Kokkari will get cameras clicking and the narrow beach causeways that lead to them are heavy with small boats and sun loungers. The main Kokkari beach has banks of stone and shingle, dropping sharply to the sea. Exposed and windy, this is also a favourite venue for windsurfers. Those looking for quieter Kokkari spots will head south-east where there are a couple of smaller coves, both shingle but much quieter than the main beach with a decent taverna on the hill behind. A further four kilometres south-east is Kedros where a signposted turn off from the main road drops down to a couple of shingle coves, neither with any facilities. The steep wooded hills behind Kokkari are very attractive and visitors should head inland for more traditional Greek village delights and the area has many splendid walking trails through the woods…

The Island of Samos:

Lemonakia: The sand and pebble beach in a sheltered bay at Lemonakia is two kilometres north-west of Kokkari. The beach is smaller and narrower than its more popular neighbour Tsamadou just around the headland so it can sometimes feel a little crowded. A couple of rows of sunbeds line the shore and there are tamarisk trees behind to shed shade while a large beach taverna sits at the western end. It is mostly pebble, both onshore and underwater, with a little sand here and there and it is an attractive spot. **Tsamadou:** North-west over the headland from Lemonakia is Tsamadou, a beautiful long sickle of sand and pebble that features on almost every advertisement for Samos. Set in a beautiful bay at the bottom of a very steep path are a couple of tavernas shaded by trees and a beach cantina that opens in the high summer. The beach is sharply sloping pebble and shingle. **Vourliotes:** The inland hills rise to the hill village of Vourliotes which has panoramic views out to the sea and over the sweeping fields of vines. This area of Samos is noted for its world-class wine making. This region produces wine, mostly Muscat, than any other on Samos with local wines winning a clutch of international awards. Fresh springs at Vourliotes help keep the landscape lush and green while the village is full of atmosphere with flower decked walls, brightly painted doors and a very pretty central square lined with tavernas serving local delicacies. Nearby are the Pnaka springs, just below the village and a favourite picnic spot with shady plane-trees, fresh spring water and a picturesque little taverna. **Manolates:** The neighbouring village of Manolates may not be as pretty as Vourliotes but it does have a magnificent position at the head of a steep canyon. The hill village is a popular starting point for treks up Mount Ambelos which looms above. The climb is not particularly difficult and walkers are rewarded with some remarkable views. Manolates village itself is set among rolling vineyards and has some excellent tavernas as well as several shops selling handmade local pottery…

The Island of Samos:

Avlakia: The sheltered beach at Avlakia, tiny and often by-passed by tourists. Only about 150 people live here and the beach is just a thin strip of white stone backed by large tamarisk trees and a wall of bamboo for added shelter. Avlakia is a beautiful spot with houses hugging the shoreline and a couple of good waterside tavernas sitting between the beach and an impressive rock outcrop headland. **Agios Konstantinos:** Agios Konstantinos is a pretty coastal village with a shoreline esplanade. The rocky village beach is considered so ugly that even the locals apologise for it. The village is a delightful mix of attractive stone houses peppered with large tavernas. In fact, there are two settlements here, Ano (upper) and Kato (lower), about 500 meters apart and both are surrounded by vineyards. **Agios Nikolaos:** The tiny resort of Agios Nikolaos stands out like a jewel. This small fishing port, home to only 50 locals. Agios Nikolaos has some excellent fish tavernas. **Karlovassi Town:** The Island's second largest town of Karlovassi is overshadowed by the other Island resorts of Samos Town and Pythagorion. It is also far more peaceful and is a good base for exploring the north coast of the Island. The town is more a cluster of villages than a town, Karlovassi can be roughly divided into four areas, each with its own character. Karlovassi waterfront is lined with tavernas and bars and has all the trappings of a rapidly growing resort. The town beach, however, is a poor pair of shingle strips between long rocky breakwaters. The new district (Neo Karlovasi) is marred by derelict factories and warehouses, a hangover from the days when this was a major industrial tanning centre. The middle district (Meleo Karlovassi) is a sprawling suburb of modern housing, redeemed in part by an attractive main square with a huge fountain and restaurants huddled beneath the shady trees. The old district (Paleo Karlovassi), which lies to the west, behind the harbour, is a picture postcard village with a hilltop church overseeing red-tiled houses horseshoed around a pleasant green valley…

The Island of Samos:

Potami: The attractive beach at Potami lies three kilometres west of Karlovasi and is a beach of pebble and some sand well shaded by trees and with a good taverna nestling in the shrubbery. It is a popular beach with Karlovassi residents and easily accessible by car or on foot. Potami beach can get busy in the high season and at weekends but it is generally very quiet. The beach has a few trees that line the shore of steeply banked shingle with rocky outcrops at both ends to add some interest. The area is also well known for its waterfalls and rock pools which attract the tour buses. A sequence of pools tumble down the hillside with a steep two kilometre walk to the top past a series of waterfalls lined with ropes for visitors to haul themselves up by and is very popular with tourists. The heavily wooded track leads to the 11th century church of Metamorfis, believed to be the oldest on Samos, and beyond along a narrow and precipitous path to a small Byzantine fortress that has splendid views back down the valley. **North-West Beaches:** The north-west coastline of Samos is wild, remote and dominated by Mount Kerkis, the Island's highest at 1,473 metres. A small farming hamlet is located at Kallithea with a small cove beyond at Varsamo. Varsamo is noted for its multi-coloured pebbles formed from volcanic ash and a couple of small caves and a beach cantina that opens in the summer. The road runs out at the village of Drakei but tracks here lead down to a couple of wild and beautiful beaches, a refuge for the rare and protected Mediterranean seal 'Monachus Monachus'. The first, and largest, of the beaches as the name suggests, is Megalo Seitani which is in a dramatic setting at the mouth of the Kakoperato Gorge. Around the bay sits the windy and exposed Mikri Seitani a small sand and pebble cove. There are no facilities on these remote beaches and coves so take your own supplies. You can also picnic in the beautiful surrounding countryside….

The Greek Island of Santorini

Santorini, also called Thira, or Fira, lies south of the central Cyclades group of Greek Islands. Santorini is fairly easy to get to as there are many daily flights and ferries to Santorini in the summer. There is also good connection between Santorini and other islands, such as Mykonos, Paros, Naxos, Crete and more, making it easy to island hop from one destination to the other. It is considered to be one of the top holiday hotspots in the Cyclades and is famous throughout the World as a home of the ancient Minoan Civilisation. The Island was born, or should I say re-born, long ago, in a centuries old massive volcanic eruption, the fumes are still rising offshore today. Cruise ships ferry in visitors by the thousand to gasp at the Island's romantic sunset skies. The best views can be found from the Santorini's cliff-top tavernas and bars in the capital town of Fira which is perched precariously on top of vertical cliffs. The view over the caldera and the romantic pull of those sunsets make this a favourite spot for honeymoon couples. The main Santorini resorts of Fira and Imerovigli are lively and if you want a quieter time then stay a little bit further north along the caldera rim. Santorini beaches are mostly confined to the south-east coast where a long strip of black volcanic sand runs from Kamari to Perivolos. Not everyone takes to the grey and gritty volcanic sand which can sizzle with trapped summer heat. The western side of the Island rings the caldera, the flooded volcano crater, and it is just one long crescent of near-vertical cliff. There are a few beaches north-east and south-west but they tend to be small, with few facilities…

The Island of Santorini:

Thira: The Island capital of Thira, variously spelt as Thera or Fira, overlooks a magnificent caldera atop some 300-metre high cliff in colours of black, red and brown. Holiday cruise ships anchor by the dozen in the deep bay below and most dock at the port of Athinios, built in the wake of the 1956 earthquake where a winding path snakes up the cliff in a series of hairpin bends. The old port of Ormos lies directly below Fira in water so deep that ships' anchor chains don't reach the sea bed. The ships moor to specially built giant buoys. Dis-embarking tourists can take a mule ride up a steep, zigzag staircase but most opt for the sedate Austrian-built cable car to take them to the top of the cliff. Some will tackle the 600 or so steps up to Fira on foot but the staircase path is heart-stoppingly steep and walkers risk being brushed aside by mule teams as they pick their way over the droppings of the donkey. The white cube houses and blue-domed churches of Thira spill down the cliff terraces in an appealing mish-mash of styles. The staggering views over the caldera from the restaurants while enjoying a romantic sunset meal is a popular holiday pastime. Old kafenia, bakeries and grocery shops have long been supplanted by trendy boutiques and bars. The most expensive shops flank the main road and most nightclubs cluster near the Fira main staircase. The north of the village is less volatile and well worth exploring. The Catholic cathedral dominates and the convent sells hand-made rugs. The fabulous Minoan frescos found at Akrotiri is now housed in Athens but the Megaron Gyzi museum has old maps of the Cyclades and photos of Thira before the devastating 1956 earthquake. **Firastefani:** The road north out of Thira leads immediately to Thirastefani, also spelt Firastefani, which was once a separate village but is now so swallowed up by its neighbour Thira that they are indistinguishable. Firastefani is marginally less busy than its neighbour and slightly less expensive. There is no village centre in Firastefani as such. It is now almost entirely composed of holiday hotels, pools, villas and apartments with a few restaurants and cafes perched precariously along the top of the cliff…

The Island of Santorini:

Imerovigli: Holidaymakers who prefer sunset views over the caldera away from the swarms of camera wielding trippers will head to the village of Imerovigli. It may be little more than another extension of Fira but it tends not to fill up quite so quickly. At three kilometres from the capital, it can be a little too far to venture for the cruise boat passengers on shore leave. This is the highest spot along the caldera rim and those awe inspiring views peak at the clifftop site of Skaros, an imposing ruin of the citadel fortress that the Venetians once crowned the Island capital. Much of the village was destroyed in the 1956 earthquake, Imerovigli is still classed a 'Traditional Settlement', protecting it against over development. The buildings that did survive have been tastefully restored, notably the traditional 'cave' homes that were deeply carved into the hillside. Homes here are among the most sought after in the Greek Islands and a typical 'cave' house will set buyers back at least €1 million. A cliffside footpath runs from Imerovigli back to Thira and offers some fine views over the caldera. **Oia:** If Thira is trendy, the phonetically challenged Oia (pronounced Eea) is upmarket trendy. Oia has splendid views over the caldera rim and a winding staircase down to a small quay. Many homes here survived the 1956 earthquake and most have been tastefully restored. Some are in bright, rich colours but most are brilliant white, clinging to the red and grey cliffs so closely that one family's roof is another's courtyard. Oia shops tend to sell more authentic goods and the food is more traditional Greek. Oia village is the place for designer jewellery, arty galleries and swish boutiques. The main square in the village of Oia overlooks the caldera and therefore, acts as a gathering point for sunset watchers who sometimes offer an implausible round of applause as the sun sinks down beyond the horizon. Worth a visit is the Maritime Museum in the village. Unlike Thira, Oia has access to the sea at Amoudi and Armeni where there are small quay sides with waterfront tavernas. Both are at the bottom of very steep stone staircases of about 300 steps. Visitors can walk or opt for a donkey ride down to the sea…

The Island of Santorini:

Cape Koulombo: The far northern coastline of the Island of Santorini is virtually inaccessible until you reach Baxedes through an area of low rolling hills. The beach here, also called Paradisos, is a long swathe of pebble but the seawater is fairly shallow. Another gritty black beach is found a little further south at Cape Koulombo, a long but narrow strip of coarse sand backed by looming cliffs that wouldn't look out of place in a sci-fi movie as the wind has carved the cliffs into weird shapes. About four kilometres offshore is an underwater crater which is the remnants of a volcano that devastated Santorini in 1650. Further south still is a small beach at Pori, set in a tranquil bay beneath hillside vineyards. It as has a small fishing quay and a couple of tavernas. Swimmers should take care as the currents here are notoriously strong off these beaches. **Vourvolos:** The village of Vourvolos is an inland continuation of Firastefani but much quieter with extensive views to both sides of the Island. A number of small beaches lie along this stretch of the east coast. The most northerly is Xiropigado, a narrow strip of pebble off the main east coast road. Just south is Vourvoulos beach itself and is a strip of stone and sharp black sand. It has a small harbour and a taverna. The exposed, the beach can attract debris. A coastal path lined with beech trees leads to a beach at Kanaraki, where dark grey and ochre bluffs of volcanic rock loom over a narrow beach of black pebbles. Nearby are Exo Yialos caves that have been hollowed out into the rock. **Monolithos:** Monolithos is a seaside village about eight kilometres from Thira that takes its name from an impressive rock outcrop now topped by the church of Agios Ionassis. The grey sand and shingle is long and deep and backed by brooding cliffs and the sand dips very sharply at the sea edge but after that the waters are shallow enough to wade so it's fine for families with children. Monolithos is a fine spot to escape the throngs of other beaches. A few trees dotted along the beach offer natural shade and a rough track that runs south of the airport fence opens out onto beaches all the way to Kamari…

The Island of Santorini:

Karterados: Inland from Monolithos and in the centre of the Island of Santorini is the village of Karterados. The village makes a fine base to explore the rest of Santorini. Built between two rivers it is almost invisible from the surrounding countryside, the name means the 'hiding' or 'ambush' spot, and acted as a hideaway from marauding 17th century pirates. The village square has a restored windmill and the notable 'Steps of Galaios' that lead into a neighbourhood of cobbled streets, traditional Captain's houses and 'cave' houses built into the rock. The village of Karterados is only a 20-minute walk from Thira so it is nicely situated between the popular capital to the west and the beaches of Monolithos to the east. The village is quite large and boasts a couple of bakeries. Several tavernas and cafes as well as a number of shops. There are daily local buses to Fira, Messaria, Megalochori and Emporio as well as services to the beaches of Perissa, Perivolos and Kamari. **Messaria:** Inland from Monolithos, near Karterados, and about four kilometres south-east of Thira in the centre of the Island and the heart of Santorini's wine making area is the village of Messaria. Surrounded by vineyards, Messaria village retains a lot of its traditional Greek village charm and has two fine churches both built around 1700. **Pyrgos:** High up the 566 metre high Profitis Ilias Mountain sits the village of Pyrgos, one of the oldest and most picturesque villages on Santorini. It sits on the northern slopes of the mountain about eight kilometres from Thira. The village is very popular for holiday excursion tours, thanks to a good road, a Venetian fortress and for having some fine examples of the Island's traditional barrel-roofed houses. Pyrgos is set among vineyards that crawl up the side of the mountain. Near the top is the small Monastery of Profitis Ilias, built in 1712, which has paintings of entrances to heaven or hell. There is also an interesting, if small, museum. It's unfortunate that the monastery must share the mountain with a rash of ugly TV and radio masts alongside the disfiguring communication towers of a military base. Oh well they say that God moves in mysterious ways…

The Island of Santorini:

Kamari: Kamaris is Santorini's main beach resort. Black stones dominate the beach which is about two kilometres long, generously strewn with sunbeds. Kamari is a modern resort, completely rebuilt after the 1956 earthquake with wall-to wall hotels, tavernas, bars, cafes and tourist shops. The black gritty sand and stone can get very hot at the height of summer, there is a sharp drop into the seawater and strong currents further offshore, so it's not ideal for families with children. **Perissa:** The Mountain at Profitis Ilias looks down on the long, black sands of Perissa Beach. The sands which stretch south for around five kilometres. The black shingle and sand gets very hot. The large headland to the north keeps Perissa well sheltered from the wind. Perissa beach shelves steeply into the sea and slippery slabs along the shore make it less than ideal for children. There is a large campsite here, an excellent bakery and several mini-markets. Eucalyptus groves provide some shade in the resort centre. Perissa is also a popular day trip target for those based in beaches Thira. There is a waterpark nearby. **Perivolos:** The beach resort at Perivolos is on the south-eastern side of the Island. Loud music bars and tavernas line the back of the beach. The sand drops sharply into the sea, so families with children must take care. Further south the beach blends into Agios Georgios which marks the southern tip Santorini. Nearby Vlychada where there is a small marina and a beach backed by eroded cliffs and strangely sculpted rock and sand formations; like a landscape from another planet. **Kokkino Paralia (Red Beach):** Just below the Minoan archaeological site at Akrotiri is a string of small beaches, the best know of which is Kokkino Paralia or Red Beach where sunbeds sit on pebbles beneath startling blood-red cliffs of lava that plunge almost vertically to the black sand shore. The beaches narrow and shelves steeply into the sea. Boat trips to other beaches leave here such as White beach, Kambia beach and Mesa Pigadia beach with its lighthouse and unusual rock formations and caves…

The Greek Island of Skiathos

Skiathos is one of the Sporades group of Greek Islands that lie just off the east coast of mainland Greece and it is the nearest Islands to the mainland. Skiathos has its own international airport and good ferry links to nearby Islands and the mainland. It is Susie and my personnel favourite Island of all of the Greek Islands. The Island was one of the first to cash in on the Greek holiday boom thanks to having an international airport. Skiathos has remained, over the years, one of the most popular Greek Paradise Island holiday destinations. We have holidayed at the beautiful Troulos Bay Hotel in Troulos on this Island numerous times. The Island of Skiathos is a small and compact Island, just 12 km long and about 6 km wide, and it has a plethora of large, deep, sandy beaches strung right the way along its southern coastline. Recent years have seen an explosion in tourist facilities and, nowadays, a virtually unbroken line of hotels, apartments and neon-lit tavernas flank the once rural road that runs the length of the south coast. The closely-packed Skiathos holiday beaches are sandy and safe for children, making this an ideal Island for family holidays. Most of the interior of Skiathos is hilly, heavily wooded and almost totally deserted with a few less crowded beaches on the north coast of the Island. Skiathos is noted among the Greek Islands for its profusion of soft sandy beaches. The whole south coast of this small Island is a succession of sandy coves. Quiet and deserted coves are few and far between, with the Kalamaki Peninsula offering the best chance of a day away from the crowds. The few north coast beaches are much more remote and have avoided the crowds because are less easy to reach. There is a very good local bus service from Skiathos Town down the full length of the south coast of the Island …

The Island of Skiathos:

Skiathos Town: The main Island resort of Skiathos Town bristles with tavernas, bars and nightclubs all lying within a deep double bay on the south-eastern edge of the Island. This is a busy and bustling resort where cosmopolitan harbourside bars play music and the air is punctuated with the whine of passing mopeds. Planes swoop in low over Skiathos Town bay to land at the nearby airport and ferries pull in regularly with arrivals from the mainland. The background noise may not be to everyone's taste but it's not unpleasant to lounge the evening away in one of the busy quayside cafe watching the tourists stroll by. We love sitting in the Mythos Café in the Old Port having a drink (or two) whilst watching the World go by in the daytime or evening. It is time well spent and the friendliness of the locals is great. Or you can join the throngs of holiday shoppers cruising the Skiathos Town boutiques and trinket shops that line the traffic-free central shopping street. Skiathos Town has two quays split by an outcrop of rock called the Bourtzi. Dozens of cafes run the length of both harbours with the old port to the west and the new harbour to the east. Cafes in the old harbour are bigger, many of them 10 or 12 tables deep. The old harbour is also traffic-free, offering a pleasant evening stroll for visitors. It is here that the Skiathos Island caquies pitch the display boards touting barbecue trips around Skiathos and daily jaunts to neighbouring Islets. The main Skiathos Town shopping street leads inland from just opposite the ferry entrance gates beside the Bourtzi. Even more shops, cafes and tavernas are jammed along either side of the narrow street, with the occasional whiff of sewage from the drains that run beneath. Many new cafes, tavernas and restuarants have sprouted in the last few years. Tavernas overlooking the bay to the west tend to be the most expensive, as are the cafes that line the old harbour. We have tried most of them and always enjoyed our meal. One of the delights of staying in Skiathos Town is that when you want to enjoy a change of scenery there are plenty of ferry or boat trips you can go on. Or you can just catch the local bus and be on a great beach in next to no time…

The Island of Skiathos:

The Beaches on the South Coast: Most of Skiathos' golden sandy beaches are strung along the Island's south coast. Well sheltered from the northerly meltemi wind, many are set in medium sized coves and backed by pine draped hills. They are all serviced by the single good asphalt road that runs the length of the Island. Some beaches are backed by low rise hotels and many get very busy with tourists. Most enjoy deep sand, shallow seas and the usual tourist facilities. **Xanemos:** Xanemos is one of the Island's naturist beaches and it's found off the end of the airport runway near Skiathos town. It can get very windy here and there is not much in the way of shelter. Xanemos beach is deep and flat but with more shingle than sand. A cantina opens in the summer with a dozen or so sunbeds for hire. Nevertheless, Xanemos is easily reached from Skiathos Town by bus or taxi or on foot around the eastern end of the Island. The village of Kalyvia is nearby, a pretty spot in the hills above Xanemos on the road to the Evangelistra monastery. It is isolated with no bus service and a long and steep walk to Skiathos Town. The supermarket is a 20 minute walk away. A couple of tavernas on the road to Skiathos Town open over the summer. **Megali Ammos:** Another beach within walking distance of Skiathos town (but in the opposite direction) is Megali Ammos; a mixture of sand and shingle that slopes gently into the sea and makes up part of the same beach as neighbouring Vassilias. The name Megali Ammos means 'large sands', although the beach is quite narrow, especially when covered in sunbeds. So close to Skiathos Town, the beach at Megali Ammos fills up early in the day and it can be full by lunchtime. The road to the beach is steep but the hill behind does offer protection from northerly winds. There are all the usual facilities here including plenty of watersports. The pretty waterfront is lined with tavernas and cafes and there is a small quay for fishing boats. Inland are several more tourist shops, cafes and a clutch of bars. For walkers there is a road to the right of Villa Ella that peters out into an old coastal footpath leading to Katsarou, Platanias, Kolios, Livetakia and Kechria…

The Island of Skiathos:

Vassilias: The narrow sand and pebble beach at Vassilias (it translates as the King's beach') lies west of Skiathos Town and is an extension of the busier and more popular Megali Ammos beach. The best of the sand is at the eastern end of the beach where there are sunbeds and plenty of natural shade from the trees that border the back of the beach. Vassilias sits below steep hills that protects the beach from northerly winds. At the western end it is hardly a beach at all actually, just a very narrow strip of sand and rocks hugging the steep cliffs that rise almost vertically behind and a steep road that winds down to the shore past a small taverna. Vassilias is a pleasant place to avoid the crowds, especially to the west. The steep cliff gives hotels and apartments here some outstanding sea views.
Katsarou: South-west of the resorts of Megali Ammos and Vassilias is the coastal village of Katsarou. Katsarou is a typical Greek sleepy village of cobbled streets and whitewashed houses just above the main road on the steep pine-carpeted hillside. The elevated position makes it cooler but the relative isolation will not suit everyone. It is a steep one kilometre walk downhill to the beaches at Vassilias and Kassandra Bay. There are a couple of pleasant tavernas in the village.
Achladies: Achladies, or Achlaidies, is not the easiest beach to find, unless you are a resident of the large Espirides hotel that backs onto the sands and pretty much monopolises the shore. To get to the beach there is a steep track to the east or some zig-zag steps through an apartment complex. An alternative is to walk through the hotel itself or to take a fenced concrete path to the west that leads through a friendly taverna. Achladies beach (the name means 'Pear Trees') is long and narrow but the sand is very fine and the waters shallow. Tavernas at the western end provide good food and a romantic setting. The beach is set at the end of a small valley floor, planted out with olives and citrus trees. There are views from Achladies beach to the Islet of Tsougria offshore and on the horizon you can just make out the Island of Skopelos. There are more tavernas and mini markets are up on the main road above the beach…

The Island of Skiathos:

Tzaneria: Small and sometimes heavily crowded, Tzaneria is the 'gateway' to the Kalamaki peninsular and dominated by the huge Nostos hotel complex whose apartment blocks climb all over the nearby hill. Tzaneria beach is not very wide but it's deep and the fine sand is regularly raked flat by staff from the hotel. Sheltered by cliffs, the seawater here is often mill pond still. A small taverna backs onto the beach and nearby woods offer shade along the edge of the sand. For the more sporty visitors there is a scuba diving school on the beach. Nearby, down a dirt track from bus stop 11 is the small and delightful beach of Sklithri, hemmed in by hills and with a small traditional taverna. The small bay provides very good shelter for boats. **Kalamaki:** The pine cloaked Kalamaki peninsula juts out into the sea between the resorts of Tzanaries and Kolios. Kalamaki remains one of the more exclusive areas of Skiathos, dotted with up-market homes and apartments. The area is also noted for its walking trails through the pines with fine sea views especially between Tzanaries and Kanapitsa. The road from Bus stop 12 to 13 goes right around the peninsula. Beaches in the small bays around the Kalamaki coast may not be the most spectacular and not easily reaches but they benefit from being far less crowded. **Kanapitsa:** The main beach resort on the Kalamaki peninsula is at Kanapitsa which has two stretches of beach, both long and narrow but very sandy and with shallow water. A large beach taverna provides refreshments and there is an hourly water taxi service to Skiathos Town which is a 20-minute journey away from a jetty on the beach. There are many small coves around the coast of Kalamaki. Half-way around the peninsula and down a very steep footpath, is the small beach of Koutsouri. Around some rocks at Koutsouri brings you to the tiny but beautiful beach of Delfiniki which translates as 'Little Dolphin'. It can be reached from the road but it is a difficult scramble so most arrive by boat. The western side of the Kalamaki peninsula tends to be hotter, away from the prevailing northeast breeze, but there are spectacular views across the sea to the Island of Evia and to the Greek mainland beyond to enjoy…

The Island of Skiathos:

Vromolimnos: The beach at Vromolimnos is very popular with young people thanks largely to a beach bar that blasts out loud music all day long and even throws the occasional foam party on the sands. It has all the usual watersports and plenty of beach facilities for the young but, as the sands are both popular and narrow, it may feel claustrophobic at busy times of the day. Vromolimnos is a splendid beach with powder-puff sand and some pleasant swimming in the shallowsea water and an ideal spot for children. Being west facing, the beach both escapes the prevailing north-east winds and offers some fine sunsets. **Kolios:** Kolios sits in a small and attractive bay and has a narrow beach of sharp sand. Boats regularly tie up to the small jetty and there is a pleasant and shady taverna up some steps at the back of the sands. A popular destination, both for beach visitors and day trip boats, Kolios beach can get crowded in the high season. Most of the time though Kolios is pleasantly low-key. The sands shelve gently and there is good swimming to be had, making this a fine beach for families with children. Tree-covered headlands both west and east also makes this a sheltered spot. A short walk in either direction reveals many small and attractive coves where the lucky ones could end up with their own 'private' beach all day. **Platanias:** The large valley at Platanias is about six kilometres from Skiathos Town and has a pleasant stream that runs throughout the year. Several tavernas and snack bars have been added to accommodate the annual influx of visitors. The long and sandy Platanias beach (also called Agia Paraskevi) has a couple of beach tavernas that open in the summer. The beach lies in the same large bay as the beaches at both Vromolimnos and Kolios. The sand at Agia Paraskevi is fine and soft but does shelve quite steeply into the sea so it is not ideal for families with young children. The beach has a range of watersports on offer as well as boats for hire. There are several good walks in the area, the most notable from bus stop 16 to Kechria beach, with an abandoned monastery on the way, or a right turn takes walkers over the hills to Skiathos Town…

The Island of Skiathos:

Troulos Bay: The big, sandy beach at Troulos Bay is a popular holiday centre and has plenty of tourist facilities, including a couple of decent tavernas and a very good small hotel called Troulos Bay Hotel that is right on the beach. We stay at this hotel every time we visit the Island. The wide sands at Troulos Bay (the name means "Dome' and there is a dome-shaped Islet offshore) leave plenty of room for everyone with some low dunes behind. There is also a river that flows down to the beach that has terrapins and fish in that visitors like to feed. There are lots of sunbeds and umbrellas on the beach and the sand slopes gently into the sea. Being south facing the beach can get very hot at mid-day but there are several good tavernas that offer good shade and food so you can escape the heat. The Troulos Beach Hotel also has a fine restaurant and several good lunchtime snack bars so you can also enjoy a lunch or evening meal accompanied by a great sea view. There are secluded coves along the coast for those who are prepared to explore the wooded headland, but the going can be difficult on foot and it may be better to hire a boat if you want to explore these. The Troulos village resort is some way inland, and purpose-built for the tourist trade. Visitors based here face a long trek to the sea, although new apartments are being built nearer to Troulos Bay beach every year. The village of Troulos itself is located inland on the coast road and has supermarkets, car hire, petrol station and some very good tavernas. There is also a well known dog shelter located near the monastery inland above the village and the dogs there love being taken for a walk so if you fancy something different to do during your holiday this could be for you. Either as you walk the dog or just take yourself out for a walk you can head off right from the village centre crossroads, passing the dog shelter, before heading down the dirt tracks that go to the northern beach at Asselinos, passing the Kounistra Monastery on the way. Troulos Bay offers not just the sea, sand and sunshine but lovely walks and great views as well…

The Island of Skiathos:

Maratha: The secluded bay at Maratha lies below the Skiathos Palace hotel just beyond the beach resort of Koukounaries and has virtually been commandeered by the hotel. However, it is just a short walk down from the bus stop to a small sandy bay, well protected beneath pine covered slopes where trees reach right down to the shore. There are sunbeds and a good beach taverna in the woods behind. The water at Maratha is quite shallow so the beach is good for families with children and there is plenty of natural shade from the pines that overhang the back of the narrow beach. Marathi is a peaceful alternative to neighbouring Koukounaries which tends to attract the big crowds, especially in the high season.

Koukounaries: Regularly voted one of the top ten beaches in the world, Koukounaries boasts a kilometre-long sickle of golden sand backed by a wooded nature reserve and a large lagoon. Impressive at first light, the rising sun soon lures the visitors to the sunbeds and the sea is littered with motorboats and the air is humming to the whine of jet skis. The resorts nature reserve status of its lagoon has helped curb tourist development and there are just a couple of beach tavernas. The sands are also overlooked by two hotels. The nearby lagoon is a haven for mosquitoes and virulent squadrons of wasps regularly patrol the overflowing waste bins. That said, Koukounaries is still a spectacular beach. The deep long sands and shallow water will appeal to families and there are some lovely walks in the surrounding woodland. Three watersports centres offer all manner of fun and there are toilets and changing facilities nearby and an attractive harbour at the eastern end of the beach. Large crowds cluster for a teatime scramble aboard the half-hourly local buses back to Skiathos Town and no quarter is given as homebound tourists elbow aboard in a stampede for seats. Crammed to sardine-tin capacity the buses lumber away in a cloud of dust back to Town. There is no village in Koukounaries, just a scattering of small scale hotels and tavernas strung along the road behind the Koukounaries lagoon. A horse riding centre is also near the bus stop…

The Island of Skiathos:

West and North Coast Beaches: Exposed to the winds, the west and north coasts of Skiathos are wilder and less accessible than the south. There are also far fewer beaches and all are more difficult to reach. Good roads lead to Agia Eleni in the west and to Megas Asselinos in the north but other beaches can only be reached by boat or on foot. Those that venture north are rewarded with less populated countryside and some wonderful walks through the pine forests.
Banana Beach (Krassas): Between Koukounaries and Agia Eleni is the popular Krassas that is better known as Banana Beach. It's signposted from the car park at Koukounaries but it is quite a long trek through the woods so some prefer the water taxi from Skiathos Town. Banana has two beaches. The main beach is deep, long, sandy and heavily decked with sunbeds with beach bars tucked away in the pine and scrub that lines the small cliff behind. The soft sand shelves steeply into the sea and Banana Beach is hugely popular with young people. Beach parties can erupt in high season and it can get very noisy. The second beach, called Little Banana, lies just around a rocky headland. It's the Island's semi-official nudist beach. Small and flat, it's bound by steep, rocky cliffs that offer some privacy. There is less well known, but equally attractive, beach nearby called Spartacus by tourists but known as Apelakia among Greeks. It lies further round the rocky headland. **Agia Eleni:** The secluded beach of Agia Eleni is at the western end of the Island, just a short walk from the bus stop before the Koukounaries car park. The road forks right over a small hill to the small bay. Two small cantinas sit of the northern end of a narrow beach of sharp sand and fine pebbles. The water is shallow and Agia Eleni is popular with families. West facing, it has great sunset views. A rough track leads around the headland to other small bays. Signs point to Krifi Ammos (Hidden Beach) a 15-minute walk to a lovely cove with a sand and pebble beach. A beach cantina sits on the hillside but the drop into the sea is very steep so it's not really suitable for children. There is also no room for turning cars so they are best left behind…

The Island of Skiathos:

Mandraki: The densely wooded area of Mandraki offers, after a 40-minute walk from Koukounaries, the three lovely beaches of Xerxes, Elias and Agistri. The beach at Xerxes, often referred to as Mandraki, is the furthest west and is backed by a cliff of red sandstone. It has calm, shallow seawater and sunbeds around the beach cantina. The central beach of Elias is long, deep and sandy and, although it drops sharply at the western end, it is far more shallow to the east where the dunes roll up behind. A small cantina is sited on the edge of the wood overlooking the beach. Elias merges into the cove at Agistri or Angistros and there is often enough driftwood lying around for visitors to build complex and arresting sun shelters. This is a popular port of call for excursion boats but the relative isolation keeps numbers down and this north coast beach trio makes a fine alternative to the south shore beaches. **Megas Asselinos:** The big, wild and windy beach at Megas Asselinos is the most accessible northern beach on the Island with a new road through the woods from Troulos. It has a huge taverna and a large campsite nearby. In August the meltemi wind can blow your socks off. It is a huge beach with plenty of deep sand and some pebbles but there is little shade. A fork right on the approach road to Megas Asselinos takes you to Mikri Asselinos, a much smaller, much more secluded beach that is a favourite with naturists. **Lalaria:** The lovely beach at Lalaria (see above) is accessible only from the sea and is famed the world over for its white pebble beach, turquoise seawater and spectacular rock arches. The bleached white stones and undersea marble slabs are responsible for a dazzling aquamarine seashore. Lalaria beach is on the itinerary of almost every pleasure boat on the Island and scores of visitors embark in the hourly boat landings. Some boats will anchor up for two or three hours and there are no facilities on Lalaria Beach. It is a very pretty spot but there is nothing to do but avoid the crowds and more pleasure might be gained from the ubiquitous postcards of Lalaria beach that are on sale in almost every shop on the paradise Island of Skiathos…

The Greek Island of Skopelos

Located between the Islands of Skiathos and Alonissos, Skopelos is the second largest of the Sporades Island chain after Skyros. Most visitors fly into Skiathos airport then take the ferry over to the Island. Skopelos is virtually covered in forest, with 80% of this hilly Island cloaked in pine trees while several sleepy resorts lie scattered around the deeply indented shoreline. Sandy beaches are relatively scarce on Skopelos; the rugged north and east coasts have few resorts whereas the hillsides in the south and west slope more gently to the sea into reach several pleasant bays. Olive and plum groves also help make up much of the lush, green interior of Skopelos and there are many pleasant walks along forest trails to enjoy. Skopelos is popular with day-trippers escaping the crowds on nearby Island of Skiathos and with those who prefer a quieter Greek Island holiday retreat. There are regular daily ferries from nearby Skiathos where the airport gets regular international charter flights landing. It is a short ferry trip to Skopelos Town or to Loutraki, the Island's other port. The Island has cashed in on the popularity of the hit musical movie 'Mamma Mia', starring Meryl Streep, which features many of the location shots that were taken on Skopelos including the beach scenes at Kastani. Less well endowed with sandy beaches than its neighbour Skiathos, the beaches on Skopelos are of stone and shingle and are mainly confined to the south coast between Stafylos and Loutraki. Most are served by an Island bus, although some require a longish walk as well. Good sand and with fewer visitors gives the promise of greater tranquillity. The further beaches are from the capital the more peaceful they become. A boat is needed for excursions to the north of the Island…

The Island of Skopelos:

Skopelos Town: Skopelos Town is a picture postcard place with roofs of blue slate and red tile stepped down the steep hill to the harbour like an amphitheatre. The focus of activity is the long, waterfront promenade of restaurants, bars and shops located beneath trees of plane and mulberry. A cliff wall brings the northern end to an abrupt halt with a row of chapels pitched precariously beneath a warren of cobble stoned streets that lead up to a 13th century Venetian Kastro. Now a designated preservation area, the streets have more than 130 churches hidden away. Most of the houses are delightfully embellished with balconies, wrought iron trellises, brightly painted shutters and flowering plants. The shops are stuffed with the usual tourist items but a higher than average shelf space is also given to locally produced crafts such as beautiful ceramics and intricate wood carvings. There is also a small Museum of Folk Art. To the south the sand and shingle beach looks inviting from a distance but the sea has a lot of flotsam floating in it from the busy harbour. Fresh water trickles down to the sea from a culvert and shore has wading birds in spring. In the high season, the beach can get packed with holidaymakers who are mostly Greeks. Another beach sits in the bay to the west at Glyfoneri, a narrow string of shingle although it does have a very good fish taverna. **Glysteri:** Daily boat trips to Glysteri beach are widely advertised in Skopelos Town. The beach lies about two kilometres north of the port and can also be reached by road. The small, stone and shingle beach is set in a deep and secluded bay with a large taverna set back in the trees and a waterside cantina that opens in the summer months. There is also a campsite among the olive groves for those who prefer being under canvas. The only drawback for those trying to escape the crowds are the fairly regular visits from caiques which drop off day trippers en route to the sea caves at nearby Tripiti. The more adventurous visitors head a little further north to the small bay at Vathias which has a wild and unkempt feeling with a steep winding road down to a scrap of rock and shingle…

The Island of Skopelos:

Sares: The narrow beach of stone and shingle at Sares has the distinction of being the first and the last beach that holiday visitors see as they arrive at or leave Skopelos on the ferry. The beach is located on the east side of the Island around the headland from Skopelos Town. Sares means 'steep' and the great grey cliffs that loom over it live up to the name. Rock falls have made Sares beach virtually inaccessible without a boat and there is not much to enjoy other than a remote strip of stone and shingle with no facilities. **Velanio:** Velanio beach is a long-time favourite of naturists who now mostly frequent the far eastern end beyond a rocky outcrop. More public than pubic these days, Velanio is about five kilometres south of Skopelos Town and to the east of the resort at Stafylos. Most visitors walk across Stafylos beach and climb over the small headland to reach Velanio which is longer, steeper and deeper than its neighbour. The mix becomes more stone than shingle as visitors head south but the seawater is clean and clear everywhere and ideal for swimming. There are sunbeds laid out on the best bits of what little sand there is. Velanio resort is said to take its name from old Roman baths 'valaneia' that were once reputedly sited here but locals insist 'venanio' simply means acorn and dismiss the Roman link. **Stafylos:** The Island's main beach at Stafylos, or Stafilos, is popular with families and the nearest to Skopelos Town at five kilometres directly south of the capital port. Access to Stafylos beach is down steep stone steps. There are tavernas at the top and bottom of the hill. The narrow strip of sand and shingle at Stafylos basks beneath high scrub-covered cliffs. The beach is deep enough for only one or two rows of sunbeds and the seawater is shallow and beach shoes will help with the underwater stones. A rocky outcrop on the beach houses the tomb of a former Cretan general Stafylos, who gives his name to the beach. Among the treasures unearthed at the tomb was a 15th century gold-plated sword now on show in the National Archaeological Museum in Athens…

The Island of Skopelos:

Agnondas: About three kilometres west of Stafylos and eight south of Skopelos Town is the pleasant fishing harbour at Agnondas, also spelt Agnontas, enclosed by hills of pine trees. Tavernas hug the shore providing good food, especially fresh fish makes this romantic spot for a seashore meal. A very narrow strip of sand and shingle sits in front of the tavernas before widening to stone and curving around the bay where trees tumble right down to the seashore offering plenty of natural shade. The gently shelving beach and protective wooded hills on both sides make this a good beach for families with children. A mini market is nearby and a small tourist gift kiosk opens in the summer. Nearby, are the secluded coves at Amarandos where pines sweep down to the water's edge offering some welcome shade. **Limnonari:** This large crescent of white sand at Limnonari is considered one of the best beaches on Skopelos, about nine kilometres from the capital and a favourite for the round the Island boat trips. Waterside tavernas offer a good variety of meals. The long, wide beach at Limnonari is of sharp white sand and it can shelve steeply into the seawater in places. Bathers must also negotiate a sloping slab of slippery rock that runs the length of the beach. It keeps the water crystal clear but forces bathers to adopt an inelegant slide in and out of the water. The sand is dazzling white and almost blinding at midday while the underwater reflections from the white stone can turn the sea a beautiful luminous turquoise. **Panormos:** As the name suggests, Panormos is a beach with a view. The beach has no sand, just plenty of pebbles that shelve sharply into a sea that is notably colder than on other beaches on the Island. Skopelos Town is 12 km away. There are tavernas along the shoreline and several shops joined by a couple of mini-markets. Panormos was once the site of an ancient city and sections of old wall can still be seen whilst walking through the woods to the west that lead to the area known as Adrina or Adrines and several coves of shingle, often deserted, and enclosed by pines are located here...

The Island of Skopelos:

Milia: Milia is considered by many to be the most beautiful beach on Skopelos. The holiday visitor is greeted by three silver swathes of tree-lined pebble and sand beaches with crystal clear seawaters and a large taverna behind the central beach. To the south is a long, deep swathe of white stone and pebble, backed by groves of bamboo. Large slabs of rock lie underwater along the shoreline. Those seeking more solitude can find small coves further south. In the centre of Mila beach is an attractive rocky outcrop, great for snorkelling, with sunbeds dotted around the tiny inlets and a shady summer cantina on the headland rock above. To the north is yet another swathe of stone. Out to sea is the small, pine clad Islet of Dasia which can easily be reached by boat. Milia lies about 14 km south-west of Skopelos Town and a similar distance east from Glossa, the Island's second largest village. **Kastani (Mamma Mia) Beach:** A kilometre or so north of Milia is the splendid beach of Kastani. One of the Island's sandiest beaches. Kastani was used for beach scenes in the hit musical movie of Mamma Mia. Kastani lies in a pretty bay of fine, sharp sand with rocks at both ends and pines that roll their way right down to the shoreline offering lots of leafy natural shade. The wooden jetty that featured in the Mamma Mia movie was only a mock-up and has since vanished, just like the film crews and movie stars. The only thing that remains of them ever being there is the war of words with neighbouring Skiathos over the Island that featured the most in the movie. The truth is it was Skopelos and this beach in particular. North along the coast are several more coves, all difficult to reach and usually visited only by boats. All are stone and shingle and their main attraction is that they are so peaceful and secluded. The best coves are at Neraki and Ftelia, each side of a small, attractive bay, and further north still are the coves at Ekatopenindari and eventually Hovolo on the outskirts of the village of Elios…

The Island of Skopelos:

Elios: Eleos means mercy and Elios is where the Island's patron saint Agios Reginus is believed to have delivered his flock from a fearsome dragon. He left behind a scruffy, unkempt straggle of stone and scrub and some deep, earthy rumblings. The village was built after the 1965 earthquake had distroyed the nearby hillside village of Klima just along the coast. The village beach of dark sand and scrub is backed by a bare tarmac road while above the village has a few tavernas and some mini-markets. There are many shingle coves along this part of the coast, notably to the south at Hovolo, although access is not easy. Several kilometres to the north there are shingle coves at Karkadzouna, Kalyves, Amenopatra, Dafni, Kalyves and Amenopetra. **Klima:** Before climbing the hillside to the mountain village of Glossa, the main road passes through the Klima - actually two villages Palio Klima and Neo Klima although the whole area is also confusingly called Elios-Klima. After the earthquake in 1965 the hillside houses of Klima were left derelict. The derelict houses were snapped up by mainland Greeks and foreigners at knockdown prices to be rebuilt as holiday homes. Today, the renovated homes are untenanted for most of the year and Klima now has the air of a dormitory village of foreigners, which is basically what it is. It is a pretty enough place to visit and visitors get some spectacular views over the bay. There is a small shingle cove at Kosta. **Loutraki:** Loutraki is the small port for the hill village of Glossa and the first port of call for ferries from Skiathos and the mainland. The port has a long quay, a few houses with some imposing cliffs behind. This quiet fishing village has kept to its traditional ways and has Loutraki although cafes and tavernas are plentiful. There are beaches nearby, the largest is a pebble beach right behind the pier and some quieter coves within walking distance, the most notable being a shingle beach at Katalakou in the south and at Glystra to the north. Loutraki was known as Selinounda in ancient times and there are ruins aplenty such as a Roman bathhouse, the remains of a temple to Athena and an ancient agora (market place) for the visitor to wander around…

The Island of Skopelos:

Glossa: The main tourist draw apart from Skopelos Town is the picturesque hillside village of Glossa, home to 1,200 people and views to die for. The traditional village way of life has so far managed to stand fast against the annual and ever growing holiday visitor influx and the place oozes charm. Many houses in Glossa have wooden balconies and the surrounding fields are full of plum and almond trees. Several dirt roads provide walks to nearby sights of interest. These include the monastery of Agion Taxiarchon, built on the ruins of a 7th century Byzantine church and the Gourouni Cape lighthouse. Tracks lead down to often deserted beaches with coves at Myrtia and Koutria to the north-west and Perivoli, Pethameni, Hondrogiorgi, Keramoto, Mavraki and Spilia in the north-east. Many however are difficult to find and only Spilia and Perivoli have roads leading to them. Pethameni is at the bottom of a precipitous path but Hondrogiorgi has easier access and is popular with locals. At Spilia there is a cave and a chapel to Agios Ioannis built on a spectacular headland above a double coved beach. The headland was created when the cliffs collapsed into the sea and the pretty chapel featured strongly in the hit movie musical Mamma Mia. Many of today's visitors can be seen running up or down the many steps that lead to or from this chapel waving their arms around and singing. Some are even in tune…

The Greek Island of Skyros

The Island of Skyros is the odd one out in the Sporades chain of Islands that lies off the east coast of mainland Greece. the island. The Islands airport receives only domestic flights from Athens and Thessaloniki. There are no ferries from Athens to Skyros. Ferries to Skyros depart only from Kymi, a small port town on the eastern side of Evia Island. It is one of the largest Islands in the Sporades. It is also the most remote and somewhat off the main tourist trail and thus the least visited of this Island group. Skyros' isolation has helped it preserve its distinctive Greek character and customs. For example, foreigners are banned from owning houses here. Tourist beds also number only around 1,000 and the resolutely traditional Skyros Islanders seem intent on having no more, although visitors who make the effort to mix are very warmly welcomed. Skyros stands so much apart from the rest of the tourist-hungry Sporades group that there is no direct ferry link from the neighbouring Islands. The landscape of the Island is green and densely wooded in the north; much more dry, rocky and barren in the south. Traditional festivals and occupations play a large part in Island life and Skyros has long been noted for its arts and crafts, its beautiful pottery and for its hand-carved furniture. Most inhabitants live in and around the Island capital of Chora and Skyros has a permanent population of around 3,000 people, mostly engaged in farming and fishing. A tomb in the southern half of Skyros Island is renowned as that 'corner of a foreign field that is forever England'. It is where the verse's author, the poet Rupert Brooke, was buried in 1915, brought ashore from a passing ship. It is notable that his grave is now one of the Island's main tourist attractions…

The Island of Skyros:

The Beaches on Skyros: The heavily indented coastline of Skyros is peppered with sand and pebble beaches, secluded coves, rocky inlets and sea caves. The main beach resorts are below Chora where sands link the resorts of Magazia and Molos. Those looking to escape the crowds have a number of splendid coves to choose between but access can be difficult and several can be reached only on foot or by boat, especially in the south. **Skyros Town:** The Island capital of Chora lies on the east side of the narrow waist that divides the Island of Skyros, north and south. Visitors arriving from the port of Linaria. The town has an attractive hillside location where whitewashed cube houses stack their way up to the summit of the hill in a fiendish maze of narrow streets. It is all crowned by the Kastro, a Byzantine fortress with Venetian trimmings built over an ancient acropolis. The main street of Chora is a narrow strip of tourist shops, travel agents, cafes and tavernas that eventually opens out into a square overlooking Molos beach and the sea. Perched on a terrace, is a bronze 'Statue of Immortal Poetry' erected in 1931 to commemorate the English poet Rupert Brooke, who is buried on the Island. Beneath the square is the small archaeological museum with exhibits of local copper artefacts and a striking ceramic ring decorated with ducks and snakes from around 900 BC. **Molos:** The sprawling tourist development below Chora and behind Magazia beach now blends into neighbouring Molos village, about four kilometres north from the capital. It is an attractive, long and sandy beach that snakes out north to a headland and a small, picturesque harbour with a stone breakwater. An old mill, now turned into a taverna, is a reminder of times past when Molos was less developed as a tourist destination. Lobster is the local specialty and there are many fish tavernas in Molos as well as bars and cafes, a bakery and a mini-market. Further north, past the harbour and around the headland, is Grysmata beach, sheltered by a strip of offshore rock. It has a few tavernas…

The Island of Skyros:

Magazia: A 10-minute walk down the hill and stairway from Chora, leads visitors past the Island's official campsite and onto the fine dark sands of Magazia beach, to the south of Molos. The long, sweeping beach is named after a gunpowder magazines that were stored here in Venetian times. Magazia has plenty of beach facilities including watersports and beachside tavernas. Long and sandy it blends in with neighbouring Molos and rarely gets crowded even in the high summer season. Sunbeds are laid out on the most popular stretches and the seawater is quite shallow. A trio of rock breakwaters have been put offshore to the south. At the northern end of the beach the rock has been carved and quarried into bizarre shapes, with a church and cave-like houses hewn from the stone. **Papa Ta Chomata:** The road south beyond Magazia leads to Papa Ta Chomata beach, sometimes referred to as Papa Ta Houma. The name translates roughly as 'land of the priest' but visitors may find little of the cloth here as this is the Island's unofficial naturist beach. The sands at Papa Ta Chomata are fine and the seawater is clean, although it can be a difficult descent down a narrow cliff path to the beach. Further south of here is Aspouss which is a pleasant spot with a couple of nice beach tavernas. **Ormos Achillis:** Further south still is the beach at Ormos Achillis. Set in a deep bay this once boasted a pleasant, if remote, beach until it was earmarked by developers for a new yacht marina. The marina project failed and, apart from a few fishing boats, the place is currently deserted. South of the bay at Ormos Achillis the coast becomes very rocky and virtually inaccessible except for the tiny Islet of Sarakiniko which has a tiny beach of white sand and shingle called Nisi tou Despoti, or sometimes Glyfada. A boat is the only way to reach the beach which sits on almost the most southern point of Skyros and it has no facilities. This heavily indented stretch of coast is a popular target for boat trips, not only to see the grave of the English poet Rupert Brooke at nearby Tris Boukes, but to explore the spectacular caves and inlets on the south-east coast…

The Island of Skyros:

West Coast Beaches: The west coast of Skyros is where the Island ferries dock at the main port of Linaria. A number of attractive beaches line the heavily indented shore. Many lie at the head of sheltered inlets and are surrounded by thick forests of pine. **Linaria:** The functional fishing village of Linaria is also the main port for Skyros. It lies on the west coast at the Island's narrow waist, tucked into a small bay about 10 km from the capital at Chora. The only other major settlement on Skyros apart from Chora, Linaria is basically a cluster of squat buildings packed around a tiny, picturesque, harbour. Linaria has some good tavernas and a small beach within walking distance at Aheronnas. The church of Agios Nikolaos, on a hill above the port, offers some spectacular views. Linaria is also the base for boat trips around the Island. A great favourite is the islet of Skyros Goula which has a couple of small beaches and dramatic caves and the islet of Sarakiniko which has a small beach. **Kalamitsa:** Kalamitsa lies to the south of Linaria, just over the headland, and lays claim as one of the best beaches in the south-west. It is a long swathe of shingle, the sand does peep through the stones at the northern end which is fronted by tavernas and a windsurfing club. Nearby is a well-preserved stone sarcophagus and an upright Doric column. To the south Kalamitsa blends into the long, white shingle beach of Kolimbades which is good for swimming. There are coves with shingle beaches further south, although none have any facilities and most can only be reached by boat. **Aheronas:** The road north out of Linaria heads into the hills and a barren landscape of low scrub. The road forks right to Chora and left around the bay to Aheronas, also spelt Acheronas or Acheroaunes. The pleasant long, sandy beach is at the head of a well protected bay with clear shallow water that makes it a good choice for families with children. Two tavernas offer the basics and a cafe serves ice cream and drinks. Aheronas beach is only a 10-minute walk from Linaria, although the prettier beach of Agios Pefkos is only just over the headland…

The Island of Skyros:

Agios Pefkos: This is the beach many visitors head for on the west coast of Skyros. Agios Petros lies over the headland from Aheronas at the head of a deep bay, about 11 kilometres west of Chora. Pine trees tumble down to the sand and shingle shoreline at the wide and attractive bay. Rocky outctops appear at both ends and a long line of trees backs the beach to the south. A couple of cantinas open here in the summer season. Once the site of a small but productive marble quarry, the small harbour that lies to the south of Agios Pefkos is where the Syrian marble used to be shipped out. Also nearby is the charming chapel of Agios Panteleimonas, which enjoys some spectacular panoramic views over the coast of Skyros. **Agios Fokas Bay:** North from Agios Pefkos and down a steep bank is the smaller, but even more attractive bay of Agios Fokas. Despite being prettier than its neighbour fewer make it down the rough track that snakes down from the road above. Once cloaked in pine forest, a fire in 2008 denuded much of the area but this remains a picturesque spot in a beautiful bay and the reward for going the extra few miles is well worth it with a beach of sand and white pebble and the small chapel at the end of the beach. **Beaches on the North Coast:** The far north of Skyros has the best of the secluded beaches, but they are not easy to find and few have any facilities. This coast also takes the winds and heavy seas that batter the cliffs over the winter as well as the northern 'meltemi' that blows through in July and August. **Atsitsa:** Set in a peaceful wooded bay Atsitsa lies on the north-west coast about 19 kilometres from Chora and is mostly rock and stones with a couple of ramshackle wooden quays where boats can tie up. Named after the offshore islet, Atsitsa is set in densely wooded coves and has some iron mine installations dating from the 19th century. Pine trees plunge down to a shoreline that is rocky enough to make swimming difficult but there is a good fish taverna here. To the north, at Markesi, is the chapel of Theotokos erected on the site of a former temple to Poseidon where ancient tomb carvings have been found…

The Island of Skyros:

Agios Petros: Just north of Atsitsa are a couple of small beaches of sharp sand and shingle at Kalogrias and at Krya Panagia, the latter of which has a tiny chapel and a summer taverna. The best of the beaches in this area is Agios Petros, a pale sand beach with a few pebbles backed by magnificent dunes. Access to Agios Petros is down a track through the dense pine woods. Like the others beaches in the area there are few facilities at Agios Petros. **Markesi:** There are several sand and pebble beaches along the stretch of coastline that makes up the northern tip of Skyros. The two that are most worth a visit are Markesi and Theotokos, although you may have to contend with the drone of jet aircraft taking off from the nearby military air base. Although neither has any facilities both have good shallow seawater, a little sand and shingle and rocky outcrops on either side. There are some ancient engraved tombs near Markesi for those interested in archaeology near the chapel of Agios Theotokos. **Palamari:** Palamari is most noted for the interesting, if rather neglected, site of a Bronze Age settlement which still shows the layout and pattern of the original streets and houses. It was first built around 3,000 BC and flourished for a millennium. The total area covers about five acres, although the eastern part is now under the sea. The main reason for the ancient city's growth was the metals that were once mined in the Palamari area. Below the archaeological site is a very pleasant sandy beach but care must be taken not to wander too near the military base which is a restricted area so be aware…

The Greek Island of Symi

The Island of Symi, sometimes spelt Simi, is one of the smaller holiday Islands in the Dodecanese group just 9 km off the Turkish coast north of the Greek Island of Rhodes. As the Island has no airport, the best way to travel to Simi is by ferry from Rhodes. Symi is a popular destination for day trippers and there are regular daily excursions from the Rhodes port of Mandraki. Once famed for boat building and for its sponges, the trees have long been hacked down and the sponges been killed off by disease. Symi today is noted more for peace and tranquillity than for its beaches, which are in short supply, mostly shingle with larger stones underwater, have little shade and very few facilities. The Island of Symi is also noted for the very high summer temperatures, which can soar to 40°C or more in July and August and make the sheltered main port a sizzling cauldron of heat. In the early morning and late evening the bay is a haven of calm but for most of the day it is thronged with day trip visitors. One of the big tourist attractions on Symi is the monastery at Panormitis, a favourite with the boat day trippers who find a spectacular building in a large bay on the southwest tip of the Island worth the long journey. Symi is one of the hottest Greek Islands. It lies just off the Turkish coast and most visitors stay in the steep sided horseshoe bay of Gialos where summer temperatures can soar above 40°C. Even the Greeks say Symi is hot. Pastel painted neoclassical houses climb up the Gialos hillside, a reflection of the days when Symi was a thriving Island made wealthy by shipbuilding and sponge diving. Today, the Island of Symi relies almost entirely on tourism; mostly day trippers coming over from the Greek Island of Rhodes…

The Island of Symi:

Gialos: The cameras start clicking the moment the ferries pull into the harbour at Gialos, also spelt Yialos. A semicircle of Venetian mansion houses stagger down the steep hillside and ferry hoots echo around the beautiful bay. Gialos is a favourite of day trippers with three or four big ferries arriving every day spilling passengers onto the long quayside that encloses the deep harbour. Sponges and spices are displayed on waterside stalls that are backed by souvenir shops and tavernas. There are at least 25 tavernas in Gialos alone. The resort is split between the harbour of Gialos and the hillside town of Chorio. The harbour is huge, helping Symi prosper as a former trading centre for sponges and for shipbuilding. Mansion houses around the bay fell derelict as traditional trades died but have since been snapped up by foreigners and many have been tastefully restored. The amphitheatre hillside creates a colourful display but also traps the heat and prevents any sort of breeze, giving Gialos harbour a reputation as a cauldron. There is plenty for the day visitor to see. The Nautical Museum has old maps, model ships and maritime stuff while the Folklore Museum has displays of paintings, photographs and traditional costumes. At the entrance to the harbour is the Roloi clock tower, built in 1881, while the Cathedral of Timios Prodromos, built 50 years earlier, has an impressive pebbled courtyard. South-west of Gialos is the church of Moni Agiou Michail Roukounioti built by the Knights of St John in the 14th century on the ruins of a 5th century monastery with frescoes and religious icons. **Chorio:** Above the harbour of Gialos is the hillside village of Chorio. Chorio can be reached from Gialos either by road or by climbing steep steps that are called the Kali Strata that rise up from the harbour. Many of the houses in Chorio have been well restored after years of neglect. Houses are often crammed together, creating archways and alleys in all directions and it is easy to get lost wandering the Chorio streets. Visitors will find a maze of whitewashed alleys and stepped streets, with little traffic and tremendous views over the bay. Tavernas, cafes and mini-markets are found, mainly in the vicinity of Chorio village square…

The Island of Symi:

Pedi: The east road out of Gialos leads to the small fishing village of Pedi which has a narrow beach of shingle and a little sand, a trio of tavernas, a hotel and a small shop. Once a thriving fishing village, very few live there now. Pedi beach has sunbeds and natural shade from a long line of tamarisks trees. Just three kilometres from Gialos, Pedi is easy to reach by foot, car or boat and the daily local bus from Gialos stops right by the beach. Set in a large sheltered inlet, the quay is big enough to take the boats that carry fresh water over from the Island of Rhodes, a necessity as Symi has no natural freshwater springs of note. A steep and rocky, but well-marked track leads to a stone and shingle beach at Agios Nikolaos beach, about a 20 minute walk, or visitors can take a taxi boat that also stops at Agia Marina beach. A short distance inland is a catacomb complex known locally as Dhodheka Spilia. **Agia Marina:** At the mouth of the Pedi inlet, on the northern side, is a tiny Islet that lies just offshore from the beach at Agia Marina. It can be reached by water taxi, and there are several each day from Gialos. On the beach sunbeds are laid out along a concrete slab that curves around the bay. A little natural shade is provided by a couple of trees and there is a taverna nearby. The main attraction of this beach is that it is one of the few beaches on Symi that has sand underfoot for some distance from the shoreline. The sand is also gently shelving and the seawater shallow, so it offers safe swimming for children, although there is not much to do here other than paddle in the sea or lie on a sunbed or build a sand castle. Well someone has to do it…

The Island of Symi:

Agios Nikolaos: Well served by taxi boats but within walking distance of Pedi is the shingle and coarse sand beach of Agios Nikolaos, on the opposite southern side of the inlet from Agia Marina. Agios Nikolaos also has the advantage of having sand and tree shade from a neat line of tamarisks trees at the back of the beach. At the furthest end, near the chapel to Agios Nikolaos, the sea is very shallow, warm and gently shelving so it's a popular spot for families with children. A beach taverna and the tamarisks offer shade for goats as well as people on sunbeds. A water taxi to the beach from Gialos takes about 20-minutes. **Agios Giorgios:** Heading south along the east coast is a narrow inlet at Dissalonias and a tiny beach at Agios Giorgios. It has no overland access and is visited only by those in their own boat or by water taxi. The beach is a narrow strip of shingle and pebble and there is no shade. There are no facilities here so bring food and water if you intend to stay. Agios Giorgios beach is backed by a sheer 300 metre vertical cliff drop that was used for a location for filming the famous 1961 war movie 'The Guns of Navarone'. **Nanou:** Nanou is another Symi beach that is 'blessed' with a more than usual share of goats. They often sit under the trees in the picturesque bay on the attractive but steeply sloped pebble beach. The bay is larger than most and has a sense of wide open spaces, although steep cliffs tower each side of the east-facing inlet. A steep drop into the sea means it's not particularly good for families or for weak swimmers but the shore is great for snorkelling as the seawater is very clear. Nanou beach has a small beach taverna, fenced in from the goats, toilets and a few sunbeds. The beach is a regular stop on round the Island boat trips but can also be reached on foot. However, the overland route is long and difficult across the centre of the Island and the walk takes about three hours from Gialos. So good walking boots are essential…

The Island of Symi:

Marathounda: Just south of Nanou is a narrow bay of bright seawater with a shingle beach at Marathounta, sometimes spelt Marathounda. Visitors come to the beach by the daily water taxi service. Marathounta is set in a very attractive bay with a beach of pebble and shingle. The stones are steep and the seawater gets deep very quickly so any children will need watching. A beach cantina is fenced off to stop the goats pestering guests at the tables and there are a few sunbeds on the stones and a small jetty for visiting boats to tie up. Just a little way south of Marathounta is an even less visited bay at Faneromi with another strip of pebble and stone but with no facilities. **Agios Vasilios:** The west coast of Symi is almost entirely composed of rocky and inaccessible cliffs. There is only one small beach of any note at Agios Vasilios, about halfway down the coast. This beautiful but remote shingle and stone beach has no facilities but a few cypress trees offer a little shade. It lies south-east of Gialos and well off the main Island road. A long walk and a scramble down a rocky gorge is required to reach it. Water taxis do drop off here, but it is usually only visited by weekly round-Island cruises as it is the furthest beach from Yialos. Agios Vasilios is an idyllic spot but lonely and isolated, hemmed in by rocky cliffs and scree with underwater stones and shingle. **Agios Emilianos:** The only other beach of note on the west coast is at Agios Emilianos, a favourite spot for round the Island boat trips where the attraction is the dramatic setting of the monastery on an Islet linked to the shore by a small causeway. Agios Emilianos has a small, shingle beach below the whitewashed chapel. The monastery is not as attractive as the setting with its whitewashed cube buildings is enclosed by bare high walls. There are a few other strips of shingle to be found around the nearby bays of Skoumisa and Maroni…

The Island of Symi:

Nimborios: Sometimes called Nimporio, Emborio or Niborios, the beach is set in a large bay and has a small beach of pebbles. It's popular with visitors from Yialos as there is a good road from Yialos and it takes only about 20 minutes to walk there on foot. Visitors can get to Nimborios by following the coast road past the Gialos clock tower or by heading inland, following the steep path that rises behind the town square. Nimborios is an old fishing village but it has no shops. A taverna provides sunbeds as well as food and drinks and it is a regular port of call for water taxis. Nimborios beach is only a narrow strip of pebbles but has fabulous views across the bay. **Nos:** The popular sand and shingle beach at Nos is close to the harbour at Yialos and so often referred to as the town beach. The beach is reached by walking past the Yialos clock tower and then heading along the Emborios coast road. Nos beach is also called Paradise beach which is probably used to encourage tourists to come to the beach. The beach is a narrow strip of shingle and sand with a double line of sunbeds. There is a pleasant taverna at one end overlooking the beach and rocky outcrops at the other end that add some interest for adults and children alike. The main road is just behind and above, so Nos beach is not particularly private and traffic noise can be disturbing for those trying to relax…

The Greek Island of Thassos

Thassos is the most northerly of the Greek Islands in the Aegean Island group and it lies just off the Macedonian coast in the north-east of mainland Greece. The Island has no airport and visitors usually arrive at the mainland airport at Kavala and get over to the Island by ferry. Fabulously wealthy in ancient times, thanks to large deposits of gold and marble, Thassos nowadays lies outside the top league of Greek holiday Islands but it still has as much to offer the visitor. We have holidayed there several times and loved the main town and the beaches on the Island very much. An excellent coast road almost rings the whole Island, providing easy access to the many sandy beaches that pepper the attractive coastline. Strangely, Thassos fails to feature in many holiday brochures so it is something of a hidden gem and spared the holiday crowds that mar some of the other Greek holiday Islands. The extensive pine trees that carpet most of Thassos have led to it being rightly dubbed the 'Emerald Isle' of Greece. Beaches, mostly sandy, are dotted all around the coast with a wide variety on offer, from large, deep beaches with plenty of facilities to small, idyllic hideaway coves. Side roads branch inland to charming hill villages and to extensive tracts of dense woodland, criss-crossed with walking trails. We found that Thassos may be off the main tourist trail but regular ferries from Keramouti are only a 10 minute ride from the airport at Kavala makes it easy to get to. Thassos is a favourite with families looking for a beach holiday with an authentic Greek flavour. Beaches are dotted all round the coast of this near-circular Island and all are easily reached from a good coast road. The large bay at Golden Beach is the most popular but good beaches are found all around the coast of Thassos. Limenaria, in the south, has four good beaches while less crowded resorts lie both east and west with good sandy beaches…

The Island of Thassos:

Thassos Town (Limenas): Thassos Town, known locally as Limenas, is the Island's main town, but not its main port which lies to the east at Ormos Prinou. Once split in two with a pretty port to the east and a wasteland to the west but much has been done in recent years to improve the whole area. The lorries laden with marble that once lumbered through the Town centre now go west and the new town port has been re-paved and planted with attractive shrubs. The prettiest part of Thassos Town is still the old port where a traffic ban paves the way for taverna tables and street stalls piled high with the wonderful Thassos honey. It has many busy tavernas but nevertheless enjoys a warm, rustic atmosphere where the brightly painted fishing boats bob against quays strewn with fishing nets. The sandy beach lies east of the old harbour and it is long and deep with shallow seawater and sunbeds. Tavernas line the road behind the beach where tamarisk trees offer plenty of natural shade. Limenas has several archaeological sites. The Agora, next to the revamped Archaeological Museum has impressive Roman foundations while an amphitheatre in the hills above hosts summer performances against a backdrop of fabulous views over the bay. On the hill ridge above the Town are well-restored city walls and the remains of an Acropolis, with temples to Apollo and Athena. West of Thassos Town a coastal track leads to a string of small beach coves known collectively as Agios Vasilios. Each cove has a beach bar, taverna or small hotel; an attractive lure for those who want to stay close to town. **Beaches on the North East Coast:** The more mountainous east coast of Thassos is covered in thick pine forest, liberally criss-crossed with hill tracks and fire breaks. The main road from Limenas cuts inland and rises steeply through tortuous bends to the hill villages of Panagia and Potamia before dropping down again to Golden Beach (Chrisi Ammoudia) and Skala Potamias (Chrisi Akti). Mountain villages such as Panagia and Potamia are a big draw for both ad-hoc visitors and organised coach parties…

The Island of Thassos:

Makryammos: The sandy beach at Makryammos lies to the south-east of Thassos Town and looks delightful when approached by boat with steep, pine-clad hills sweeping down to the crescent bay of white sand. Closer inspection, however, reveals leaves from the surrounding trees coagulate into great black mounds, slumped like beached whales on the shoreline and attract swarms of flies. Makryammos is a good family beach of sharp white sand and shallow seawater. It's also a favourite target of day-trip boats which tie up at a breakwater. Access from the main road above is through the holiday camp complex where 'Private Property' signs give the impression that Makryammos beach is private - it is not.
Panagia: The east road out of Limenas climbs steeply to the picturesque hill villages of Panagia (pronounced 'Panahia') and Potamis, or Potamia, both big tourist draws thanks to their woodland position above the coastal resorts of Skala Potamias and Golden Beach. In Panagia village centre the cafes and tavernas cluster round a central square with a fountain which gushes water from local springs. Paved streets head into the hills where there are several walking trails through wooded hillsides and valleys. The more adventurous can tackle Mount Ipsarion which looms above at over 1,000 metres, the rest can enjoy the lush countryside and walks that offer fine views over the bay below. **Potamia:** Potamia, also called Potamis or Potamias, is quieter than Panagia mainly because the main road by-passes the village. It has a soporific air with a few small cafes on the narrow village streets. The Greek American artist Polygnotos Vagis was born in Potamias and a small museum devoted to his works can be found in the village. Like Panagia, the Potamia area is a favourite for walkers, with many woodland paths up into the hills. Trails also lead down to the popular sands at Skala Potamia and Golden Beach, which lie about four kilometres away…

The Island of Thassos:

Golden Beach: Excursion boats on the quayside at Limenas head out daily for the long, sandy bay at Golden Beach, or Chrysi Ammoudia to give it its proper Greek name. Golden Beach is very long and deep, with low dunes and large areas of scrub stretching out over the large, flat plain behind. The beach sweeps right around a huge bay, with the hamlet of Chrisi Amoudia at the northern end, ostensibly the beach resort of Panagia, and Skala Potamias to the south, serving Potamia village. The long sands narrow in the middle of the bay and disappear beneath rocks and shingle before emerging to the south. Both ends of the beach get fairly crowded while the centre remains empty. A road runs along the back of the beach to serve the holiday apartments and occasional tavernas that lie scattered across the flat plain behind. **Skala Potamia:** The southern end of Golden Beach opens out into a deep triangle of good white sand edged by a small harbour at the popular resort Skala Potamia, or Skala Potamias. Some claim the sands at Skala Potamis are the best on Thassos, with its large beach of pale sand sliding gently into shallow blue seawater. Others find the sand too 'gritty' for their taste and point out the lack of any natural shade. An arcade of tavernas and bars lines the back of the Skala Potamis beach. **Paradiso:** The hamlet of Kinira is located on the east coast about 24 kilometres from Limenas and has two small beaches of white pebble called Loutro and Kinira and also the ruins of a Byzantine baths and an early Christian basilica found nearby. South over the headland is the beach at Paradiso, hidden in a beautiful cove and hedged by steep wooded hills. Paradiso beach is deep and long with soft sand and a very shallow shoreline shelf into the sea. The offshore Islet of Kinira adds interest and there is a taverna among the dunes at the back of the beach providing sunbeds and basic food and drink. Sheer cliffs at the southern end offer some shade from the afternoon sun and trees encroach on the shallow dunes behind. Paradiso is a family beach and a great place for bucket and spade holidays…

The Island of Thassos:

The Beaches on the South Coast: The south coast of Thassos is a very popular holiday area, particularly around Limenaria and at Potos and Pefkari. The landscape is not as impressive as in the north of the Island and fortunately the area has now recovered from a series of devastating forest fires. **Alyki:** Once a secret gem, Alyki is now visited by a large number of daily visitors and a car park has been carved out of the cliff above to accommodate all of the day trip coaches. Alyki has two small coves, set back-to-back of a narrow wooded promontory. The southern beach is a small crescent of fine sand at the end of a long and narrow inlet of shallow seawater. Half a dozen tavernas sit on a ridge behind nestled beneath shady trees. Narrow tracks lead over the headland to the northern beach, a much smaller and stonier affair. It is jaw-droopingly wild and on windy day's large spectacular wave's crash through the narrow entrance to the bay and pound onto the stony seashore. Between the two beaches there are ancient marble quarries and a small archaeological site that includes a couple of early Christian basilicas. **Astris:** South of the monastery at Archangelos, the road winds around several headlands before dropping to a small coastal plain and an excellent sandy beach at Astris. Astris beach is a long strip of golden sand bisected by an outcrop of rock where a taverna stands among the trees. A working boatyard stands behind the trees at the northern end of the sands, which are soft and pale and shelve gently into the sea, making this a very good beach for families with young children. The beach at Astris rarely gets crowded and makes an ideal spot for those who prefer more peaceful surroundings. Inland is the village of Astris, noted for its tiny stone built and slate-roofed houses…

The Island of Thassos:

Psili Ammos: Marble slabs slope down to the beach at the beautiful resort of Psili Ammos. The beach is a deep arc of rich, golden sand and it has a couple of tavernas behind, one decked out to resemble a cowboy ranch and belting out all-day pop music; the other is more traditional. Good sand and beach facilities make Psili Ammos a popular beach for families. The sand, however, dips very sharply into the sea and children must be watched. The steep beach can bring in big waves and there are strong underwater currents here. This beautiful spot is also favoured by watersports enthusiasts who love the howl of their jet skis and a dive centre sits on the hill. Family crowds make Psili Ammos is a busy, noisy beach in the high season. **Potos:** The popular tourist resort of Potos is where more than 30 tavernas, cafes and bars line the short sea wall above a narrow strip of sand. The crescent of good sand turns to shingle at the harbour end. The beach shelves steeply in parts so children must be watched. The many boats pulled onto the beach near the harbour add even more colour. The village is a maze of back streets full of shops and cafes. To the south of Potos is Ossegromos Beach where there is a small stretch of sharp, white sand. **Pefkari:** Paddle boats, surfboards and jet skis are prominently parked on the manicured white sands at the popular beach resort at Pefkari. The beach is of gently shelving sand and shallow seawater. This is an ideal spot for families with children. The nearby headland offers splendid cliff side walks. Tavernas and cafes line both sides of the shady, quiet lane that runs along the back of Pefkari beach. The beach is long and deep with soft white sand that is kept very clean by the taverna owners. There are masses of sunbeds and a wide range of watersports on offer…

The Island of Thassos:

Metalia: Metalia beach lies just east of the big south coast resort of Limenaria. Metalia is a quiet and attractive beach with a small beach bar. Some rate this beach amongst the best beaches on Thassos. Metalia is a notably quieter alternative to Limenaria. **Limenaria:** Limenaria is the second biggest resort on the Island after Limenas. It has a long waterfront promenade is backed by dozens of tavernas, bars, cafes and shops. The west end of the promenade is lined with large boulders and a narrow beach. The eastern end has a small arc of pleasant sand overlooked by a small, square shaped harbour full of fishing boats. Visitors tend to use Limenaria as a base to explore the south of Thassos and there are good walks in the pine-carpeted hills. **Trypiti:** Trypiti, sometimes spelt Tripiti, lies to the west of Limenaria, two kilometres from the resort. There is no village here, just a long, deep and sandy beach. The sands sweep right around a huge bay with beach bars at both ends. To the west is a small sea cave and shallow pool that shelves steeply inside the cave and waves come crashing in on windy days. The sand also shelves rather steeply into the sea but Trypiti is still a big pleasant beach with sunbeds at both ends, near the beach bars. **West Coast Beaches:** The west coast of the Island of Thassos is much flatter than the east, with rolling farmland and small inland hamlets. The beaches may not to be as good as those in the east but there are some very pleasant resorts on this part of the coast of the Island…

The Island of Thassos:

Skala Maries: Skala Maries is an isolated resort set in a deep crescent of a bay. The resort climbs a small hill overlooking the sands. The beach is a crescent of sand with the occasional hulk of a boat pulled up on the shore. **Skala Kalirachis Harbour:** Skala Kalirachis is a huge harbour with a couple of small beaches of sand on either side. **Skala Sotiros:** Skala Sotiros, sometimes called Skala Sotirou, has a pleasant beach. The beach has a good stretch of sand with sunbeds near the short jetty in front of the main taverna. The southern end of the beach quickly turns to shingle and stone but there is good swathe of sand at the northern end and the seawater here is sheltered and shallow. **Dasyllio Prinou:** Dasyllio Prinou, or Dasyllios Prinos, is the name now given to the whole area and includes a long beach backed by several resort hotels as well as a very large camping site. Dasyllio Prinou stretches from the main port of Skala Prinou for two kilometres south with a 300-space camping site that is the biggest on Thassos. The land around Dasyllio Prinou is heavily wooded, with about 250 varieties of trees recorded here. But then, Dasyllio is the Greek name for little forest and the trees reach right down to the seashore. **Skala Prinou:** When we have stayed on the Island of Thassos we have based ourselves at Skala Prinou. It is a first-rate beach resort. Skala Prinou, or Skala Prinos, is just the place to catch a ferry over to the mainland. It is a fine base for exploring the rest of the Island but it is, in fact, little more than a bus and ferry stop. That said, we enjoyed our stays here and found the clutch of cafes, tavernas and shops offered us everything we needed for a great holiday. There is also a long, narrow beach that stretches north with a shallow sloping bay backed by a line of trees…

The Island of Thassos:

Skala Rachonis: The beach resort of Skala Rachonis, or Skala Rahoni is a good long stretch of sandy beach and a small harbour. The beach is also dotted with small stands of pine for some good natural shade. Although very popular this is still very much a laid back resort with just a few tavernas and cafes. Horse riding is offered at the nearby at Pine Tree Paddock. Skala Rachonis itself is complemented by another good sandy beach that lies about two kilometres to the north. **Pachis:** Just north of Skala Rachonis is Pachis Beach, a long stretch of golden sand backed by some tamarisk trees. There are a couple of large tavernas and some beach bars. Many opt for the far end of the beach which has the best of the sand, and a pleasant cantina under the trees. The sand here is soft and golden and it is fairly shallow offshore and good for families with children. Tamarisk trees and pines provide plenty of good natural shade. Over the headland to the north is a tiny beach of Glyferoni at the head of a small bay. **Glyfada:** The road from Pachis follows the coast around the headland before turning south-east and back towards Thassos Town. It passes a few small beaches. One is called Perasama which has small sandy cove with a summer beach cantina. There are tiny patches of sand at Papalimani and Agia Irini on either side a rocky headland. The road eventually reaches Glyfada where there is a strip of sand. The sands are pleasant enough, although rather narrow in places with trees that offer plenty of shade. **Nysteri:** A small but splendid tree-lined beach lies below the hotel at Nysteri, just outside Thassos and a kilometre east from Glyfada beach. There is plenty of parking on a large patch of ground off the main road at the eastern end of the beach where a rough track leads down through woodland to the seashore. Nysteri has a fine sandy beach with shallow seawater and sunbeds. Trees behind the sands offer plenty of good shade and a small cantina opens in the woods during the high season…

The Greek Island of Zakynthos

Zante is what the Italians call the Island Zakynthos is its Greek name. It is one of the most southerly of the Ionian chain of holiday Islands that sidle down the coast of western Greece. The Island has an international airport and also has numerous ferries docking at the towns main port daily. Susie and I have holidayed on this Island several times and have always enjoyed our stays. The Island of Zante is one of the most popular of the Greek holiday Islands. Zante is an Island mix of busy beaches, quiet family coves, wild and rugged cliffs, green forested hills and fertile plains in roughly equal measures. The notorious beach resort of Laganas, for example, has been justifiably likened to a stage set on the movie Blade Runner while the idyllic Port Vromni beach is seen as a haven of peaceful tranquillity. Two major events shaped modern-day Zante. The catastrophic earthquake of 1953 which destroyed almost all of the Island's elegant Venetian mansions while the construction of the airport gave easy access to the Island of Zakynthos. The busiest beach resorts are north-west of the capital city of Zakynthos Town and along the huge bay of Laganas, to the south. Elsewhere, visitors can expect pretty village tavernas, quiet beach coves and lots of fine scenery, especially along the wild western coast. On such a large Island as Zante you would expect a wide variety of beaches and Zante certainly lives up to these expectations. The biggest beach strips are north-west of Zakynthos Town and around Laganas Bay. Those seeking more sedate spots will head south-east to the peninsula at Vasilikos or resort like Keriou Limnou in the south-west…

The Island of Zakynthos:

Zakynthos Town: The small, port resort of Zakynthos Town was rebuilt after the 1953 earthquake. The capital town is in a magnificent setting in a large bay with the Bochali hills behind. The main Solomu Square, thronged by holiday strollers on mid-summer evenings, with tavernas and cafes lining the triangular marble-paved piazza. A statue to the Island's favourite son, Dionysius Solomos, dominates the square. He wrote the Greek national anthem but, although born here, he lived and died on the Greek Island of Corfu. Tavernas also line the busy Strada Marina, part of a one-way system and the main route to the ferry port. Zakynthos Town has three interesting museums. The Byzantine Museum, arguably the best, has some 17th century paintings of the Ionian School and some very good icons. The renovated church of Agios Nicholas dates from 1561 and the spectacular Agios Dionysius, often lit up late at night, has a magnificent silver coffin said to house the relics of the Island's patron saint. The road north out of Zakynthos Town runs behind a beach backed by vineyards and orchards.
Beaches on the North East Coast: The long stretch of coast north-west of Zakynthos Town is one of the most visited. Good, sandy beaches and shallow seawater make it popular for family holidays. **Tsilivi:** North from Zakynthos Town is Tsilivi, a family resort with a long, wide beach of good sand. The sea is very shallow and safe for children. Heavy winter rains can wash sand away from the western end to reveal rocks and stone; much better sand is to be found at the eastern end of the beach. Being north facing the beach can get very windy and good for windsurfers. Low sand dunes and scrub help give Tsilivi beach a wide-open feel. Tsilivi resort is packed with restaurants and menus lean towards British tastes and you will even find a chip shop and a McDonald's here. There is plenty of family-type entertainment here with karaoke bars, crazy golf, bowling and so on. Tsilivi is about 10 km from Zante Airport…

The Island of Zakynthos:

Tragaki: To the north of Tsilivi is a clutch of pretty beaches at Tragaki, Limanaki, Ampoula and Bouka. The low-key attractions of beach tavernas and music bars help make this area of Zante increasingly popular with families. The proximity of the capital to the resort and the regular local bus service promises visitors a quiet day on Tragaki beach followed by a lively evening out in Zakynthos Town. The village of Tragaki is built on the side of the Kavelaris hills, set amongst olive groves and with panoramic views over the bay. Bouka has a long and pleasant stretch of sand with an attractive little fishing harbour at one end. The long, thin sand and pebble beach at Ampoula is nearby. The seawater at Ampoula is shallow near the shore, so it is good for children, but there is a steep incline a little way out. Beaches get quieter as you head west. Close by is the remains of a Venetian observatory, which is worth a visit. Inland at Sarakinda is a small water park. Tragaki is 12 km from Zakynthos Airport. **Alykanas:** The resort at Alykanas sits at the head of the huge sandy bay that sweeps around to neighbouring Alykes. Soft sand shelves gently into the sea. The beach is backed by low dunes, some scrub and olive groves. The sand narrows and turns to pebble nearer Alykes. The shallow water make Alykanas beach good for family holidays. Fishing boats use the small harbour at one end of the beach. Bars, tavernas, shops and mini-markets, line the resort's main street. The resort has a relaxed atmosphere and the popular 'Trainaki' train tour that runs between Alykes and Alykanas takes in the hill village of Katastari, the Vertagias Caves, the folk museum at Pigadakis and the church of Ag. Panteleimona with a snack stop at the Kaki Rahi taverna. Alykanas is 18 km from Zakynthos Airport…

The Island of Zakynthos:

Alykes: Alykes is a three kilometre stretch of golden sand that sweeps around the bay from Alykanas and is many say it is the best beach to be found north of Zakynthos Town. Alykes, sometimes spelt Alikes, gets it name from the large, flat salt pans that lie behind the sand at the southern end. The seawater is very shallow for several metres out but then dips sharply, making the beach fine for children close to the shore, and great for surfers who ride big breakers whipped up by northerly winds. The centre of Alykes beach is the busiest part of the beach but more peaceful spots are in either direction although pebbles are more prevalent to the east. Alykes village is very compact with the usual tourist shops, tavernas and cafes. There is even a tourist train from Alykes to Alykanas. Alykes is 17 km from Zante Airport. **Agios Nikolaos:** Beyond Alykes the north coast of the Island of Zakynthos changes into a long series of cliffs and rock, dotted with small pebble coves, many of them difficult to reach except by boat. The cliffs get wilder and steeper until they reach the tiny port of Agios Nikolaos 30 km from Zakynthos Town. Not to be confuse with the resort of the same name in the south of Zante. This Agios Nikolaos has a small pebble beach and there are some nearby rocky coves. The setting is idyllic and the port has ferry links to Kefalonia and caiques often pull in on their way to the famous Blue Caves of Zante. Agios Nikolaos is also a popular mooring point for visiting yachts and boats and has a good tavernas and cafes in the village. **Volimes:** Volimes is the largest of Zante Island's hill villages made up by three smaller hamlets. Prepare for the step back in time as each village is a cliche living museum, with some of the best preserved buildings on Zante, survivors of the 1953 earthquake. The villagers have local embroidery, cheese and exceptionally good honey for sale…

The Island of Zakynthos:

West Coast Beaches: The west coast of the Island of Zakynthos is as dramatic as the east is flat and soft. As a result, few Zante visitors make their way there. Those that do can enjoy sheer limestone cliffs, sometimes plunging 1,000 feet or more straight into the sea. The roads on the west coast are often steep and winding and driving can be rather tiring. **Porto Vromi:** Steep limestone bluffs rise on each side of a narrow inlet at the small and beautiful, village of Porto Vromi. The sheltered harbour is often full of fishing boats and the inlet is tipped by a narrow beach of white sand and shingle. Porto Vromi means 'Dirty Port' and the name derives from the natural tar that stains the beach. The tar is is not a real problem for visitors and the flecks of tar can be easily avoided. Above the Porto Vromi harbour is the 15th century monastery of Panagia Anafonitria, noted for its fine frescos, and there are regular boat trips to the nearby Blue Caves of Zante. **Kampi:** High on the western cliffs perches Kampi, the destination of many day trip coach parties. Cliff top tavernas offer romantic sea views from the 300-metre-high cliffs and many visitors come to watch the sun setting over the waves. Kampi is remote enough to ensure the views can usually be enjoyed in comfort but visitors may be unlucky if their visit coincides with the arrival of an evening coach party. The local tavernas can quickly fill up, especially on the popular Greek nights held regularly for the coach visitors. Kampi village is little more than a cluster of stone-built houses linked by narrow streets. There are attractive alternative cafes and tavernas away from the sunset-watching crowds on the cliff top. Kampi village also has a small and interesting folk museum stuffed with domestic and agricultural paraphernalia. This is a great place to spend the day and linger to see the setting sun…

The Island of Zakynthos:

Beaches on the South Coast: The huge bay of Laganas accounts for most of the south coast beach resorts, along with the peninsula at Vassilikos which has picturesque coves and lovely green vegetation. **Limni Keriou (Keri Lake):** Limni Keriou, also called Keri, sits on the southern tip of the Island of Zakynthos on the western side of Laganas Bay. There was a lake here once, now drained, and the area is often referred to as Keri Lake. The steep, narrow beach has more pebble than sand but it is still very attractive, with warm shallow seawater and a small river running over the beach and into the sea for added interest. The picturesque village has many pre-earthquake buildings and the view from Limni Keriou beach is impressive, with high cliffs flanking both sides and the turtle nesting Islet of Marathonisi lying offshore. From here the paths along the coast lead to secluded coves and a cliff top lighthouse where a small car park near the taverna offers spectacular views of nearby limestone sea arches. Boats can be hired off the beach to visit the turtle nesting Islet of Marathonisi but ecologists warn that the swarms of visitors frighten the shy loggerhead turtles away and fewer nest there each year. Marathonisi Islet has reefs that link it to the cape of Marathias and there are two small beaches on the Islet. The turtles nest on a long sand bank which it a protected area in the wider marine park but that doesn't stop turtle watchers scaring the creatures off before they even get there. Just inland of Keriou is the pretty village of Lithakia, one of the oldest on Zante and built on the lower slopes of Megalo Vouno. Lithakia has changed little over the years and the village church of Agios Ioannis is a fine example of traditional Zakynthian church architecture…

The Island of Zakynthos:

Agios Sostis: The resort of Agios Sostis has attracted holiday development to give visitors an alternative beach location to the hugely busy and popular Laganas resort which lies two kilometres around the bay to the east. This pleasant resort has a wide gently shelving sand and pebble beach backed by a couple of tavernas with low cliffs at the southern end where the beach turns to rocks before meeting the wall of its large harbour. The beach is named after the chapel on the picturesque Islet that sits out in the bay to the south, connected to the resort by a dramatic wooden bridge. The resort of Laganas is only a 20-minute walk along a coastal track and five minutes by car or bus. Excursion boats offer turtle spotting trips to the offshore Islet of Marathonisi. This is not a good idea because the tourists disturb these shy creatures. They are seriously disturbed by the daily swarms of trippers and often fail to lay their eggs. Agios Sostis is about 10 km from Zante Airport. **Laganas:** By far the biggest and most commercialised resort on the Island of Zakynthos, Laganas heaves with bars, cafes and shops, all offering an indiscriminate diet of junk food fry-ups, bargain booze and tacky souvenirs. Laganas is not the place for a peaceful break as the young party around the clock here. The evenings are full of flashing neon signs along the Golden Mile of deafening music bars full of young revelers. There are at least 100 bars on the main Laganas strip and they outnumber restaurants by about ten to one. The beach is the biggest on the Island and stretched for nearly nine kilometres. The sands are firm, hard packed with shallow seawater all make this an ideal beach for families but also for nesting turtles. The meeting of nature and holidaymakers has not been a happy one. The tacky turtle trinkets and t-shirts and the ruthless exploitation of the rare turtles is slowly killing them off as nests are bulldozed to make way for sun loungers and glass-bottom boat trips scare the creatures away. Frankly, anyone who cares about nature should avoid Laganas. There are plenty of places to stick a beach brolly other than through a clutch of turtle eggs or preventing them nesting there altogether just to get a photo. Laganas is 8 km from Zante Airport…

The Island of Zakynthos:

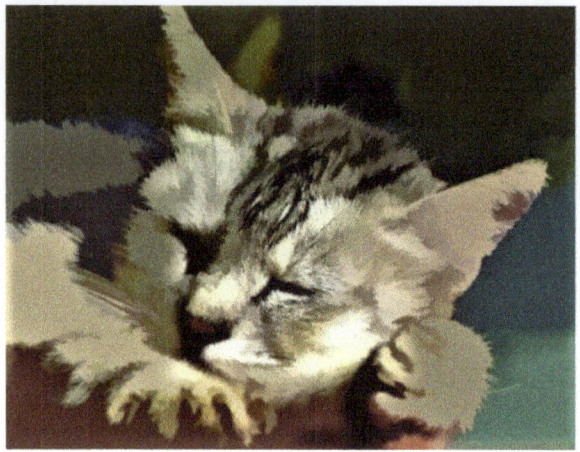 

Kalamaki: The dark sands of Kalamaki are equal to its neighbour Lagansa but the atmosphere on the beach is nowhere near as raucous. The sand is soft on the long beach and the seawater is very shallow, with some impressive rock formations along the shore makes Kalamaki is a family holiday destination. The resort is enclosed by olive and citrus groves with the backdrop of Mount Skopos in the distance. Planes fly in low over the beach to land at the nearby airport. Kalamaki nightlife mainly consists of touring the tavernas and bars and those looking for something more lively will head for the bright lights of Laganas just a short distance down the coast. Kalamaki beach is also a favourite with egg-laying turtles. Visitors are asked to stick to designated paths. Wildlife protection is more in evidence here than at nearby Laganas but depressing reports still come in of nest sites being destroyed. **Vassiikos Peninsula:** Vassilikos has some of the best countryside on Zante and great beaches too. **Gerakas:** On the eastern side of the Vassikos peninsula at Gerakas, also spelt Yerakas, is a long, crescent of golden sand and shallow seawater backed by sandstone cliffs with views across the bay to Laganas. Often voted among the best beaches in Europe, Gerakas gets it share of tourists during the day but, being also a major turtle breeding ground, it is off limits from dusk to dawn. Wardens based at the information centre above the beach patrol the nesting areas where sunbathing is banned. There are no watersports here and beach visiting hours are restricted. Thankfully, Gerakas conservation area status has spared it the ugly fate of resorts like Laganas. A trio of tavernas provide visitors with food and cold drinks and there is car parking near the mini market on the way to the beach. The cliffs at the southern end of Gerakas beach turn to white clay that years ago visitors used the clay as a natural sun block but the cliffs have now been closed off following several rock falls. So buy your suntan cream from the shops and do not venture to the cliffs for it…

The Island of Zakynthos:

Porto Roma: At the tip of the Gerakas peninsula is the tiny cove of Porto Roma which has a narrow sandy beach with a taverna overlooking the sea. A sublimely beautiful spot with olives and pines touching the shore below cliffs covered in rich vegetation. The beach gets very busy in the summer months. Porto Roma has a couple of beach bars, three tavernas and some small shops. **Agios Nikolaos:** Agios Nikolaos beach is a small, attractive stretch of good sand split by an outcrop of rock and crowned by a small chapel. The resort is named after the chapel and should not be mistaken for its namesake port in the north-west of the Island. Inland of Agios Nikolaos there are lush pine forests and olive groves. **Vassilikos:** Vassilikos village is reached by a very scenic drive through pine patterned hills to a tiny hamlet above a narrow beach of sand and pebble. To the north is the popular Banana Beach. The Vassilikos area has long been a nature reserve. Vassilikos is a quiet resort and is 17 km from Zante Airport. **Porto Zoro:** Porto Zoro is one of the most spectacular beaches on the peninsula. The beach is a small crescent of sharp sand with offshore rocks to the east that are ideal for snorkelling. The Porto Zoro beach is gently shelving but can be steep near the rock formations. **Argassi:** The shingle beach at Argassi which is so narrow in places that visitors are hard put to lie down without getting their wet feet. The seawater is very shallow for many metres out making Argassi a safe beach for children. Beyond the shingle shore it is sandy underfoot. Argassi is a popular family resort with a good selection of shops and tavernas. Smart hotels hug the shore intertwined with tavernas and bars, although greater choice can be had in Zakynthos Town which is only three kilometres north. Argassi is about 6 km from Zakynthos International Airport…

Acknowledgement

Having reached the end of our tour of the Greek Islands I would like to thank all the people, of all the Greek Islands featured: Aegina, Agistri, Alonissos, Andros, Corfu, Crete, Evia, Hydra, Ikaria, Ios, Ithaca, Kalymnos, Kefalonia, Kos, Lefkas, Leros, Lesvos, Lipsi, Maganissi, Mykonos, Naxos, Paros, Patmos, Paxos, Rhodes, Samos, Santorini, Skiathos, Skopelos, Skyros, Symi, Thassos and Zakynthos for making every visitor feel welcome and for giving them a great holiday to remember on their respective beautiful paradise Greek Islands. I would also like to thank my publishers Rainbow Publications UK. For publishing this book and for giving me the opportunity for my words to be read once more. Finally I wish to thank my wife Susie for the love and support that she gives me in all that I do every day of my life.

Susie… 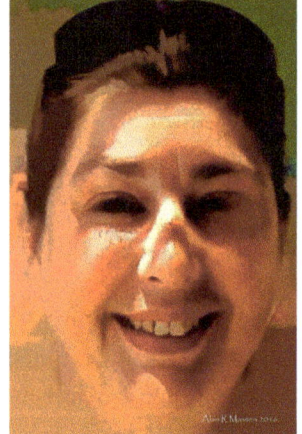  **…Alan**

Copyright © 2019 Alan R. Massen

To ALL a very BIG
Thank You...

www.ingramcontent.com/pod-product-compliance
Lightning Source LLC
Chambersburg PA
CBHW061925290426
44113CB00024B/2824